God's Old Testament People

Teachers Guide for Grade 9

Prepared by:
Thomas Buck
Margaret and Fred Trinklein

Edited by Board for Parish Services Staff
Editors: Arnold E. Schmidt
Jane Haas
Editorial Secretary: Phoebe Wellman

Publishing House
St. Louis

Contents

Write to Library for the Blind, 1333 S. Kirkwood Road, St. Louis, MO 63122-7295 to obtain God's Old Testament People (Teachers Guide) in Braille or sightsaving print for the visually impaired.

3558 S. Jefferson Avenue, St. Louis, MO 63118-3968
Manufactured in the United States of America

To the Teacher

God's Old Testament People, designed for ninth-grade students, provides a chronological overview of the Old Testament. It contains a strong emphasis on God's covenant people and on their responses to His covenant.

This course may be taught in grade 10 or (with adaptation) in grade 11 or 12.

God's Old Testament People is a 90-session course, providing resources for one semester. We recommend class five days per week. However, if the class meets less often, you might (a) extend the material in this course over a longer period of time, (b) assign certain sessions to individuals or small groups for reports in class, or (c) select sessions or units in accordance with class periods available.

THE LUTHERAN HIGH SCHOOL RELIGION SERIES

This is one of 12 courses for Lutheran high schools. The courses have been designed to permit use with a variety of scheduling programs. Four courses contain 90 sessions each and provide materials for five sessions per week for one semester. Each of the other eight courses contains 45 sessions, and is designed for one quarter (half a semester).

Following are the topics of the 12 courses:

Grade 9

Fitting In: Relationships with God and Others (45 sessions)

"For God So Loved . . .": A Study of the Gospel of John (45 sessions)

God's Old Testament People (90 sessions)

Grade 10

New Testament History--Including Early Church History (90 sessions)

The Church in Paul's Epistles (45 sessions)

Christian Ethics (45 sessions)

Grade 11

Christian Doctrine (90 sessions)

Later Church History: Luther and the Reformation; Lutheranism (45 sessions)

Christian and Non-Christian Religions and Cults (45 sessions)

Grade 12

Personal Christian Living (90 sessions)

Engagement and Marriage (45 sessions)

The General Epistles and Revelation (45 sessions)

This design was prepared after a survey of all high schools affiliated with the Association for Lutheran Secondary Schools and after extensive conversations with high-school and college teachers. Thus it reflects both current practices and theory. The Parish Services staff wishes to express special thanks to the ALSS administrators for their cooperation and assistance.

While any course assumes a certain background and maturity of the students, each course can stand alone--a previous course in this series is not an absolute prerequisite. The Student Books contain no grade level designations; therefore courses can be adapted to other grade levels.

MATERIALS

In addition to this guide, you will need a copy of the accompanying Student Book and a Bible. (This course generally quotes the New International Version of the Bible. We recommend that you select a translation commonly used in the congregations of your students.)

The students will need a copy of the Student Book and a Bible. They will also need access to other resources, such as Bible commentaries, dictionaries, concordances, and maps.

USING THIS GUIDE

Some sessions suggest more activities than can be accomplished in one period. Be selective. You know your students. Use the activities and materials that will be of most value to them.

LAW AND GOSPEL

The plans in this guide help you structure sessions so that students see both Law and Gospel. You will want the Holy Spirit to work in them as they hear God's words of accusation, forgiveness, and guidance. As you begin to plan the course, you might reread The Proper Distinction Between Law and Gospel by C. F. W. Walther. This is good reading for all who work with youth, especially teachers.

Once **(John 12:20-21)** some Greeks came to Philip and said, **"Sir, we would like to see Jesus."** Your basic goal as you teach each day should be to bring students to "see Jesus." Confront them with their spiritual needs; then lead them to see Jesus their Savior as the Answer to those needs. Let His love permeate all relationships in your classroom as you grow together in grace by the Spirit's power. Establish this as your primary goal and let all other objectives grow within this goal.

We invite you to write the editors about God's Old Testament People. Share the joys and frustrations you experienced as you taught this course, offer suggestions for other courses, etc. Please send your comments to:

Editorial Services Unit
Board for Parish Services
The Lutheran Church--Missouri Synod
1333 South Kirkwood Road
St. Louis, MO 63122-7295

Unit 1: Getting Started

This unit will establish rapport among the students and with the teacher. High school freshmen are pressured to "fit in" or deliberately "exclude." Peer acceptance becomes a primary goal. The activities of this unit will help students adapt to the Lutheran high school and will motivate them to serious study of the course contents.

If the students and teacher have been together for a previous class, some of the activities will need to be adapted.

PLANNING THE UNIT

Session 1: Obtain or draw a poster that says "Remember, God Doesn't Make Junk," "Be Patient--God Isn't Finished with Me Yet," or something similar. Make copies of the autobiographical forms needed in the session. You will also need a supply of 3 x 5 cards.

Session 2: Reserve the suggested reference books in the school library. Obtain a supply of small-denomination foreign bank notes or foreign-language coupons for a store or restaurant. Place as many versions of the Bible as you can locate on reserve in the library.

Session 1: Getting to Know Each Other

BIBLE BASIS: Matt. 22:37-40; Matt. 18:20; Prov. 16:28; 2 Cor. 5:17

CENTRAL TRUTH

God loves each of us just the way we are. He has no second class citizens in His kingdom. Jesus' message to His followers was clear and simple: **"Love each other as I have loved you" (John 15:12).**

OBJECTIVES

That the students will:

1. Get to know the other students and the teacher
2. Begin to establish a routine for this class (bring materials needed, sit at proper places, etc.)
3. Explain Bible passages that reinforce their feeling of self-worth and that admonish them to love others
4. Recognize that this course will focus on God's covenants as found in the Old Testament

BACKGROUND

Many adolescents have low self-esteem. They manifest this painful situation in many ways: Some bluster and brag. Others are shy and withdrawn. Cliques--all too prevalent--can devastate life for many and can make a mockery of the Christian walk of joy and enthusiasm.

This lesson focuses on the Christian imperative to love our neighbors as ourselves. Love begins with the teacher. Each student should feel that the teacher is pleased to have him or her in the classroom and regards each student as one of God's special persons of possibility.

You might open the class with a prayer something like this:

Dear Heavenly Father, God of Abraham, Isaac, Jacob, and me: We acknowledge You as our Creator and Redeemer. We thank You for the privilege of gathering together here in freedom and peace to learn more about You and Your will for us.

Not even a sparrow falls to the ground without You being aware of it. And because we are precious in Your sight, we trust You to care for the needs and frustrations and hopes and fears of everyone in this room, including me. You have brought us together for Your special purpose. Grant me wisdom and insight to be a good teacher. Grant each person in this room, my brothers and sisters, the grace to feel Your unconditional, unending love. Increase our love for You and for one another. For Jesus' sake. Amen.

Prepare an autobiographical form to help you learn more about the students--to the end that your teaching will be more effective and sensitive. Ask questions about students' families, interests, joys, problems, etc. Distribute the forms at the end of the session as an assignment for session 2. Assure the students that only you will read the autobiographies and that you will return them at the end of the course.

To encourage students to be open and honest in this opening session, share your own interests and family background. Use a little humor. Do not present yourself as someone who never does anything wrong. Be yourself.

You may want to apply the Golden Rule to the class requirements. In other words, everyone will be prompt, well prepared and equipped, courteous, friendly, etc., because this is in the best interest of everyone present. It is a way to communicate love to one another.

INTRODUCTION (Objectives 1, 2, and 4)

Bring the class to order and pray the prayer provided or another prayer. Welcome the students to the course, explain the seating plan, and make necessary housekeeping announcements--including the topic and scope of this course: God's covenants with His people as found in the Old Testament. Read the unit introduction from the Student Book, and help students understand the idea of covenants.

GETTING TO KNOW EACH OTHER (Objectives 1, 2, and 3)

Briefly affirm that a gathering in Jesus' name, such as this class, is honored by His presence. Jesus is here! He calls us His brothers and sisters! He wants us to love each human being.

Ask volunteers to read the Student Book Bible passages aloud to the class. Allow those who wish to share what these words mean to them.

Option 1: Use this option (adapt as appropriate for your class) if most students in the class don't know one another.

Announce that the next part of the session will be relatively informal, because your goal is for them to get acquainted with one another.

Ask those who feel they know three -fourths of the class members to raise their hands. This will be group 1. Those who feel they know one-half of the class members will be group 2, and all others will comprise group 3.

Use these three groups to help you create clusters of three students each in such a way that, if possible, none of the three is known to the other two (except by name and face). If groups 1 and 3 are small, they may be combined.

Ask each cluster to write their three names on a 3 x 5 card and hand it to you.

During the next 10 minutes have each student give a short get-acquainted description of himself or herself (interests, family, likes, dislikes, strengths, weaknesses) to the other two students in the cluster. At the end of this time, ask one person in a cluster to introduce another one, giving as much information as time will allow. Since the students will not know in advance which classmates they will be called upon to introduce, they will need to pay close attention when the original self-portraits are presented.

Obviously, this procedure will require careful timekeeping. For example, allow three minutes for each autobiography and one minute for each introduction by another student. Use the filled-out 3 x 5 cards as guides. When all have finished, each student should have assumed two roles: an introducer and an introducee. Both the person being introduced and the one giving the introduction should stand. Class size will influence how much time you will devote to this activity. You may need to finish the introductions during session 2.

Option 2: Use this option if the students already know one another quite well. Use the class time to discuss one or more of the following texts, which relate to building up the individual and the body of Christ:

1 Cor. 3:10-17 (individual)
Eph. 2:19-22 (corporate)
Heb. 3:1-6 (individual and

corporate)

1 Peter 2:1-17 (individual and corporate)

If you have time for only one passage, use **1 Peter 2:1-17.**

Session 2: Getting the Message from God's Word

BIBLE BASIS: 2 Tim. 3:16-17; Luke 24:27; Acts 4:12

CENTRAL TRUTH

God has given us His Word in the form of the Bible for our benefit and instruction. It reveals His love for us as manifested in the redeeming sacrifice of Jesus Christ and thus provides a basis for successful living and eternal salvation.

OBJECTIVES

That the students will:

1. Recognize the importance of studying the Bible
2. Identify difficulties involved in communicating accurately the important concepts in the Bible
3. Demonstrate an awareness of the different styles of writing contained in the Bible
4. Realize the importance of using a good translation of the Bible
5. Identify differences among translations (e.g., a literal translation over against a mere paraphrase)
6. Declare that the Bible is the Word of God
7. List the fulfillment of God's covenant in Jesus Christ as the central message of the Bible
8. Begin a program of daily Bible reading

BACKGROUND

The Bible is unique. It has long been a best-seller and it has been translated into more languages and dialects than any other book. (There are more than 70 versions of all or parts of the Bible in English alone.) Even in schools where the teaching of religion is prohibited, the Bible is often studied for its literary value.

Archaeology and other sciences have shed much light on the Bible. Time after time, the truth of God's Word has been verified through excavations, dating methods, and archaeological discoveries. The Biblical Archaeological Review, an authoritative joint publishing venture of Christian and Jewish scientists, provides excellent information in connection with this topic. (See the appendix for bibliographic information for this and other references.)

The efficacy of God's Word, however, does not lie in its literary value or in the fact that archaeological discoveries support its truthfulness. We can't ask God for this type of verification; He expects us to believe even though we have not seen. The basic reason for studying the Bible is neither literary nor scientific. It's much bigger than either of them. The Bible might be called "God's love letter" to the human race. Adolescents readily understand that a love letter is a meaningful document and that the recipient is apt to pore over it, savor it, memorize parts of it, and reread it many times. God's love letter deals with His love for us as revealed in the life and sacrifice of His Son. As with any human love letter--and even more so, because of its vital importance in our lives--the Bible should become a treasured and daily part of our existence.

We dare not assume that each student is familiar with the Bible. We will want to use an interesting approach to help them learn to know it better, but we need to avoid a trap--the use of gimmicks for the sake of novelty. They tend to blur our goal: to make the Bible clear to the students and to explain the reasons for which it was written. With that purpose in mind, the whole Bible becomes exciting and important, including all of the Old Testament.

We recommend Halley's Bible Handbook for both teachers and students. Though not an exhaustive commentary, it correlates Bible topics with other disciplines. And above all, it treats the Bible with the reverence that should be accorded it by those who know it to be God's revealed Word.

Finally, only two things in the universe are trustworthy--God and His Word. The Bible is His Word. It can be trusted.

Open the session with the following prayer or one of your own: **Dear Heavenly Father, I thank You for the privilege of teaching Your Word. Bless each and every student here with a hunger to learn, and the joy that comes from having that hunger satisfied. In Jesus' name. Amen.**

IMPORTANT MESSAGES (Objectives 1, 2, and 3)

The stories in the Student Book show that a seemingly unimportant document can have great meaning in a person's life. As a follow-up to these stories, give each student a foreign bank note (of very small denomination) or a small gift certificate to a Chinese restaurant or the like. (A bank or stamp dealer should be able to supply an Arabic or other mysterious-looking paper suitable for this purpose.) Tell the students that the documents have value and that it is up to them to find out what they are for and to cash them in.

DIFFICULTIES IN COMMUNICATION (Objective 2)

Luther once pointed out how difficult it would be for a person who had seen an exotic animal in a foreign country to describe that animal to the people in Germany, who were familiar mostly with horses and cows. In Africa, a missionary would have a hard time explaining to a person in a grass hut that many people in America live in multistoried apartment buildings. Encourage students to think of and share other examples of this kind.

A MESSAGE-WRITING EXERCISE (Objective 3)

This exercise is not meant to imply that the Bible is intentionally obscure, but rather that God spared no pains in presenting His message in various ways and for a variety of readers. As a master teacher, He allows for individual differences in the writers of the Bible as well as in the readers.

MESSAGE FORMS IN THE BIBLE (Objectives 3, 4, and 5)

In addition to the Student Book activity, arrange with the English teacher to give interdisciplinary credit for an optional report on Bible translations. They can find background information in Comparative Study of Bible Translations and Paraphrases (available from Concordia Publishing House, order No. 9-2274). They might also request information about translations from the Commission on Theology and Church Relations, The Lutheran Church--Missouri Synod, 1333 South Kirkwood Road, Saint Louis, MO 63122-7295.

GOD'S LOVE LETTER and **READING GOD'S WORD** (Objectives 6 and 7)

As in every session, the students should make the study of a section of God's Word the highlight of the class period. Ask individual students to read the three Bible passages aloud and to tell briefly what each passage means to them. If other students have Bible versions besides those quoted in the lesson, have them read the texts aloud also. Beginning with session 3, however, reading and discussion of the texts should be based on the Bible version that the teacher has selected for the course.

Emphasize the fact that the first two texts refer specifically to the Old Testament. This reinforces the importance of including a systematic study of the Old Testament in the religion curriculum.

A BIBLE READING PLAN (Objective 8)

Use **A Word of Caution** from the Student Book to introduce students to the idea of a Bible reading plan.

Then ask students to calculate the number of chapters of the Bible a person would have to read per day in order to finish the whole Bible in one year. Encourage them to ask themselves questions such as "How much time would this take every day? Am I willing to make that kind of commitment?" The idea here is not to win some kind of merit badge with God but rather to point out that reading the whole Bible is not an insurmountable task and that, as with any kind of prolonged activity, a daily schedule is the key to success. (You might suggest a plan other than beginning in Genesis and reading straight through the Bible. Too often young people who try that approach get bogged down somewhere in Leviticus.)

Unit 2: Beginnings

After Adam and Eve yielded to Satan's temptation, God in His unfathomable love, immediately promised them a Savior. The repetition of that promise through the centuries reinforces our awareness of God's love and mercy. This unit climaxes with the story of Noah and the indomitable love of God in action as He uses Noah's faithfulness to preserve the human race and keep the covenant of salvation intact even as He expands it to ensure the uninterrupted progression of seasons until the end of the world.

PLANNING THE UNIT

Session 3: Make a time line for the Old Testament, beginning about 4000 B.C. and continuing to at least 1000 B.C. Add events or characters as you encounter them in lessons throughout the course. This could be a student project, but since you need it for session 3, you will have to make at least a temporary time line. Obtain a copy of the book, The God of Science.

Session 5: Assemble several hard-rock record jackets that can be examined in class for Satanic symbols. Write to the LCMS Commission on Organizations for literature on rock music and Satanism. Place books on cults and Satanism on reserve in the library, or alert the librarian to possible student request on these subjects.

Session 7: Gather the necessary materials for the classroom-size life line of the patriarchs. (See the list in **"The Classroom Graph"** in Session 7.)

Session 9: The following books should be placed on reserve in the library: The Ark on Ararat, The Flood, and The Bible and Modern Science. (See the bibliography for publication information.) Obtain a tape or record of Bill Cosby's monologue on the Flood and a machine with which to play the recording.

Session 10: Obtain the pamphlet, "The Sky Has Fallen." (See the bibliography for publication information.) It will be helpful to bring examples of rainbows in today's culture (jewelry, pillows, mobiles, etc.).

Session 3: The Origin of Everything but God

BIBLE BASIS: Gen. 1--2

CENTRAL TRUTH

God is eternal--He has no beginning and no end. God created everything else that exists. As creator, He is the undisputable ruler of the universe. His divine love was already evident at the very beginning of time.

OBJECTIVES

That the students will:

1. Recognize that **Genesis** means "beginnings"
2. See in God's Word the importance of the refrain, "And God saw that it was good"
3. Learn that everything was created to please God
4. Discover that in **Gen. 1:1--2:3** God tells about the creation of the world, while in **Gen. 2:4-25** He tells part of the history of the heavens and the earth

5. Identify Moses as the writer of Genesis

6. Recognize that God through His people transmitted the messages of creation and salvation already in the ages before Moses wrote the book of Genesis

7. Resolve to use one day of the week for rest and worship

BACKGROUND

Do not get entangled in tangential questions, no matter how intriguing, while teaching this lesson. As God reminds us in **2 Tim. 2:14,** such digressions tend to undermine the simple, childlike faith that the Bible stresses. (See **Ps. 131:1-2** and **Matt. 18:3.**) Always keep the central truth of the lesson in mind. The approach should be as simple and direct as Scripture itself: "In the beginning, God . . ." No apologies, no dissertation, no elaborate explanations are necessary (or possible, for that matter)--just the simple narrative as given by God Himself.

If students raise questions about various theories of evolution or creationism, point out that theories are important steps in the scientific method, but that theories are only that and should not be mistaken for indisputable conclusions. The scientific method deals with facts which are gained through the sense organs and theories or explanations which are developed by the mind. The very nature of science demands that all theories, and even conclusions, must always be left open to question. A scientist who is no longer willing to question a scientific "fact," even if it is one that he or she has personally discovered, has lost perhaps the most important requirement of a qualified research scientist.

For more background to this topic, read The God of Science, by Frederick E. Trinklein. In this book, the Christian author details his personal interviews with many Nobel laureates and other leading scientists in eight countries on such questions as the nature of the scientific method, the existence of God, and the viability of miracles.

Biblical teachings and your school's approach to evolution and creationism should be discussed at a faculty meeting at the beginning of the school year. Together the administration and teaching staff need to decide how much of this subject should be covered in religion courses and how much should be treated in other courses. Make students aware that there is harmony in the school on these matters--a knowledgeable and intelligent harmony. Point out during this session that other aspects of God's act of creation will be covered in other courses and that in this lesson you intend to bring out the covenant/love themes of creation.

Gifted students might do extra work on a paper about creation and evolution.

THE JOY OF CREATING (Objectives 1, 2, and 3)

Begin with the reading of **Gen. 1 and 2.** If all students have the same version of the Bible, read the chapters in unison. Point out the rhythmic quality, punctuated with the refrain, "And there was evening, and there was morning." Then discuss the Student Book activities for this section.

WAYS OF TELLING (Objectives 4, 5 and 6)

Theologians have held long and bitter arguments as they compared the content of **Gen. 1:1--2:3** with that of **2:4-25.** Some have held that the accounts are contradictory, and that the Biblical creation account is, therefore, unreliable.

We do well to realize that God and His Word are wiser than we are. As you teach this account, focus on its central truth--God's love letter to us. As you do this, you will affirm the Bible's inerrancy--but don't let preoccupation with that concept cause you to neglect the central message of God's power and love.

The Student Book introduces the 10 history accounts suggested by the introduction to each account ("These are the generations . . ." [RSV];

"This is the account . . ." [NIV]). Commentaries such as those by Keil and Delitzsch (Commentaries on the Old Testament: Pentateuch, vol. 1) or Roehrs and Franzmann (Concordia Self-Study Commentary) provide additional background information.

Refer to a time line to show how long God transmitted His messages through His people prior to Moses.

"ON THE SEVENTH DAY HE RESTED"
(Objective 7)

Help the students to see how Satan is trying to erode the foundations of one of our most precious heritages --the family. Encourage the class to promote and expand the time available for family togetherness in their homes, beginning with Sunday worship! Discussion of the Bible passages read in the service and the theme of the sermon during Sunday dinner is an excellent habit to establish in a Christian home. Encourage the students to ask a parent or grandparent about the ways Sundays were observed when they were young. Has it gotten better or worse?

Use the following prayer, or one similar to it, at the close of the lesson:

We thank and praise You, dear Heavenly Father, for the astounding beauty and variety of Your created works: the many shades of color--and eyes capable of seeing them; the tonal richness of music and speech--and ears to enjoy each variation; the endless gradations of textures, from satiny flower petals to jagged crags of granite--and the sense of touch that lets us appreciate them; for water and air; for smiles and tears; for male and female; for blond and brunette; for varied colors of skin. For all Your messages of love that surround us daily, we respond now with humble, heartfelt thanks. In the name of Jesus, who shows us how much God loves the world. Amen.

Session 4: The First People

BIBLE BASIS: Gen. 1--2

CENTRAL TRUTH

God created people for harmony and fellowship with Him and one another and provided everything that is necessary to make this relationship both possible and pleasurable.

OBJECTIVES

That the students will:

1. Examine their responses to loneliness and become aware that true companionship involves interaction
2. Recognize that God created far more than is necessary merely to sustain life and to recognize that all of creation is an expression of God's great love for us
3. Examine the positive and negative aspects of human personality, attributing the former to being created in God's image and the latter as evidence that something has marred that image
4. Rejoice that they can see in other Christians the good works that are evidence of saving faith and that others can see these same evidences in them
5. Recognize marriage as a divinely ordained relationship in which two people become one flesh emotionally, psychologically, etc., as well as physically
6. Recognize and appreciate the purposes and importance of sexual differences in the divine plan

BACKGROUND

Surveys show that God's role as judge is more vivid in the minds of most believers than is His role as the perfect Creator who longs for a loving relationship with His creatures. To prepare the students for a ready acceptance of God's promise, they must first recognize His infinite wisdom and love. Only then will they be able to comprehend the awesome spiritual battle that is being waged for their very souls and will eagerly seek God's solution to the problems created by sin.

Godless humanism--with its emphasis on people as the central beings in the world--often infiltrates secular education today. It permeates many textbooks, television programs, novels, and even music, and has influenced the minds of all of us, especially our young people. Many have been led to suspect that if God does exist, He is vengeful, sexist, self-centered, capricious, and unreliable. Use this lesson to lay a solid Biblical foundation of evidences of God's divine love with His provision for harmonious relationships. The Bible provides a clear picture of the fortress we have against Satan, who wants to destroy our relationship with God and resultant loving relationships we have with other people.

The Bible texts provide background material against which the students can test their own biases and discover or rediscover their unalterable heritage of God's love as set forth in His Word.

INTRODUCTION (Objective 1)

Encourage class discussion on the merits and shortcomings of having a robot as a friend. You might also ask if, as children, the students were ever asked to kiss a relative they disliked and, if so, how much love they communicated by that kiss. God wants our genuine love, not a hollow imitation. The discussion should help students understand why it was possible for Adam and Eve to sin.

SETTING THE STAGE FOR HAPPINESS (Objective 2)

Ask students to tell about their favorite creations and the pleasure they derive from them. Allow ample time for comments on a black-and-white, plastic, monotone world. The students may come up with other "extras," such as steam, liquid, ice, springs, rivers, lakes, etc., or variations in seasons, aromas, tastes, and the like. Bask, with the class, in the infinite amount of evidence of God's love for us.

CASTING THE CHARACTERS (Objectives 3, 5, and 6)

Relate our positive human attributes to what we know of God's character: He created, He enjoyed "work" and "rest," He is eager to communicate love, He is wise, He is powerful, etc. Students will readily see that some human attributes are definitely not Godlike. Allow them to conclude that we no longer reflect God's image clearly.

Help the students discover that God instituted marriage as part of His perfect plan for Paradise. It provides a unique blessing in response to the special need for companionship. God could have managed procreation in some other way. But sex is part of the package designed for pleasure in the marriage relationship, which unites a man and a woman into one flesh or supernatural body, a unity that includes--and transcends--a physical union.

Lead the students to examine **Gen. 1:27-28** carefully and see that the term "man" refers to "them" and that Eve was included in God's total plan. Both were to subdue and rule the earth. Marriage before the Fall was free of stresses caused by jealousy, greed, and fear. Adam and Eve were created to be completely free of psychological hang-ups and could enjoy perfect harmony in their activities.

HAPPINESS TOGETHER (Objectives 3, 4, and 5)

Put two headings on the board, "Adam and Eve" and "Married Couples Today." Have the class suggest ways the couples in each column reflect the image of God. Adam and Eve, for example, enjoyed work, were always happy, and never sinned. Married couples today might forgive each other, worship God, and give food to hungry people. While the list for Adam and Eve may be longer, the list for married couples today should demonstrate that Christians living in the bond of wedlock can, in fact, really reflect some of the image of God to each other!

Lead the class to evaluate the preponderant one-sidedness of God's command to Adam and Eve: God gave them the entire universe and perfect fellowship with Him as a free gift.

In response they were to refrain from eating the fruit of the tree that would lead them to know evil and death. What a bargain! Encourage class reaction to this situation.

Be sure the class understands how clearly God spelled out the results of breaking His command. He offered no recourse--no negotiation or plea bargaining. The penalty for choosing evil is death.

Note God's words in the institution of marriage. When husband and wife unite, they shall become one flesh. Ask students to talk about this relationship, to describe the unity and mutual responsibility of marriage partners. Then talk about ways today's "new morality" encourages husbands and wives to disregard God's design for marriage.

Most adolescents are idealistic. With God's blessing you can bolster this characteristic by giving them knowledge and appreciation of God's system of morality. As one bumper sticker says, "Wise men still follow Him." Encourage the students to follow God's morality (found in Scripture) rather than secular humanism's new morality (which can be compared to accepting some wiseacre's advice to lubricate a fine watch with chunky-style peanut butter).

Ask a student to read **Eph. 5:28-33** aloud. Point out how this passage undergirds the concept of the marriage covenant and use it as a way of communicating the closeness of our relationship with Christ: He is the head and we are His body, a supernatural reality brought about by another of God's promises. Talk briefly about the blessings we enjoy because of this relationship.

You might close the session with the following prayer: **Precious Father, Almighty Creator, how good and gracious You are to us! Help us to feel Your love more surely and clearly every day--and to reflect it to each other. In Jesus' name. Amen.**

Session 5: Satan and the Beginning of Evil

BIBLE BASIS: Gen. 3

CENTRAL TRUTH

Satan, our foremost enemy, seeks to upset God's plan by destroying our allegiance to Him. Satan's tactics are very effective, but we can be sure of victory over sin, death, and Satan because God is more powerful.

OBJECTIVES

That the students will:

1. Discover the description of Satan as a serpent in Scriptures
2. Recognize Satan and his angels as rebellious creatures who were cast into hell--out of God's grace and blessings and presence
3. Identify overt and covert Satanic influences in the world today
4. Relate their own temptations to those that Eve experienced
5. Take comfort in God's power and the promises of salvation through Jesus that are found in God's Word

BACKGROUND

In any contest, whether it is in sports, chess, or the battlefield, we gain a great advantage when we become familiar with the game plan and strategy of the opponents and the motives under which they operate. This lesson teaches about the wiles of Satan. The students should be required to read the lesson in advance so that they will, hopefully, be "psyched up" to discuss Satan's modus operandi. In today's "I'm OK, you're OK," demythologized society, we need to underscore the reality of evil forces battling for our very souls and bodies. Secular humanists have relegated the existence of Satan to a credibility roughly on a par with Santa Claus. How convenient for Satan!

A few students, however, may become so intrigued by demonology that they spend more time reading books on Satanism and cults than they do reading Scriptures. Some may even visit gatherings where participants plan seances, practice voodoo, use Ouija boards, and the like. This is spiritually dangerous! Playing with fire can be devastating, and you should warn against such preoccupation with Satan's work. We need to focus on God, not on Satan. (Both extremes are dangerous--ignoring Satan's existence and becoming preoccupied with it.)

For the serious, well-grounded student who wants to pursue the topic of Satanism and other cults further, place appropriate books and pamphlets on reserve in the library. Be sure to assign a Christian adult to meet regularly with students as they study. How to Repond to the Eastern Religions, by Philip Lochhaas (St. Louis: Concordia Publishing House, 1979), provides an excellent and succinct description of Hinduism, Hare Krishna, TM, and Buddhism. You might write to the Commission on Organizations of The Lutheran Church --Missouri Synod for a more complete and current listing of resource materials on the subject of cults.

To encourage the study of angels, and especially the archangel Michael, who is referred to in this lesson, have students consult a concordance or Bible dictionary.

After developing a healthy fear for Satan as the enemy and a powerful foe in an ongoing battle, you will place this fear in proper perspective by referring to the weapons that are described in Scriptures and that are ours to use against the enemy. Point to the victory over Satan and sin that Christ Jesus has won for us.

INTRODUCTION (Objective 1)

Open with the following prayer (or a similar one): **Oh, precious Savior, how helpless we would be against the tricks of Satan if You were not by our side. His plans for us are so evil and Your promises are so beautiful. Keep us alert to Satan's distortions of the truth. Make us strong to resist him through faith in You and the study of Your Word. Thank You for defeating Satan with Your life, death, and resurrection. We love You. We praise Your holy name. Amen.**

Referring to material in the Student Book, ask a student to write names for Satan on the board as other students supply them. Use this time for a cursory check of the assigned homework.

THE SOURCE OF EVIL (Objectives 2 and 3)

Lead the class in a discussion of Satan's relationship with God before and after being cast into hell. Help them to recognize Satan's current, ongoing activity--his contest with God for our souls. We have a free will; no one is forced into heaven. Satan wants us to choose him instead of God. And that happens when we turn our backs on God's promise--the free gift of salvation in Christ Jesus.

Satan brought death; Jesus brings life. Point out that the evil spirits that Jesus and His disciples cast out were Satan's emissaries.

Because newscasts sometimes include gruesome stories of atrocities resulting from Satan worship or "black masses," which may involve the torturing and maiming of animals and/or humans, you ought to discuss the reality of these events in class. The forces of evil are real, powerful, and not to be taken lightly. "Friends" do invite teenagers to participate in seances, Tarot-card readings, and the like, "just for fun."

Take time to share some of these experiences. Ask, **How do we know that fortunetelling is wrong?** Tell students to look up **Acts 16:16-18.** Paul cast out a fortunetelling spirit in the name of Jesus. **Isaiah 8:19-20** provides further teaching on this matter. Jesus said, **"He who is not with Me is against Me" (Matt. 12:30).** Warn against unhealthy preoccupation with Satan and cults. Encourage the students to focus on Jesus.

HOW TEMPTATION WORKS (Objective 4)

Ask if any student can think of a "perfect" character in the Bible. We need heroes with clay feet, else we might despair. We learn a great deal about God and His love through these episodes.

Lead the class to see that **Gen. 3** could be subtitled, "Helpful Hints on How to Overcome Temptation." Ask for other subtitles, perhaps listing them on the board and adding the one quoted above only if needed.

If time permits, you might dramatize the temptation and the fall into sin, but do this after you discuss the Student Book material. Help students identify with all the steps of Satan's approach. Adolescents are quick to say to their parents, "Everyone else is allowed to . . ." Other aspects of Eve's temptation involve exaggeration and half-truths. The students should readily identify with Eve here.

Be sure the class recognizes that Satan often tries to make us doubt God's love for us--to suspect His motives rather than to see His omniscience and tender mercy. In every trial of life we tend to respond, "Why me?! It's not fair!" Ask the students whether they have every heard anyone crying, "Why me?" after not getting a good grade on a test or after suffering an injury in an accident. Point out humanity's threefold vulnerability--physical ("Your eyes will be opened"), spiritual ("You will be like God"), and intellectual ("You will know good and evil"). Satan still works on all three levels.

LIVING WITH JESUS (Objective 5)

Satan will use every available approach, even to the extent of using a person like St. Peter (as was pointed out earlier). After discussing the Student Book material, you might roleplay the following:

Setting: A Friday night party in a home with a bar. The parents are next door playing bridge.

Characters: Students from school: Austin, the host, who is a devout Christian but is eager to please; Kurt, an amiable neighbor; Steve, a shy, new student in school; Beth, a shy, devout girl; Sharon, who is eager to be popular; Tina, a girl who is looking for excitement.

Roleplay: The evening has been going well, but there is a lull in the conversation. Tina suggests a new drink she has tasted. Kurt shows interest. Sharon doesn't want to be considered a nerd. Austin, Steve, and Beth are cautious. Everyone knows that the liquor cabinet is off-limits to Austin. How might the conversation proceed? The three people who are in favor of the "experiment" might use the kinds of approaches that Eve listened to in this lesson. How can Austin, Steve, and Beth follow their consciences most effectively--without making enemies? Identify the motivations exemplified by each character in the drama. Do these motivations make him or her hopelessly evil? Or unquestionably sinless? Or is there some of each in all of us?

The roleplaying should lead to a statement of belief in and a commitment to Jesus and His teachings. Let the students reach the conclusion that without a "higher power" to draw up guidelines, we are like a ship without a rudder. The Bible helps us to live this life well and shows us the final outcome of our battle with the powers of darkness --our victory in Jesus Christ. **"The One who is in you** (Jesus) **is greater than the one who is in the world** (Satan)" **1 (John 4:4).** Praise God!

This would be a good time to discuss the "armor of God" **(Eph. 6:10-18).** You could assign this as a written report.

Session 6: Saved--by the Grace of God

BIBLE BASIS: Gen. 3:4-21

CENTRAL TRUTH

Even in the face of their rebellion, God continued to show His love for Adam and Eve and promised them a Savior.

OBJECTIVES

That the students will:

1. Identify with Adam and Eve in the story of the fall into sin and the promise of a Savior

2. Describe the total helplessness of their natural spiritual condition

3. Identify Satan as the source of all that is evil and see disease, hatred, wars, etc., as "gifts" of Satan

4. Verbalize parallels between Satan's promises to Eve and today's hedonism

5. Thrill to the agape love of God as He announced to Adam and Eve a the sure promise of a new birth through the victory of Christ Jesus over Satan

6. Face the certainty of God's pronouncements--both those that result in punishment and those that result in salvation

7. Discover the purpose of life in Christ

BACKGROUND

In these days of plea bargaining and "easy" paroles, students may well think that that this is the way God acts toward us. Nothing could be further from the truth. God establishes the terms for fellowship with Him (which Scripture describes as Life), and they are absolute. By eating of the forbidden fruit, Adam and Eve broke their perfect relationship with God. They chose to trust Satan rather than God; thus they became Satan's subjects. The result was immediate and irrevocable: death. Their peaceful relationship with God was shattered beyond their ability to repair it because they were spiritually dead. Physically, death was also immediate in that the aging process began at that point.

We see overwhelming evidence of God's agape love when He made an immediate provision to deliver us from the clutches of Satan through spiritual rebirth. He promised to act to restore life to the corpse of humanity.

This lesson leads the students to recognize their natural helplessness and God's mercy in offering them new life--a sure promise that provides salvation for all as a free gift. The introductory story clearly demonstrates the infallibility of God's pronouncements and the universal, inescapable, ugly scars that result from following Satan.

INTRODUCTION (Objective 1)

Use the first part of the Student Book material to set the stage for students to reflect on and perhaps to share incidents when they were burdened with guilt. You might want to encourage this by briefly sharing such an experience of your own.

Review what had happened in Paradise. Adam and Eve lost a perfect universe and perfect fellowship with God because they chose not to abstain from the fruit of a single tree. Emphasize the infallibility of God's pronouncements and the certain consequences of sin. See **Is. 59:2.**

DEAD IS DEAD (Objectives 2, 3, and 4)

Ask the class what they can get for nothing these days. Jot some sayings on the board (e.g., "You get what you pay for" "There is no such thing as a free lunch"). Students may suggest others. This reflects the philosophy of secular humanism. We like to feel we've earned our way. The idea of a "self-made man" appeals to our egos.

Have a student read **Eph. 2:1-3** aloud before considering the questions posed in the Student Book. Help the class to see in **2:3** that we were all born spiritually dead (a consequence of the Fall) and that in this condition we were all followers of Satan **(2:1-2)**.

Ask what the Bible might mean in today's terms by "gratifying the cravings of our sinful nature." List some "cravings" on the board (e.g., money, power, fame, gluttony, drunkenness, thrills, revenge). Today's secular humanism insists that "it's your body--do with it whatever feels good." Lead the class to compare this with Satan's urging of Eve to taste the forbidden fruit. Conclude this discussion with a return to the fact of the universal helplessness that was ours because we're born spiritually dead.

GOD'S LOVE NEVER WAVERS (Objective 5)

Draw attention to the unwarranted kindness of our Creator as He responded to Adam and Eve cowering the bushes. (a) God called to Adam **(Gen. 3:9)**. (b) Adam "plea bargained" **(3:10)**. (c) God directed Adam's attention to the source of his trouble by saying, "Who told you?" **(3:11a)** and invited his confession and repentance **(3:11b)**. (d) Adam blamed Eve--and God **(3:12)**. (e) God invited Eve to confess **(3:13a)**. (f) Eve blamed the serpent but did admit to having been deceived **(3:13b)**.

THE RESULTS OF SIN (Objectives 1 and 6)

As you examine **3:14-19**, contrast the perfect universe of Paradise with the environment that resulted when Satan got his way, emphasizing Satan as the source of all evil. The serpent was cursed and condemned to crawling on his belly. Even as rainbows remind us of promises of God, so serpents remind us of sin, its dangers, and its consequences.

Ask the girls to react to Eve's lot and the boys to Adam's. A lively exchange may result. Emphasize that God did not tell Eve that she could not have a career and did not tell Adam to "lord it over" Eve. God simply foretold how things were going to work out as a result of sin polluting all of creation. Everything was painful and stress-ridden.

Although spiritual death was immediate, physical death is a process. Adam and Eve, created perfect, began to age but lived for centuries. Clothing made of skins necessitated the death and dissection of an animal. These must have been traumatic developments for Adam and Eve.

NEW LIFE IN CHRIST (Objectives 1, 5, 6, and 7)

Contrast our reaction to a deliberate slap in the face (or obvious social snub) to God's merciful promise of salvation through Jesus Christ, the seed of woman. And He did this even before he said one negative word to Eve or Adam!

Ask the students to read **Eph. 2:4-10** in unison. Students should recognize that God is our only hope. His love and mercy motivated Him to resurrect us by grace--a gift of God! Take a little time to revel in this marvelous truth, reflecting with awe and wonder on God's agape love. God has made us corpses alive in Christ! Why? Examine **verse 7**. What joy is ours in Jesus!

Lead the class to see that God asks us to respond--to accept His love and to love Him in return. When we do this, our love will also overflow to our fellow humans and in the "good works" of **verse 10**. Life now has a purpose! We are created new in Christ Jesus. **"If anyone is in Christ, he is a new creation" (2 Cor. 5:17)**. We have been "born again!" **(1 Peter 1:3)**.

ADDITIONAL ACTIVITIES

1. Encourage the students to examine the indications of the plurality of the Lord God in **Genesis 1:26** and **3:22**.

2. Help the class to conclude that eternal life in this sin-ridden world would be hellish. Preventing Adam and Eve from eating of the tree of life was an act of love. Physical death ends our battle with evil and allows us to enter eternal bliss. You might ask, **Have you ever visited a nursing home? Do you know anyone who looks forward to death? Can you picture the misery that would surround us if no one could die? In view of these facts of life and the promise of resurrection for all of us (John 5:28-29 and Rev. 20:12), can you see how physical death has lost its sting and is actually a blessing?**

Session 7: Preserving the Promise

BIBLE BASIS: Gen. 5:1-32; 11:10-26

CENTRAL TRUTH

God used the longevity of the patriarchs to preserve His messages --including His promise of a Savior --during the years before He inspired Moses to record His message in the Bible.

OBJECTIVES

That the students will:

1. Identify an important purpose of longevity in pre-Abramic history --the transmission of God's messages

2. Plot on a graph the lifelines of the patriarchs (ancestors of Jesus) from Adam to Abram

3. Discover that God used the wide overlapping of life-spans to accurately transmit the message of salvation

4. Thank God for sustaining the lives of the patriarchs so they could transmit the message of salvation to several generations

BACKGROUND

Many people, particularly those who emphasize the Darwinian theory of the evolution of the human species, relegate the historical figures in Scriptures to little more than mythology. However, an increasing number of scientists today are voicing their objections to Darwinism on scientific grounds and are proposing a sudden, or catastrophic, emergence of life forms rather than the gradualism of Darwin. The "missing links" required by Darwinism have simply never been found.

Unfortunately, this relatively recent scientific attitude has not filtered down sufficiently into most science textbooks, although the number of references to evolution has been drastically reduced in most recent high school biology texts. Several good references on the new attitude on Darwinian evolution in the scientific community are listed in the bibliography in the back of this book. Not all of these reflect the Biblical approach to the emergence of life, but they do show clearly that Darwinian evolution is not the firmly established and universally accepted "truth" that many people think it is.

Students should understand that a scientific theory is a proposed answer to a question that arises from observations in nature. A theory is a working tool. Scientists use theories to organize further observations and experiments. But a theory is not intended to be an article of faith. One does not "believe in" a theory the way that one believes in God or in love or in brotherhood. In fact, a scientist may propose and work with two contradictory theories at the same time! And even when a theory is confirmed by more observations and becomes a so-called law, it is still not an absolute fact. New observations may at any time contradict a theory and make it necessary to reject it altogether. This is exactly what is beginning to happen to the Darwinian theory of evolution.

A dictum in science states that "no amount of observation can ever prove a theory absolutely, but a single observation can disprove it." This continuous quest for new knowledge makes science challenging and exciting. But we dare not forget the limitations of the scientific method. The personal interviews of famous scientists in chapter 2 of _The God of Science_ make this point forcefully.

The reliability of Scriptures, on the other hand, is an article of faith. We can use archaeology and other sciences to verify the accuracy of many Biblical accounts, but we really accept the messages in the Bible by faith. When you believe something, it is an absolute truth for you.

INTRODUCTION (Objective 1)

After opening the class with prayer, ask the students to turn to session 7 in the Student Book so that you can check their homework. (The students should have filled in columns A and C. Some may have completed columns B and D as well. Make a note of the latter as possible leaders for the last part of the lesson.)

The Student Book introduces the topic of oral communication and its pitfalls. To underscore this concept, start two conflicting messages at opposite corners of the room. Tell two selected students to whisper the message to the person seated next to them and continue the process until everyone in the room has received it. Use any item of current school interest. Or invent a completely fictitious message. Here is a possibility: "Disneyland in California will be tripled in size because it has been found that Disneyworld in Florida was built on a contaminated landfill and will have to be leveled before the end of the year." The conflicting message at the other end of the room could be "Disneyworld in Florida is three times as large and so much more popular than Disneyland in California that the California site may be sold for a children's museum."

The last student to receive each message will give that message, as he or she received it, to the entire class. In all probability, this activity will demonstrate the inaccuracy of oral communication.

HOW GOD KEPT THE MESSAGE STRAIGHT
(Objectives 2, 3, and 4)

Briefly discuss the seeming impossiblity that the message of salvation could be clearly passed along for some 2,000 years. Lead students to recognize that with God nothing is impossible. He may have used means we know nothing about, but the information He gave us in **Gen. 5:1-32** and **11:10-26** shows one means God used.

Point out to the students that by adding the figures in columns A and B for an individual in the Student Book, they can determine the figure in column B for the next person. By adding columns B and C for a given person, they obtain the figures for column D. Choose a student who understands this method and who may already have completed the columns as homework, and have that student explain the computations to the class. Choose another student to write the figures on the board. All students should enter the resulting figures in their books.

See **Gen. 5 and 11** for answers for columns A and C.

The corrects answers for "Date of Birth" are 0, 130, 235, 325, 395, 460, 622, 687, 874, 1,056, 1,556, 1,656, 1,691, 1,721, 1,755, 1,785, 1,817, 1,847, 1,876, 1,946.

The correct answers for "Date of Death" are 930, 1,042, 1,140, 1,235, 1,290, 1,422, 987, 1,656, 1,651, 2,006, 2,156, 2,094, 2,124, 2,185, 1,994, 2,024, 2,047, 1,995, 2,081, 2,121.

Next, have several students cut ribbons to represent the length of each life span (1"=25 years) while others mark the birth date of each man on a previously prepared wall graph. (Instructions for the preparation of this graph are given below.) Then tape each ribbon in place. Another approach would be to assign one patriarch to each student. He/she should cut a ribbon to the proper length and tape it in the correct position on the graph. Those who finish first could be assigned a second patriarch if there are more patriarchs than students in the class. Students would use any spare time by entering birth dates on their Student Book graphs and filling in the lifelines for future reference.

Discuss the resulting insights. These should include the following:

1. Several of the patriarchs were alive at any given time. Lamech, father of Noah, was 56 years old when Adam died. Noah was a contemporary of all the preceding patriarchs except Adam and Seth. Noah's son, Shem, lived until Abram was 150 years old! Abram's father was 128 years old when Noah died.

2. Methuselah died the year of the Flood.

3. Life spans declined rapidly after the Flood.

THE CLASSROOM GRAPH

Materials: A roll of brown wrapping paper, 30" wide; a measuring stick with metric and English markings; a black marking pen that makes heavy lines; tacks or tape for fastening graph to the wall; red ribbon, 1" wide and 50'long; cellulose tape; scissors.

Cut a 10' length from the wrapping paper and lay it on the floor horizontally. Draw a line along the complete length of the paper 5" from the top. Beginning at the right of this line, mark off 24 4" segments and label them as follows from left to right: Creation, 100 AC, 200 AC, and so on, up to 2,400 AC. (AC stands for "After Creation.")

In a column at the left under the horizontal line, print the names of the 20 patriarchs from Adam to Abraham. Leave a vertical space of 1" for each name. This will facilitate the use of 1" ribbons to show the life span of each patriarch.

Title the graph: Lifelines of the Patriarchs.

Hang the graph where it is easily visible by all the students and readily accessible for adding the ribbon life lines.

Announce that the Student Book graphs will be checked during the next class session.

Session 8: Sin Grows and Grows (Cain and Abel)

BIBLE BASIS: Gen. 4

CENTRAL TRUTH

Left to ourselves, sin would separate us from God and would move us toward total rebellion. But God delivers us from our sin and gives us peace.

OBJECTIVES

That the students will:

1. Compare the struggle against sin with the struggle of a person mired in quicksand
2. Describe the consequences of sin in Cain's life
3. Identify faith as the means to please God
4. Describe the sorrow we experience here on earth because of sin
5. Rejoice in the peace that God gives them

BACKGROUND

Probably most students have heard or read the story of Cain and Abel many times. Therefore this lesson focuses on only one aspect of the story--the effect of sin in the life of Cain.

Society tends to foster the idea, "Don't worry about one little sin. It won't hurt you--especially if you don't get caught!" People also avoid terms like sin. We talk about mistakes, goofs, errors, etc.

Sin is real. Sin does damn. Therefore we need to face it head on. We need to confess our inability to fight against it on our own. Thanks be to God, however, He has rescued us. Through faith in Christ we enjoy His forgiveness and have the power to resist the temptations of Satan. Through faith in Christ we enjoy real peace. That's the message you will want to leave with your students today.

INTRODUCTION (Objective 1)

Have someone read the opening paragraph in the Student Book. Then invite the students to share their own experiences--real or vicarious--with quicksand. Try to get them to describe the completely helpless, panicky feeling of someone who realized he or she is mired deeply in quicksand. Then ask, **What comparisons can you make between quicksand and sin?**

Check the Student Books for graph completion during the **"Sin--Again"** discussion. The graphs will be needed for session 10.

SIN--AGAIN!

If this incident is new to some in your class, ask one who knows the story to summarize it for the others.

Help students see the degeneration that had occurred. **Gen. 2** described complete happiness--perfect intimacy with God. **Gen. 3** told how this intimacy was broken. Adam and Eve disobeyed God, and then lied to Him. Now, in **Gen. 4**, we find other sins, including murder. Ask, **Can you give an example of the same thing happening nowadays--of some "little sin" leading to "bigger" sins, and maybe some serious consequences?**

When confronted with our sins, what does our response revealabout our relationship with God? Emphasize that God holds us individually and personally responsible for our daily decisions. No one can make our decisions for us. When confronted with our sinfulness, we usually repent or resent; we yield to God's love or we resist it.

Following are suggested answers for this section:

1. Shepherd.
2. Farmer.
3. Cain.
4. God did not look with favor upon His offering.
5. Faith.
6. He belonged to the evil one; his own actions were evil.
7. God told the Israelites to bring first fruit offerings, and not to bring anything with a defect for an offering.
8. Answers might include the call by a parent for someone to stop doing some kind of sin.
9. He killed Abel.
10. No.
11. Undoubtedly God wanted Cain to confess his sin.
12. In **Gen. 3:9**, etc.
13. Answers will vary.

SIN BRINGS SORROW (Objective 4)

Before you begin this section, review the greatest sorrow sin brings--eternal separation from God in hell. Also review the Good News: through faith in Jesus we have been saved.

When we look at life here on earth, we can't always tell what caused a given sorrow. At times (as when someone who has been drinking has an accident) we clearly see a cause-effect relationship. At other times, however, "sinful" people seem to prosper, and "good" Christians have all kinds of trouble. Emphasize that all sorrow is caused by sin, but that it's foolish to try to analyze a specific cause for each problem we face. Point out that God loves us--very much--and will take all sorrow away when we get to heaven.

Suggested answers for this section:

1. The ground would not yield crops for him; he would be a restless wanderer.
2. Despair.
3. God put a mark on Cain to keep others from killing him.
4. God loves everyone, including our enemies, He sends them rain and sunshine; being "rich toward God" is much more important than being rich with earthly goods; limitless earthly wealth is nothing compared to the salvation of our souls.
5. When we live according to the Spirit, we desire spiritual blessings.

GOD BRINGS PEACE

After reading the first paragraph together, talk about recent news items that demonstrate the lack of peace within people who have achieved great possessions, power, or pleasure. Ask, **Why do you think this person (these people) did not find peace? What advice would you give them?**

Have someone read **John 16:33** aloud. Ask, **What's special about the peace Jesus is talking about here? How can you be sure YOU can have this peace?**

Then ask someone to paraphrase **Phil. 4:4-7**. Close by basking in the joy that is ours because God first of all created us, then redeemed us, and now keeps us faithful to Him.

Session 9: New Courage (Noah)

BIBLE BASIS: Gen. 6--8

CENTRAL TRUTH

God-fearing people are not "pushovers"; God gives them the courage of their convictions in the face of all odds because they know that He always keeps His Word and protects His people with His gracious power.

OBJECTIVES

That the students will:

1. "Walk in Shem, Ham, and Japheth's sandals" as they experience the derision and mockery of their peers
2. Face for themselves the options that confronted Shem, Ham, and Japheth
3. Express trust in God to give them the courage to stand firm in their convictions as Christians
4. Identify with the exultation of Noah's family as God "remembered" them
5. Identify Jesus as their Savior

BACKGROUND

The story of the Flood continues to capture people's imagination. Curiosity about Noah's ark has stimulated numerous expeditions to Mount Ararat, especially in recent years. Among the most prominent of these searches are those of former astronaut James Irwin. But so far the findings of all the Ararat expeditions are inconclusive. The Ark on Ararat, by Tim LaHaye and John Morris, summarizes the searches for Noah's ark. One chapter, "An Engineer Looks at Noah's Ark," provides other interesting information. You might use the book for extra credit reports by interested students.

Nearly every tribe and nation on the face of the earth alludes to a global flood in its mythology and writings. (The Ark on Ararat gives a comprehensive list of these accounts.) Secular humanists relentlessly attack the Biblical account of the Flood, and Satan tries to use such attacks to weaken, if not destroy, the childlike faith of the uninformed student. Pray that through this lesson God will strengthen the students' faith in Him and His Word as they carefully examine the Biblical record and deal with several typical objections to it.

Chapter 3 of The Bible and Modern Science, by Henry Morris, provides particularly helpful background material for teachers.

PEER PRESSURE IN NOAH'S DAY (Objective 1)

Begin with prayer. Use the materials in the Student Book introduction to lead into a discussion of the peer pressure Noah and his sons must have experienced.

Point out that the climate before the Flood must have been considerably different from today's climate. For example, **Gen. 2:5-6** indicates that streams (RSV: "mist") watered the earth, and rain had not yet been sent by God. This would account for the fact that rainbows were apparently unknown before the Flood **(Gen. 9:12-17)**.

Conclusion: God sometimes arranges unexpected and unusual happenings. So we should take warnings against wickedness seriously (but never doubt God's love or His power to save from earthly troubles those who are "righteous" in His sight).

PEER PRESSURE TODAY (Objective 2)

We do not need the explanations that appear in this section, since we accept the entire Bible by faith, including the things we cannot understand. However, as students confront some of the objections they may face in the academic world, God may use these thoughts to help them resist temptations.

Many recent books and articles written by competent scientists repudiate the anti-Biblical theories of secular humanism on scientific grounds. The Flood, by Alfred Rehwinkel, contains a wealth of geological and archaeological information relative to this lesson.

In connection with the objection that the ark could not house so many animals, you might point out that all races of humanity stemmed from Noah; hence many varieties of animals could derive from a single pair as well. Also, the animals that God preserved in the ark could very well have been young, thereby requiring a minimum of space, food, and care. So there is really no valid objection to fitting the necessary animals into the given space. It is even possible that, if dinosaurs were still alive at the time of the Flood, baby dinosaurs could have been preserved on the Ark.

With regard to objection 2 in the Student Book, **Gen. 1:6-8** refers to an expanse of water above and below the sky. The Canopy Theory suggests that (1) a thick layer of water vapor enveloped the earth before the Flood (much like the dense atmosphere that even now shrouds Venus and some of the other plants), (2) this canopy obscured the sun and prevented the formation of rainbows, (3) such a canopy produced better living conditions than we have today, such as moderate temperatures throughout the world, and (4) the canopy was the source of much of the waters of the Flood.

Some have calculated that the water on earth today would cover the entire globe to a depth of over a mile if the land masses were leveled. Surely, when the "springs of the great deep burst forth" **(Gen. 7:11-12)**, there was a tremendous upheaval. Perhaps the tilt of the earth's axis resulted from the catastrophic events that accompanied God's terrible wrath at the time of the Flood. In fact, if the earth's axis was perpendicular to its orbit during pre-Flood times, there would have been no Arctic ice. Also, Scripture first mentions mountains in the Flood account. Could the first mountains have been formed during that cataclysm?

Gen. 8:1 clearly states that God sent a special wind to make the waters recede after the Flood. Even with that "special" wind, it took at least seven months before Noah's family could leave the ark. The waters could diminish only by evaporation, since there was no place to which they could drain. The water that did not evaporate remained as oceans, which today cover some 2/3 of the earth's surface.

Regarding the objection about the extent of the Flood **(Gen. 7:18-24)**, a flood that lasted 150 days before land became visible again had to be global. What kind of "walls" would confine it to a given area? The presence of flood narratives in most cultures also testify to a universal flood.

NOAH'S FAITH (Objective 3)

It's difficult to comprehend the trauma of the experience of Noah's family: the derision of the crowds, the frustration of not being able to convince anyone else of the gravity of the situation, being sealed in a watertight vessel for an unknown period of time, hearing the screams of the drowning people and the cacophony of animal sounds, the violence of natural forces that were unleashed, the tossing of the rudderless ship, the stench of excrement, the seemingly endless waiting. God, in His mercy, used extraordinary means to speed up the processes of global flooding and evaporation, but Noah's family still suffered some strong side effects of the world's wickedness.

Have students read **Matt. 24:36-42** aloud in unison. Discuss briefly its clear and relevant message.

GOD'S LOVE NEVER FAILS (Objective 5)

Noah's story is another part of God's love letter to us. God even saw to it that Noah had "clean" animals to sacrifice as an act of worship in response to His invitation to leave the ark a year and 10 days after He sealed them into it. What joy they must have experienced! Alone in the flood-ravaged world, they were living proof of God's love to His obedient children!

This loving God promised that He would never again curse the ground with a flood or destroy humanity, and that as long as the earth endures the seasons will continue their life-supporting cycle.

NOAH IN THE NEW TESTAMENT (Objective 5)

Compare Noah's warnings of the Flood with Jesus' warnings about the end of the world. In this way Noah was a type of Christ.

Rejoice with the students in the power to save that God gives through Baptism. Jesus' resurrection assures that He has the power to save.

You might end this session with a spontaneous hymn of praise.

Session 10: A New Day Dawns

BIBLE BASIS: Gen. 9--10

CENTRAL TRUTH

At times God deals with His people in new ways, but He always deals with them in grace.

OBJECTIVES

That the students will:

1. Examine the new aspects of the relationships between God and Noah and his family

2. Consider possible causes for shorter life spans

3. Trace the descendants of Noah to better understand Noah's prophetic pronouncements

4. Discover evidence that God's mercy continues through all times and circumstances

5. Discuss the spiritual significance of rainbows

6. Identify Jesus as the saving Light, who makes rainbows in our times of sorrow

BACKGROUND

The data collected and graphed in session 7 will be reexamined as the class considers the "new day" that dawned after the Flood and the instructions God gave to Noah and his sons.

Since the Fall and God's promise of salvation, much of our life on this earth is a training ground for eternity. All of history is "His story"--the story of God's redeeming work on earth--and it will end when He chooses. The Flood is a major event that marks the beginning of a new era. The supplementary readings listed in session 9 highlight the catastrophic occurrences that accompanied the Flood.

Before the Flood, God clearly stated that man's days will be 120 years **(Gen. 6:3)**. The average life span up to that time was nearer 900 years. So it is abundantly clear that God's purpose prevailed!

As students examine possible "natural" causes for this change, help them focus on God as the author and sustainer of nature. Pray that God will strengthen the students' faith through new insights into His wisdom, power, and infallibility.

A NEW LIFE SPAN (Objectives 1 and 2)

Open with prayer. Include the request for childlike acceptance of God's Word and a healthy intellectual curiosity.

Ask the class, **What was the root cause of the Flood?** They should quote **Gen. 6:3-5**, among other verses. Help them to see that everyone but Noah and his family ignored God's commands. God is patient, but He is not forgetful --then or now **(2 Peter 3:9-10)**.

Refer to the graph the students made during session 7. Using a blue marking pen, draw a vertical line to represent the Flood (1,656 A.C.). Observe how life spans shorten gradually but decidedly from that point onward. Observe that God can act outside the "laws of nature" since He ordained them in the first place. But, more often than not, God acts through natural laws to bring about His purposes. Use the materials in the Student Book in the search for the "natural" causes of shorter life spans after the Flood.

The canopy that was mentioned in session 9 may have been the source of the extraordinary amount of water required to flood the entire earth and would explain the absence of rainbows before the Flood. Here are some additional points regarding the life-shortening side effects of the Canopy Theory that are given in the Student Book:

1. Data from numerous space flights indicate that ultraviolet, X-ray, and cosmic radiation is even more dangerous than had been previously thought. Astronomers continually monitor the sun for disruptive flares that spew life-threatening particles and rays into space. Scientists may even reschedule space voyages to avoid passing through these outbursts.

2. The weight of the vapor canopy around the earth before the Flood could have produced atmospheric pressures approximately double that of the present day. It probably included a high concentration of healing oxygen.

3. The reduction of the so-called greenhouse effect after the Flood would result in wider temperature ranges, higher winds, and more spotty precipitation.

The pamphlet, "The Sky Has Fallen," (see the bibliography), contains a good description of the Canopy Theory.

NEW FOOD (Objective 1)

You might discuss the pros and cons of eating meat. Most people rejoice because God permits them to eat meat, but some believe that meat is, in itself, a life-shortening factor. Point out that Nick's friend may be a vegetarian for that reason.

"OLD" LOVE (Objective 4)

As students work through the this lesson, they may observe that the main differences before and after the Flood dealt with externals--a shorter life span and new food. But the "internals" remained the same; people still sinned, and God's love still abounded. (In **Heb. 11**, for example, God mentions Noah's faith but says nothing about his drunkenness.)

God did not give up on the human race. Have the class read **2 Peter 3:3-13** in unison and discuss its relevance.

SIN--AGAIN! (Objective 1)

Alcohol is not considered evil in and of itself (**Deut. 14:26** and **Ps. 104:15**), and Jesus approved of the use of wine by miraculously making it at the Wedding of Cana. But Scripture also praises abstinence from alcohol (**Dan. 1:8-17** and **Luke 1:15**). And the warnings against excessive drinking are numerous and strong (**Is. 5:11, 22; Deut. 21:20-21; Prov. 20:1; Luke 21:34; Rom. 13:13**). Alcohol is associated with God's judgment (**Ps. 75:8** and **Rev. 14:10, 19**). Today alcoholism is a major cause of death; it causes fatal accidents on the highways, prompts violence in homes, and dissipates both body and mind. The ravages of alcohol are not partial to any age, sex, race, or socio-economic level. In Satan's hands, alcohol is a life-shortening agent!

God mercifully records the shortcomings of Biblical heroes to teach and encourage us. Let us choose to "defend him, speak well of him, and put the best construction on everything," as Luther admonishes.

WHAT IS GOSSIP? (Objective 4)

Encourage a frank and open exchange on the topic of gossip. Webster's Ninth New Collegiate Dictionary defines gossip as a "rumor or report of an intimate nature." Encourage students to ask themselves two questions before passing on information: (1) Is it true? (2) Is it helpful?

Shem and Japheth's actions could have been carried out by Ham with no one else being informed. Ham was obviously titillated by the unexpected scene.

GOD SPEAKS THROUGH NOAH (Objectives 3 and 4)

Be sure the students recognize that the Canaanite nations that were driven out by the Israelites are named after and descended from this same Canaan, the grandson of Noah. God frequently denounced idolatry and accompanying sexual perversion as the reason for the destruction of these nations.

Lest the students take the fatalistic stand that the Canaanites were predetermined by Noah's curse to a life of wickedness, note that not all of Canaan's descendants are named among the nations to be wiped out.

The migration and proliferation of Noah's descendants will be treated more thoroughly in connection with the Tower of Babel.

RAINBOWS (Objectives 5 and 6)

Gift shops have rainbows in the form of stickers, stationery, ceramic desk sets, mobiles, pillows, and wall hangings to mention only a few. Bedroom ensembles and wallpaper represent some of the more ambitious commitments to this decorating theme. Cheer Bear (one of the popular Care Bears of the 1980s) sports a rainbow on his rotund tummy. The rainbow's message of cheer and hope has permeated society. And well it should, since it was a sign given to all living creatures (**Gen. 9:9, 14-17**). Help the students to see that God truly loves and cares for all His creatures.

For the Christian, it is helpful to reflect on the dual ingredients of rainbows--sunshine and rain. God often breaks through the tears of our lives with His "Sonshine" to form beautiful "rainbows."

Session 11: Concluding Activities for Units 1 and 2

This guide will provide evaluation activities for each unit. Use them as a review, a test, or in another way that seems appropriate to you. Since classes and students vary, we urge you to adapt the activities. Always review or test concepts you covered in class--even if they differ from those that appear here or in the corresponding Student Book pages.

The Student Book activities for unit 11 have been designed to help students prepare for an evaluation activity you will provide.

MULTIPLE CHOICE

1. The main purpose of the Bible is to
   (A) explain how the universe was created
   (B) describe the origin of life
   (C) tell about God's love for us in Jesus
   (D) warn against sin
2. Which of the following is not a type of book in the Bible?
   (A) mystery (C) prophecy
   (B) poetry (D) history
3. Eve was created because
   (A) Adam asked God for a mate
   (B) Eve was meant to be inferior to Adam
   (C) God wanted Adam to have companionship
4. After the fall into sin God promised
   (A) a Savior (C) happiness in Eden
   (B) marriage (D) childbirth without pain
5. Which of the following was not one of the things God told Adam and Eve they could do in the Garden of Eden?
   (A) Eat the plants in the garden
   (B) Rule over the other creatures
   (C) Eat the animals in the garden
   (D) Subdue the environment
6. Adam and Eve could live in the Garden of Eden as long as they
   (A) tended the garden
   (B) did not eat any of the fruit in the garden
   (C) did not eat from the tree of the knowledge of good and evil
   (D) had children
7. While talking to the serpent in the Garden of Eden, God
   (A) promised a Savior for us sinners
   (B) took away Satan's power to tempt people
   (C) blamed Satan for the actions of Adam and Eve
   (D) said that He would destroy the world
8. The first people who are mentioned in the Bible as meat eaters are
   (A) Adam and Eve
   (B) Cain and Abel
   (C) Methuselah and his family
   (D) Noah's family
9. The life spans of people became gradually shorter after
   (A) the time of Cain and Abel
   (B) the time of the Flood
   (C) the time of Abraham
10. The Flood resulted from rains that fell for a period of
   (A) 1 week (B) 40 days
   (C) 100 days (D) 1 year

TRUE-FALSE (Circle T for True and F for False.)

T F 1. God created the universe so that He and His creatures will reap pleasure from it. (T)

T F 2. The marriage vow lasts for life. (T)

T F 3. By His life, death, and resurrection, Jesus took away Satan's power over death. (T)

T F 4. Once we come to faith in Jesus, all consequences of sin are removed. (F)

T F 5. After Adam and Eve sinned, God gave them a chance to confess. (T)

T F 6. Sin brought consequences to Eve, but not to Adam. (F)

T F 7. Some statements in the story of creation refer to God as a plural being. (T)

T F 8. In describing the age of the patriarchs, the term year should be understood as meaning months. (F)

T F 9. Methuselah may have died in the Flood. (T)

T F 10. Noah took exactly two of every kind of animal into the ark. (F)

MATCHING

(Some choices at the right will be used more than once; others will not be used at all.)

5 Shem
10 Abel
9 Satan
5 Japheth
3 Adam
4 Serpent
8 Noah
1 Cain
7 Methuselah
6 Eve

1. First murderer
2. Father of Noah
3. First father
4. A form Satan took
5. Son of Noah
6. First person to be tempted by Satan
7. Noah's grandfather
8. Built an ark
9. First sinner
10. First murder victim
11. Never died
12. Lived more than 1,000 years

COMPLETION

1. The most important part of God's creation is [people].

2. God told Adam and Eve that if they would eat the forbidden fruit they would [die].

3. St. Paul compares the relationship between Christ and His church to that between [husband and wife].

4. Abel's occupation was that of a(n) [shepherd].

5. To give God our firstfruits means to [give our best].

6. Before the Flood, the earth was watered by [mist--or streams] instead of rain.

7. The total number of people in the ark was [8].

8. The first drunkard mentioned in the Bible is [Noah].

9. God's sign that He will not destroy the earth with a flood again is [the rainbow].

10. God promised a Savior for us sinners when we couldn't save ourselves because [He loves us].

ESSAYS

(On a separate sheet of paper, write briefly about any 4 of the following 10 topics. Be sure to put the number of the topic at the beginning of each essay.)

1. Why can we refer to the Bible as God's "love letter"?

2. Compare the Flood and Baptism.

3. Describe the difference between the way God created Adam and the way He created Eve.

4. Describe an appropriate way to observe Sunday.

5. Tell how to overcome the temptations of Satan.

6. How is the Canopy Theory related to the life spans of the people before the Flood?

7. List evidences of God's love for Cain.

8. What is God's attitude toward alcholic beverages?

9. Tell how sin grows and grows.

10. What does God expect us to do in response to His love for us in sending Jesus to be our Savior?

Feel free to duplicate the above questions for use in testing. Please add the following credit line: Concordia Publishing House, copyright 1986. Used by permission.

Unit 3: God's Covenant with Abraham

In this unit, we will examine God's unfolding covenant relationship with His children. In so doing, we will emphasize His faithfulness and trustworthiness in spite of the foibles of His followers.

God nurtured Abraham's faith and called him to the special task of covenant-bearer. The processes of selection and separation culminated in a covenant people set apart: the children of Israel.

PLANNING THE UNIT

Session 12: Assemble advertisements that illustrate the egocentricity that secular humanism fosters in our day (e.g., cosmetic ads that say, "I'm worth it!" Get a copy of the Humanist Manifesto and highlight several blatantly anti-Christian parts. A student in the class who is interested in architecture might write a report on the amazing engineering aspects of the ziggurat.

Session 13: Make a copy of the

Ferrel story in the Sept. 12, 1984, issue of the New York Times, page A18. Alert the librarian to possible requests for articles and books refuting astrology. Refer students to pertinent articles in the Lutheran Witness, (e.g., December 1983 and May 1984 issues). Discuss with other religion teachers the possibility of a cooperative project, such as a "thanksgiving" basket for the poor or collecting and restoring old toys for needy children.

Session 14: Alert the librarian to possible requests for materials for a report on homosexuality. Bring articles from recent publications dealing with the problem of homosexuality today.

Session 17: A chick incubator and some fertile eggs could add visual dimensions to the concept of the struggle that is necessary to life. A film clip on hatching eggs might be simpler to use and just as effective.

Session 12: Tongues and Races (Babel)

BIBLE BASIS: Gen. 11:1-9

CENTRAL TRUTH

Because human disobedience and pride interfered with God's plan of salvation, He supernaturally intervened in human history to bring about a variety of races and languages. Thus God in His grace kept people humble--a prerequisite for life as His children.

OBJECTIVES

That the students will:

1. Recognize that worship and glorification of God are characteristics of His people, while pride or self-glorification are characteristics of those who are deceived by Satan
2. Examine themselves for evidence of pride or humility and discuss their reactions to pride or humility in others
3. Recognize racism and prejudice as attitudes that are displeasing to God
4. Describe God's natural and supernatural involvement in present-day events

BACKGROUND

In this "ME generation," where godless self-actualization is touted as humanity's highest goal, it is helpful to take a hard look at where that goal has led many of its seekers: drug addiction (including alcoholism), broken homes, sexual perversion, and violence. Secular humanists have negated God and every other authoritarian institution, including the traditional family, in favor of whatever is thought to promote the individual's freedom to explore and develop his or her "unique" identity. This often leads to pain and confusion.

Keeping God's ordinances, which many consider to be outmoded mythology, invites ridicule. The attacks of secular humanists are becoming bolder and more vitriolic all the time. Consider the January-February 1983 issue of The Humanist, which states that the classroom must become an arena of conflict between the old and the new, between "the rotting corpse of Christianity, together with all its adjacent evils and misery," and the new faith of humanism--"it will undoubtedly be a long, ardous, painful struggle replete with much sorrow and many tears, but humanism will emerge triumphant. It must if the family of humankind is to survive."

Many secular humanists consider disobedience to God to be a mark of clear-thinking individualists who have thrown off the shackles of traditional religion.

The story of the tower of Babel presents an all-too-familiar life-style. In direct opposition to God's command to fill the earth, the inhabitants of Babel took deliberate steps to thwart God's purpose. God reacted decisively: He confused the languages. This confusion illustrates the divisive nature and result of sin. But we also see that in His love

God "sanctified" even the results of sin for human good. The variety of languages led to mass migrations. God thus thwarted the developing pride, a characteristic that would keep people from turning to Him.

The goal of this lesson is to promote the glorification of God and and a spirit of humility toward Him and toward our fellow human beings.

PRIDE VERSUS HUMILITY (Objectives 1 and 2)

Use this section to identify God's clear teaching about pride and humility. Briefly discuss evidences of conceit and how conceit often leads to actions of braggadocio. Use the discussion to encourage the virtues of humility and compassion.

PRIDE AT BABEL (Objective 1)

Have **Genesis 11:1-9** read in class, preferably in unison. Point out that the Tower of Babel was probably similar to the so-called ziggurats, or artificial temple hills, that have been discovered in Sumeria and Babylonia. Halley's Bible Handbook provides additional information on this topic.

Emphasize that people built these structures primarily for idolatrous worship and self-glorification. People did not long remember God's message through the Flood; another supernatural intervention came about 100 years later! (See **Gen. 10:25** and **11:16**.) Enter it on your time line at 1,771 A.C.

In **Gen. 9:1** God gave instructions to "fill the earth." His plan included even the places where His children were to live **(Acts 17:24-28)**. When people followed their own selfish desires instead of God's plan, they sinned just as Eve did in Eden. Encourage students to share their own struggles to be obedient to God's will rather than to follow the world's advice to "look out for Number 1."

Help the students recognize that God's people often find benefits even in the most difficult circumstances. Ask students to give examples from their own lives and in the lives of their families. For example, the father may lose his job only to find a better one.

GOD INTERVENES (Objective 3)

Survey your class to see how many languages are represented. Ask one student to say, "Hello, how are you?" in one language and another to respond, "I am quite well, thank you," in another. A third student could then ask the previous speakers in a third language, "What are you talking about?" This activity should give an effective illustration of the plight of the people of Babel.

Briefly discuss racial differences and similarities. It was once thought that blood transfusions between members of different races were impossible. Now we know that blood types do not depend on race, and blood banks do not specify the race of a donor on the specimen. (Ask a hospital or other blood bank to verify this.) Stress the common ancestry of all races--Adam and Eve, Noah and his family--and examine the texts on racism in the Student Book.

GOD STILL INTERVENES (Objective 4)

As an outgrowth of the discussion in this session, you might talk about the work of Bible translators. For information write to Lutheran Bible Translators Inc., 303 N. Lake Street, Call Box 2050, Aurora, IL 60507-2050. Encourage students to consider becoming missionaries or Bible translators.

Read **Acts 2:1-21** in class. Discuss similarities and differences between Babel and Pentecost. At Babel God confused the languages and scattered the people. On Pentecost He empowered His disciples to speak to people who spoke various languages, thus uniting them in His church. The Pentecost beginning will finally be completed in heaven, when once again all will praise their God with one common tongue, just as was possible before Babel.

Session 13: Abram--Spiritual Giant with Clay Feet

BIBLE BASIS: Gen. 12

CENTRAL TRUTH

God moved Abram, product of an idolatrous society, to obey His call. Abram received spiritual blessings beyond his powers to comprehend, but he still had to face earthly problems.

OBJECTIVES

That the students will:

1. Recognize that God still calls people to serve Him in special ways
2. Locate the cities of Ur, Haran, Shechem, and Bethel in the Fertile Crescent of the Middle East
3. Imagine standing in Abram's sandals as he receives God's call
4. Discuss the uses that God wants us to make of our blessings
5. Distinguish between sanctification and the unscriptural doctrine of justification by works
6. Describe the spiritual giant Abram as an erring but forgiven human and accept God's forgiveness for their own failures
7. Reach out to others with the message of forgiveness

BACKGROUND

The signs of the zodiac are marketed today in jewelry and wall hangings and on clothing and stationery. Astrologers are in demand on talk shows and as guest speakers for social groups. Horoscopes are cast at prestigious resorts and are printed in countless magazines. Abram's father, Terah, would feel right at home in present day America! Young people, who face so many puzzling decisions, are drawn to horoscopes, Ouija boards, tarot cards, and the like for answers. It is important that we identify all guidance-seeking of this sort as idolatry--as turning to someone or something other than God for direction in our lives. These pursuits are not just harmless pastimes. They are wrong and they are dangerous.

Through faith Abram resisted such Satanic gods. Abram was willing to lose all he held dear in order to follow the one true God. Read **Rom. 4** and **Heb. 11:8-19** for a New Testament description of Abram's faith.

In this lesson the goal is to expose Satan's deceptive tactics and to reaffirm the eternal and temporal values that stem from obedience to our living and loving God.

INTRODUCTION (Objectives 1 and 5)

Open with prayer.

The introduction in the Student Book presents a young boy who answered God's call to help his fellowman. You can find more details in the Sept. 12, 1984, issue of the New York Times. You might follow up this story with an individual or class library project. Students may be inspired to start a similar campaign in their own school or neighborhood.

ABRAM'S ROOTS (Objectives 2 and 3)

Use a large wall map to show the Fertile Crescent. (See the latest Concordia Publishing House catalog for order information.) Help students to locate Ur, Haran, Shechem, Bethel, and Egypt. Point out that the distance from Ur to Haran is about 600 miles and from Haran to Shechem is about 400 miles--and there were no highways! Terah's destination when he left Ur was Canaan, but he paused at Haran and went no further. Perhaps he found a thriving market for idols of the moon gods, since Haran was also a center of moon worship.

Don't push discussion of astrology if there is no interest, but a lively discussion may result even without any prodding. Students are inundated today with stories about the occult. Instead of opening a conversation with, "Haven't I met you somewhere before?" one is now apt to hear, "I'll bet you're a libra, right?" Unfortunately, Christians often read horoscopes regularly. But it is significant to note that they often appear on the comic page of the newspaper!

If any of the students are amateur astronomers or have taken any courses that involve star charts, ask them to explain what is meant by the signs of the zodiac and how the sun moves through these signs during the year. Then point out that the dates that are given in horoscopes no longer correspond with the daily position of the sun in the sky in modern times. Precession, the slow wobble of the earth's axis, makes it necessary to revise star charts every 50 years or so. (An astronomy or physics text would provide more information on precession for students who are interested in studying it further.) Horoscope readers often are shocked when they find out that they are not really under the sign that they thought they were. There are some exceptions, of course, because precession has not yet shifted the stars by a whole constellation, but the discrepancy is getting greater as time passes.

Point out that astronomy is a science, whereas astrology is a religion, and that astrology is incompatible with Christianity because it looks to causes and solutions for the situations of daily life from sources other that God's Word.

Many astronomers and other scientists today are trying to expose astrology as a pseudoscience. An excellent article on this topic, "The Scientific Case Against Astrology," appeared in the November-December 1980 issue of Mercury, the journal of the Astronomical Society of the Pacific. The article cites statistical tests that have shown astrology to be unreliable. The school librarian may be able to help locate other antiastrology literature.

We should thank God for helping Abram--and us--to see through Satan's deceptions. Now we can help others by exposing the myths of astrology!

Help students to wrestle with the enormity of the sacrifice God asked Abram to make--and the nebulous promise it involved: "a country I will show you." Remind the class that Abram was already 75 years old and had no children. Where was this "great nation" to come from? Certainly Abram was a man of faith!

BLESSED TO BE A BLESSING (Objectives 3, 4, and 5)

Read **Gen. 12:2-3** aloud. Then lead the students to examine God's promises closely. While they were nebulous in that they did not give names, places, and times, they did include the following magnificent promises: progeny, prosperity, fame, purpose, encouragement, protection, and worldwide spiritual prominence. Note that both verses end with the message that these blessings for Abram were to result in the blessing of others. "A blessing to others" culminates in the promised Savior, but Abraham and his descendants were a blessing to others throughout the Old Testament.

Apply the concept of "blessed to be a blessing" to our own day. If a student asks how Gentiles can be called "sons of Abram," ask the class to turn to **Rom. 4:16-19** for clarification.

Point out the danger of confusing sanctification--the maturing process we experience as Christians that results in ever more willing obedience and in the sharing of our blessings--with the false doctrine of justification by works, which implies that we must work our way into heaven. **Rom. 3:28** and **5:1** leave no doubt that faith in Jesus--being His disciples--secures heaven for us. **John 13:35** and **1 John 4:7-8** indicate that active love for others is the distinguishing mark of those who have faith.

The possibilities for Trevorlike class projects are as boundless as the imagination and enthusiasm of the class and the leadership of the teacher. Pray together for direction. Anticipate exciting results. Work as a separate class or in cooperation with other classes.

CLAY FEET (Objective 6)

The Nile was a more dependable source of water than was seasonal rainfall. The Bible records several instances when Egypt became a refuge in times of drought.

Briefly review Abram's cowardice in asking Sarai to identify herself as his sister (which she indeed was according to **Gen. 20:12**) and to hide the fact that she was also his wife.

God turned even Abram's cowardice into a blessing as Pharaoh and Abimelech heaped material goods on Abram for Sarai's sake. Stress God's displeasure over extramarital sex--long before the giving of the Ten Commandments.

AMAZING GRACE (Objectives 6 and 7)

Even if time is short, be sure to discuss the insights the New Testament (e.g., **Rom. 4** and **Heb. 11**) provides for the Abram incidents. Church leaders then must have emphasized Abram's actions in a "work righteous" way--and this misinterpretation of Scripture certainly abounds today!

Conclude the session with a strong emphasis on God's great mercy and love (1) in sharing the shortcomings of His heroes and (2) in providing redemption freely through Jesus. Now we need never never despair and we can offer hope to even the most wayward persons.

Session 14: God's Chosen People

BIBLE BASIS: Gen. 13--15; 17:1-17; 18:1-19; 21:8-21

CENTRAL TRUTH

God's covenant with Abram assured him that God would provide for all his physical and spiritual needs and required him to respond with a life of service to God. Our loving God also provides for our needs and calls us to lives of service to Him.

OBJECTIVES

That the students will:

1. Compare the life-styles of Abram and Lot based on their priorities.
2. Discuss the various elements of God's covenant with Abram.
3. Identify ways God's people can be a blessing to others.

BACKGROUND

Christianity is all too often "marketed" as some kind of insurance policy: If we "choose" to be Christians, God "owes" us protection from the problems of this life. This lesson shows that, in marked contrast to the insurance-policy view, when God chooses (calls) an individual to a task (ministry), the individual still faces great risks, and that person's blessings are not always immediately apparent. But God's promises are always trustworthy and their fulfillment far exceeds our human expectations.

The goal of the lesson is to motivate the students to commit themselves wholeheartedly to Jesus Christ as their personal Lord and Savior--to become true "children of Abraham."

INTRODUCTION (Objective 3)

Open with prayer. Allow some time for students to react to the introductory material in the Student Book. Ask volunteers to share experiences about being chosen and finding it to be more demanding than they first thought.

CAPTAIN, PLAYER, OR SPECTATOR? (Objective 1)

As the students provide the answers to the questions in this section, walk around the room and observe which students have completed their homework.

Make sure that the students have identified homosexuality as the sin that had reached epidemic proportions in Sodom and Gomorrah and had incurred God's great wrath. The boldness and pervasiveness of gay and lesbian support groups today should make us question our own effectiveness as Christian witnesses. Point out that sexual perversion is becoming less and less shocking as we are confronted with it on all sides. Pose the question, **Will we have the courage to stem the tide of immorality in our land? If not, will our country, like Sodom and Gomorrah, become an object of God's wrath?**

The students--especially the

girls--may note that Lot's sexual standards had become so warped that he offered his own daughters to the mob to be sexually abused. (These same girls had similarly distorted sexual standards, as evidenced in their successful plot to get their father drunk and commit incest with him.) This was the country of the Canaanites --an example of what happens when sexual distortions become a preoccupation.

As the students compare Abram's and Lot's life-styles, lead them to recognize that Abram left things that he held dear to come closer to his God, while Lot deliberately chose to live near wickedness (**Gen. 13:12-13**). The evil that surrounded him disturbed Lot (**2 Peter 2:7-8**), but not enough to make him leave. Abram built altars and worshiped wherever he went; apparently Lot was so inactive as a witness to his faith that no one outside of his immediate household took him seriously when he warned of God's wrath. It appears that Abram was a blessing to others, while Lot looked out for Lot.

GOD'S COVENANT WITH ABRAM
(Objective 2)

In Ur and Haran, Abram enjoyed the comforts and security of civilized urban life. Now, as a childless nomad, the promises of descendants and land must have sounded truly wonderful. Tell the students to note the repeated emphasis on <u>many</u> descendants; a <u>separate</u> nation, land of their <u>own</u>, and <u>great</u> blessing.

In **Gen. 15:1** God told Abram that <u>He</u> is Abram's reward. <u>He</u> is the limitless source of supply for all of Abram's needs and of his fondest dreams. This seemed to cause a minor panic in Abram. Perhaps he feared that the original covenant was being superseded and that he wouldn't have true heirs after all. Hence the request for a sign. So God designed a ritual that symbolically sealed His covenant.

Point out that the prophecy in **15:13-14** referred to the bondage of the Israelites in Egypt. Explain that the covenant sign, circumcision, did not indicate that only males were under God's covenant. Women were included in the covenant relationship of their fathers or husbands.

In **17:17-18**, even Abraham questioned the way God would carry out His promise. This fact should comfort us when we begin to wonder about our own comprehensions regarding God's promises to us.

Do not dwell on the Ishmael/Isaac contrast at this point. Session 16 will focus on this topic. Instead, stress Abraham's immediate obedience to God's command regarding circumcision.

The students should readily understand that Lot was blessed by his association with Abram. The Student Book refers to Lot as a "player" because he is called a "righteous" man in **2 Peter 2:7-8** and, as such, is part of God's "team." God even blessed "spectators" as Abram rescued all those who were taken into captivity by the invading kings. Compare this to the blessings that are enjoyed by all American citizens because the Constitution recognizes the sovereignty of God and because the founding fathers of our country confessed Him.

CHILDREN OF ABRAHAM THROUGH JESUS
(Objective 3)

Stimulate discussion and self-examination in the light of the contrast between Abram and Lot. Leave ample time for the consideration of the texts at the end of the lesson. These passages emphasize the importance of sanctification--works as evidences of faith. They also contain the clear teaching that it was not Abraham's works but his faith in God that was counted to him for righteousness. **Gal. 3** is especially good as a summary of this truth. <u>Be sure to save class time for discussion of this chapter.</u> Since most people remember more of what they verbalize than of what they only hear, give free reign to student expressions of insights they have gained in this lesson. End the session with a brief summation that we become Abraham's children through faith in Jesus Christ.

ADDITIONAL ACTIVITY

1. Ask the students to list the similarities and differences between circumision and Baptism. Write the lists on the board.

Similarities: God commanded them both; they both involve physical acts; they are both outward signs of a covenant between God and the recipient, a covenant that brings people into God's family.

Differences: Only male children received circumcision whereas both male and female children are baptized. Also, God's command to circumcise applied only to the physical descendants of Abraham and those who were brought into that "family," whereas the command of Jesus to Baptize included all nations.

The discussion of circumcision should emphasize its foreshadowing of Christian Baptism (**Gal. 3:26-29**). The circumcision of infants also undergirds the Scriptural teaching of the baptism of infants. Both are means by which God bestows blessings on the recipients without their rational involvement (works). God did not tell Abraham to wait until the child was old enough to understand the meaning of circumcision and requested it. Similarly, Baptism should not be delayed until some "age of accountability." Of course, when an unbaptized adult becomes a Christian, there is no choice except to baptize him or her as an adult.

Read **Ps. 33** aloud in unison. Note in verses **18-20** whom God helps and shields. Compare this passage with **Gen. 15:1.**

2. As an extra credit activity, have volunteers tell how the following passages tell how one becomes a "child of Abraham"--one of God's chosen people: **Luke 3:7-14; Luke 13:22-30; Luke 16:19-31; Luke 19:1-9; John 8:31-47; Acts 13:26; James 2:20-24.**

Session 15: No Rejects with God (Abraham and Isaac)

BIBLE BASIS: Gen. 16; 17:18--18:15; 22:1-19; 23:1--25:11

CENTRAL TRUTH

"Abraham believed the Lord, and He credited it to him as righteousness" (Gen. 15:6). God works in us to strengthen our faith in all kinds of circumstances. He remained with Abraham through times of weakness and times of strength. And, in the powerful drama of Abraham and Isaac, He foreshadowed the sacrifice He would make through His Son to save us from our sins.

OBJECTIVES

That the students will:

1. Recognize that a gift should never be held in higher esteem than its giver

2. Recognize that God can build faith through hardships

3. Express trust in God to lead them through difficult situations

4. Seek God's help for all of life's decisions--including the selection of a mate

5. Identify Abraham and Isaac as types of God the Father and His only Son, and recognize the love that is illustrated in both instances

BACKGROUND

We often hear the lament, "I didn't get anything out of the church service today," as though worship services are meant to be all take and no give. Our goal in church, as in all of life, should be to worship and praise our wonderful God and glorify His name. Abraham understood this and practiced it, even if it meant sacrificing his long-awaited son and heir.

Abraham learned that is is impossible to outgive God. And he realized that God, the Giver, must always be held in higher esteem than His gifts. When we reverse that order of priority, we no longer hallow God's name. Perhaps you know some dedicated and gifted church workers who have lost sight of this principle and who tend to glory in their gifts, thereby attracting attention to themselves.

If you are familiar with such a situation, you know how many problems it can cause.

In this lesson, we want to encourage the students to see the wisdom of choosing the worship of God as the highest priority in their lives. They should also express a dependence on God, even at times when He doesn't answer their prayers at the times and in the ways they expect.

INTRODUCTION (Objective 1)

Ask if anyone can recall what became of the genie in the story of Aladdin's lamp. Develop this sufficiently to allow students to conclude that emphasis in this legend is on the gifts rather than the giver. Lead them to see that God is sometimes relegated to the status of a genie or some kind of year-round Santa Claus.

SARAI'S IMPATIENCE (Objectives 2 and 3)

Ask, **Do we sometimes get impatient with God and try to "help" Him to answer our prayers?** Take time to discuss examples, such as cheating to "help" get better grades or shoplifting to "help" obtain coveted Christmas presents. Do such "helps" help in the long run? Of course, God does not want us to sit idly by, either, as we wait for our prayers to be answered **(Eph. 4:28)**.

Do not spend time on a discussion of Ishmael and Isaac at this time. Session 16 will focus on this topic. Focus now on the love God showed to Hagar (saving her life and enabling her to live again among Abram's household) and to Abram (preserving his offspring, Ishmael).

Tell the class to read **Gen. 18:14a** together several times. Then tell them to close their Bibles and recite the passage.

Finally, talk about the love God continued to show to Abraham and Sarah, even though they at times showed that they doubted that He could accomplish His goals "on His own." Ask, **How does God deal with us today?**

FAITH TESTED, PRESERVED, AND STRENGTHENED (Objectives 2 and 3)

When considering God's test of Abraham, be sure that the students recognize that the Bible makes it clear that God is against the sacrificing of children **(Jer. 32:35** and **Ezek. 23:36-37)**. Unfortunately, the practice was widespread in Canaan at the time of Abraham.

Ask, **What happens to a muscle when it is tested by adding more weights to an exercise bar?** Lead the students to conclude that when God tests us with a difficult situation He causes our faith and confidence in Him to be strengthened as we trust Him to give us "the ram in the thicket."

Some students may refer to a news item they have read or heard in which someone claimed that God had told them to murder an innocent victim. Ask, **How can we know for sure that it is God who is speaking to us? Could some stranger fool <u>you</u> into thinking that he was your father? Why not?** The secret, as in the story of Abraham, is to know God intimately through daily conversations: through prayer, in which you talk to God; through Bible reading, in which God talks to you. Only those who don't know God well can be fooled by Satan's imitations.

Locate Mount Moriah (Jerusalem) and Beersheba on the classroom map. It took Abraham and Isaac about a week to make the round trip.

Although the text does not say so, Abraham may have wished to spare his servants the painful experience of seeing Isaac sacrificed, or he may have feared their attempted intervention. God's command to Abraham was a very personal message that was given only to Abraham.

Heb. 11:17-19 indicates that Abraham was so spiritually mature that he believed in resurrection, long before Jesus rose from the dead.

Point out the irony of the fact that the only land that Abraham personally owned was his burial site! See **Heb. 11:9**. Today the tract is still marked by a Moslem mosque. As to **Gen. 22:16a**, can anything be more certain than an oath that God swears by Himself?

CHOOSING A WIFE FOR ISAAC
(Objective 4)

Ask, **What makes a marriage really happy? How do you plan to choose your mate?** Write the word "LOVE" on the board and ask for a definition. In the resulting discussion, the Hollywood version of love will undoubtedly emerge, complete with the hedonistic emphasis on the right chemistry. Point out that many couples who put the emphasis on this kind of love often split up long before true love can mature and blossom.

Ask the class to read about Isaac and Rebekah in **Gen. 24.** As you examine **v. 67**, help students see that Isaac (1) accepts God's choice through Abraham and his servant, rather than resenting their "interference"; (2) marries Rebekah after giving his consent and accepting hers in return; and (3) loves Rebekah after they are married. In fact, love is not mentioned until after the marriage. If a bride and groom see their mate as God's special person sent in answer to prayer, their chances for a wonderful, evergrowing love affair are far better than those of a couple that elope because they are zapped by some kind of "electricity" at a discotheque. Isaac believed in his father's wisdom and in God's guidance. Encourage the students to ask God to lead them to the best mate for them.

GOD'S HEARTACHE FORESHADOWED
(Objective 5)

Probably no emotion is more universally understandable than the love of a parent for a child--and especially for an only child. God chose to use this vehicle to demonstrate His love for His creatures. In Abraham and Isaac, He presents a poignant dramatization of that concept.

In comparing Isaac and Jesus, point out that young Isaac would probably have been able to resist being sacrificed by his aged father had he chosen to do so. Isaac was strong enough to carry the wood up the mountain. His age has been estimated at anywhere between 12 and 38, with 25 being the most likely number, according to F. Rupprecht's Bible History References (St. Louis: Concordia, 1947, 1974). That would make Abraham 125 years old--hardly a match for a "lad" or young man.

If any student suggests that Jesus' crucifixion was beyond His control, refer to **John 10:17-18.** If the question arises, "Wasn't God cruel to send His Son to suffer and die instead of going Himself?" it would be helpful to tell the students that it has been found that a person who can endure torture will weaken if a member of his or her family is tortured. If a human being's love for his imperfect child is that great, God's love for His perfect Son must have made the Son's sacrifice more heartrending than if God the Father had died for us Himself.

Dicusss how coldhearted it is for anyone to refuse the gift of salvation, which was won at so great a price **(John 3:16)**. How blind we are if we allow Satan to deceive us with the lie that God doesn't really love us!

Session 16: Slave or Free? (Isaac and Ishmael)

BIBLE BASIS

Gen. 16-26 (selected verses); **Gal. 3:23-4:31**

CENTRAL TRUTH

God loves and constantly watches over us all, inviting us to give up our slavery to sin and to become His children through faith in the sacrificial life and death of Jesus Christ.

OBJECTIVES

That the students will:

1. Accept God's purpose for their lives as unique and perfectly suited to them
2. Identify ways God blessed the lives of both Isaac and Ishmael
3. Express an assurance of God's impartial love for all people
4. Find in **Gal. 4** a way to

differentiate between the bondage of legalism and the freedom that is ours by grace

BACKGROUND

Repeated surveys show that many lifelong members of Lutheran churches see their godly lives as the assurance that they will go to heaven when they die. There is, of course, nothing wrong with making such a statement if it is meant to point out that good works are evidences of a living faith. But, unfortunately, further questioning often reveals that this is not the case.

In this lesson, the goal is to help the students recognize that faith is a gift of God, and that it produces a life of joyful service by heavenbound, spiritually mature believers.

INTRODUCTION (Objective 1)

Open with prayer. Then, if possible, arrange for the class to watch someone use a potter's wheel. (Consider a demonstration in the art room or ask a volunteer to bring a younger brother's or sister's potter's wheel--e.g., one made by Fisher-Price.) Help the class to picture themselves as clay in the hands of God, the Master Potter. As any experienced potter knows, a stiff, unyielding lump within a large mass of clay throws the entire piece off balance and, unless it is removed, limits the possibilities for shaping the final product. Application of this concept to our lives under God is an easy transition--the more completely we yield to God's will, the more He can maximize our potentials. Without Him we are helpless--or worse yet, we are molded by the diabolical pressures of the forces of evil.

ISAAC AND ISHMAEL (Objective 2 and 3)

These are similarities that the students should find:

Gen. 16:11 and **17:19**--Both were named by God before birth. **Gen. 16:15** and **21:3**--Both were sons of Abraham. **Gal. 4:1-2**--Both were under guardians. **Gen. 17:26** and **21:4**--Both were circumcized. **Gen. 25:9**--Both cared about Abraham enough to be involved in his burial. **Gen. 17:20** and **26:3-4**--(1) Both were blessed by God; (2) both were promised many descendants; (3) both would become great nations.

Conclude this section with an observation about God's great love for slave and free alike.

As you lead the class through the differences between the two sons of Abraham, help the students to see that God gave special responsibilities along with the special privileges. To bear the name Christian is a wonderful privilege and an awesome responsibility.

The differences that should be identified are:

Gen. 21:10 and **25:5**--Only Isaac was considered an heir. **Gen. 21:21**--Ishamel married an Egyptian (thus joining his bloodline with the descendants of Ham). **Gen. 24:4** --Isaac's bride came from His own extended family (descendants of Shem). **Gen. 16:12**--Ishmael was wild, stubborn, and contentious. **Gen. 24:63; 25:21; 26:16, 17,** and **25**--Isaac was given to meditation and prayer; he was a peacemaker; he built altars and worshiped like his father Abraham.

The fact that Ishmael was born of a slave woman, whereas Isaac was born of the slave's free mistress is the key difference between the destinies of the two sons. Isaac received God's covenant (**Gen. 17:19-21** and **26:2-6, 24**). This covenant resulted in special material blessings (**Gen. 26:12-14**). It also brought great spiritual blessings, such as being the forefather of the Messiah. But there were also some accompanying trials, such as the test on Mount Moriah in **Gen. 22:1-19**.

Point out the historical impact of Ishmael's sibling jealousy and contentiousness on the Middle East even today. Allow the students to reflect on the problems caused by two nations, the Arabs and Israelis, who claim the same ancestor (Abraham) as their own and struggle to control the land of his wanderings and his final resting place. The Cave of Machpelah (the patriarchal tomb where Sarah, Abraham, Isaac, Rebekah, Leah, and Jacob are buried) is now concealed by an Arab mosque that is closed to Christians. It was formerly marked by a Christian church that was built by the Crusaders. (See Bible Reader by Walter M. Abbot, page 37, and Halley's Bible Handbook, page 101.)

This Arab-Jewish interaction can be the focus for a special report in which students trace the spiritual conflicts.

Finally, move to a discussion of the way the love of God ends conflict. In a very real sense, a mass spiritual conversion of the people in the Middle East would bring a much more lasting peace than a thousand Camp David agreements! The love of God in the hearts of the students and those they associate with also provides the key for their interpersonal relationships. When God's love fills our hearts, it overflows into loving relationships with others.

SLAVE OR FREE? (Objective 4)

Let the students share what they discovered as they worked through this section in the Student Book. Stimulate discussion with additional questions. In comparing the childhoods of Ishmael and Isaac, ask, **When we are newborn, weak, baby Christians, can a casual observer distinguish us from an unsaved person? What is the only real difference between us and the unsaved person at that time?** In recognizing that we are heirs **(Rom. 8:17)** of both suffering and glory, ask, **When did the difference between Isaac and Abraham's other sons become most apparent to the world (Gen. 25:5-6)?**

Point out that when we mature spiritually, it should also be evident to the world--in our patience during suffering (**Acts 5:41** and **James 1:2-3**), and in our willingness to suffer for others and even to lay down our lives, if necessary **(1 John 3:16-24)**. Encourage the students to see, through Paul's observation, that our sufferings are not worth comparing with our blessings **(Rom. 8:18)**, both here and hereafter.

The students who are "afflicted" with doubts about being children of God need to be comforted. Those who are "comfortable" to the point of complacency need to be "afflicted" with the admonition of James that faith without works is dead **(James 4:17)**. The final section of the Student Book is designed to do just this.

The following passages in the Student Book should provide encouragement to those who feel "afflicted" by a weak faith: God does not reject those with weak faith **(Mark 9:24)** but nourishes it **(Is. 42:1-3)**. God gives each of us our "measure of faith" **(Rom. 12:3)**.

Question 11 can both serve as a "faith inventory" and provide guidelines for living out the faith God has given us. (God's law always tends to do both.) The listed passages give the following evidences of faith: loving one another **(John 13:35)**, serving one's brother **(Matt. 25:34-40)**, not judging one's brother **(Matt. 7:1-2)**, praising God **(Heb. 13:15-16)**, helping orphans and widows **(James 1:27)**, and rejecting bad fruit while bearing good fruit **(Gal. 5:19-26)**. Any Christian who is confronted with these passages from the Word of God realizes how weak he or she really is and how much he or she needs strengthening of faith.

Finally, show the students how faith can grow. **Rom. 10:17** points out that God gives faith through His Word. **Luke 17:5** directs us to God for growth in faith. **James 1:17** and **Eph. 2:8** remind us that faith is, from beginning to end, a gift of God. Hallelujah!

Read the final paragraph of the Student Book together. If there is time, read **Rom. 11:33-36** as a closing benediction.

Session 17: A Cheat Becomes a Champion (Jacob)

BIBLE BASIS: Gen. 25; 27--33; 35

CENTRAL TRUTH

God can accomplish His purposes in any situation. When we try to impose our own plans and timetable on Him, the situation worsens. When we "give in" to His lordship, He makes us "champions."

OBJECTIVES

That the students will:

1. Concede that, also spiritually, haste makes waste, and that they should seek and wait for the Lord's direction in their lives
2. Conclude that, although Jacob did not appear to be a born "winner," God had given him the qualities for him to accomplish God's purposes
3. Recognize how God used Jacob's hardships as tools for refining Jacob's character
4. Discover new insights into prayer
5. Surrender to the lordship of the Triune God

BACKGROUND

This lesson focuses on the maturation process that takes place and the methods God uses to achieve His end--to make a cheat into a champion.

It can be argued that the covenant is hinted at to Rebekah in **Gen. 25:23**, sold by Esau in **25:31-34**, and conceded by Isaac in **27:28-29**, but the first two passages may refer to material possessions and family position and the third passage is phrased in such a way that it sounds tentative. Not until **28:13-15** and **35:9-12** does God affirm that His covenant is indeed continuing with Jacob (Israel). Rather than complicate the lesson, the first three references are de-emphasized in favor of the latter two.

Ninth-grade students are often in a state of despair over their inadequacies. Hopefully this lesson will give them hope--in God--and help them to accept adversities and setbacks as character builders.

INTRODUCTION (Objective 1)

Open with prayer. If you have obtained a chick incubator, stimulate interest in it and provide a calendar for marking the incubation period. A film clip of the hatching process would be faster and cleaner than the "real thing." Allow time for brief sharing about the hatching process.

JACOB'S YOUTH (Objective 1 and 2)

Call attention to the fact that Isaac, like his father Abraham, was childless for over 20 years. God's covenant would come to fruition only with His continuing concern and intervention. The frustration of Isaac and Rebekah increased their dependence on God.

Favoritism and family bickering occur in most homes. Let the "realism" of Isaac's family emerge as you briefly review the familiar parts of the story. Encourage students to put themselves in Jacob's sandals as he fled, a penniless heir, to a strange land. The girls may identify better with Rebekah, who never saw her favorite son again.

GOD TRAINS JACOB (Objectives 2 and 3)

If any questions about the meaning of Jacob's dream arise, point out that the ladder was a visible symbol of the real and uninterrupted fellowship between God in heaven and His people on earth.

Lead the students to see that the shepherds greeted Jacob first. When they saw Rachel, Jacob tried to gain some privacy by urging the shepherds to water their sheep and "go already!" They claimed they needed help with the stone on the well. In his impatience, Jacob rolled the stone away single-handedly--and thereby won the admiration of Rachel. This is an episode that high school students can identify with!

Following are suggested answers for this section:

1. He set up a monument to God and promised to give God a tenth of his possesions.
2. Some shepherds.

3. Rachel.
4. He welcomed Jacob.
5. That Rachel would become his wife.
6. Seven years.
7. "They seemed like only a few days."
8. His impatience.
9. Laban had given Leah instead of Rachel as Jacob's wife.
10. He would give Rachel also in return for another 7 years of work.
11. Probably very little or none.
12. He wanted to go back to his homeland.
13. He trusted a false god --perhaps astrology.
14. Yes.
15. Jacob would receive the speckled and spotted sheep and goats.
16. Laban.
17. Many speckled and spotted animals were born.
18. Laban's sons were envious of his wealth; Laban had been changing Jacob's wages.

JACOB TRANSFORMED (Objectives 4 and 5)

Emphasize the drama of the scene in which Jacob received the encouragement of the angels and faced the threat of Esau's approaching army. Note that Jacob first used his intellect and did what he could about the situation. Then he turned the outcome over to God. (His exemplary prayer is considered at the close of the lesson.)

Help the students to recognize that Jacob, who once took everything he possibly could from Esau, had now been transformed (by years of God's dealings with him) into a "giver."

The familiar story of Jacob wrestling with God needs little attention at this point other than pointing out that a "new man" emerged.

Help the students see that only after Jacob yielded completely to God did he find peace with God. He had now accepted the God of his father and grandfather as his own and took his place with them under God's covenant.

Allow ample time for "reading, learning, and inwardly digesting" Jacob's model prayer. Ask the students to share what they have discovered in the prayer. Responses should include, but not be limited to, the following insights:

a. Jacob acknowledged God as the true God of his forefathers (perhaps in contrast to the idols and household gods of Laban).

b. Jacob acknowledged God as his Lord.

c. Jacob reminded God that he was where he was (in danger) out of obedience to Him.

d. Jacob confessed his sinfulness.

e. Jacob acknowledged that all he had he owed to God.

f. Jacob pleaded for help and specifically named his needs.

g. Jacob admited his own helplessness to save himself and his family.

h. Jacob claimed God's promises for himself.

i. Jacob implied that God always kept His covenants and that, for that reason, he was trusting Him.

Close by encouraging students to privately "wrestle" with the two questions at the end of the lesson in the Student Book.

Session 18: What About Dreams? (Joseph at Home)

BIBLE BASIS: Gen. 29; 30; 35; 37

CENTRAL TRUTH

God works through us, even through our weaknesses, to accomplish His purposes--that people will believe they will be saved through faith in Jesus.

OBJECTIVES

That the students will:

1. Interpret the significance of dreams in light of God's Word
2. Identify some of the tensions that arose in Jacob's family
3. Receive God's blessings in an attitude of humility
4. Rejoice that God has revealed Himself to them through His Word

BACKGROUND

The story of Joseph and his brothers is so familiar that this lesson will touch on it only briefly. The goal will be to help the students recognize that God works in different ways with different people and at different periods of history, but His actions are always consistent with His Word as revealed in the Bible. God's love is constant; His actions fit His purposes and the needs of His people at any given time.

Christians sometimes respond to another person's spiritual experiences --especially in the area of dreams and visions--with great negativity and judgmentalism. On the other hand, some individuals who experience a personally meaningful vision exhibit an attitude that smacks of boastfulness and "super spirituality" as they insist on sharing it with anyone who will listen. By examining various possible responses to dreams, you can help students prepare for the multitude of unusual experiences they will likely face sometime in their lives.

Be sure to discuss the last section of this lesson, even if you need to skip some of the other parts to do this.

INTRODUCTION (Objective 1)

After opening with prayer, discuss the introductory story. It may spark a sharing of similar experiences in the lives of the students or of their friends or relatives. Some may be eager to share something in the supportive body-of-Christ community that they have never felt free to share with more casual acquaintances. Deal lovingly with all responses. Jot down notes about them so you can come back to them later in the session. (Tell students that you plan to talk about the incidents later.)

JOSEPH'S DREAMS (Objectives 2 and 3)

Help the students realize that God was apparently fortifying Joseph for the terrible ordeal that he was about to face as a favorite son-turned-slave by hinting at some special future events.

Develop the thought that God could have given dreams in connection with this incident to Joseph's brothers and parents also, if He had chosen to do so; but, as far as we know, He didn't. God sent the dreams for Joseph's benefit (and for ours). By sharing them rather tactlessly, Joseph did not bless others but rather broadened the already existing communication gap between himself and his brothers, which ultimately caused his exile.

DREAMS TODAY (Objectives 1, 3, and 4)

Young people usually become very interested in unusual happenings. Therefore you can expect lots of questions and discussion in connection with the opening story and the discussion in this section.

As you discuss, be sure to place your emphasis on the main truth: God ordinarily speaks to us today only through the means of grace--His written and spoken Word and the Sacraments. Most Christians do not receive a spectacular revelation from God. People who feel they must have such an experience to affirm their Christian faith may be in effect telling God, "It's not enough that You give me Your Son incarnate, forgiveness, written revelation, and visible means--Baptism and the Lord's Supper." God has indeed revealed in this way everything we need for salvation. (See **Heb. 1:1-2; John 1** and **John 3:16.**)

You should also point out the dangers involved when one seeks to go into the "beyond" by any means available. A perfect example of this is Saul, who consulted the witch of Endor **(1 Sam. 28)**. Astrologers and the occult seek special "revelations" in dreams. Satan often obliges. But contrast these demonic revelations with Jesus' strong admonition to the rich man in the parable of Lazarus, **"They have Moses and the Prophets; let them listen to them" (Luke 16:29)**.

Then, too, when young people hear about incidents that suggest someone has received some kind of special revelation, they may be tempted to think God loves that person a little more than He loves them--that they haven't prayed hard enough or haven't been good enough to receive some special revelation from God. As the passages mentioned above indicate, in Scripture we have received a fabulous revelation! You will want to assure your students that God loves every one of them, that He loves every one of them so much that He would have died for each one--even if he or she had been the only person on earth.

When students feel so very sure of God's great love for them, they're not so likely to get caught up in various charismatic aberrations, including those that focus on special revelations from God. God has brought us to faith through the Word and Sacrament, and He will keep His promise to strengthen that faith through the means of grace. We can trust that sure Word of Promise!

Having said this, however, we cannot state categorically that God will not or does not reveal Himself in special ways at special times in the lives of His people today, nor that all dreams or visions come from Satan or from our own overactive imaginations. Of course, any "special revelation" of this kind will always agree completely with God's written revelation of Himself in the Holy Scriptures.

Many rationalists and secular humanists believe that God never did and never will invade our universe to override the laws of nature. Christians know that He has, in fact, done so. And we believe that He continues to act on behalf of His children, both within and outside of His own natural laws.

1. Encourage students to focus on the wonderful things God has revealed to us through His Word. He will keep His promises to give us peace through these means!

2. Ask a volunteer to read **Heb. 1:1-2.** Then talk about some of the blessings God promises through the message He has given us through His Son.

3. When we examine the things that happened to Lillian, it seems likely that she became so engrossed with thoughts about her brother that her dream occurred as a result of the power of suggestion in her subconscious mind, though we cannot rule out the power of God or Satan to give a dream. And both God and Satan work through natural means.

4. It seems that God also led Lillian to use this incident from her own life to comfort her friend. In a similar way He did not cause Joseph's brothers to commit the sin of selling Joseph, but in His remarkable power God "turned to good" that sinful act to accomplish His purposes **(Gen. 50:20)**. God's use of Rebekah and Jacob's deceit **(Gen. 27)** falls into the same category. Having said this, we again cannot ignore the possibility that God had sent the dream **(Joel 2:28-32)**. The third Student Book choice ignores the power that God has in the lives of Christians. His Spirit does live in us, and as a result we do act in response to His love and power rather than "on our own." Be sure to talk about d. We can offer much stronger comfort than, "He didn't have to suffer that awful thing"!

5. It should be obvious that God's sure promise can bring much, much more comfort that we would receive from Lillian's story.

6. Encourage students to discuss this section as you read it together. Add your own insights and information from above as seems appropriate for your class at this time. As time permits, you may also want to discuss Jesus' warnings about false prophets with their signs and wonders **(Matt. 24:5, 11, 23-27; Mark 13:21-22)**. Also be aware that in **1 John 4:1-6** God admonishes us to test the spirits, not ignore them. As Paul says in **1 Thess. 5:19-24: "Do not put out the Spirit's fire; do not treat prophecies with contempt. Test everything. Hold on to the good. Avoid every kind of evil. May God Himself, the God of peace, sanctify you through and through. May your whole spirit, soul, and body be kept blameless at the coming of our Lord Jesus Christ. The One who calls you is faithful and He will do it."**

Session 19: Concluding Activities for Unit 3

Use the following questions as a review, a test, or in another way that seems appropriate to you.

MULTIPLE CHOICE

1. Another word for pride is
   (A) shyness (C) conceit
   (B) humility (D) self-pity
2. The process by which we are made righteous in the eyes of God through the life and death of Jesus Christ is called
   (A) sanctification
   (B) justification
   (C) self-righteousness
   (D) glorification
3. The land of the patriarchs is in the part of the world that is called
   (A) the Far East (C) Eden
   (B) Africa (D) the Fertile Crescent
4. Which was not a part of God's covenant with Abraham?
   (A) many descendants
   (B) a separate nation
   (C) a land of their own
   (D) freedom from trouble
5. Jesus told Nicodemus that to get into the kingdom of heaven he must
   (A) obey the Law
   (B) be born again
   (C) become a full-time missionary
   (D) be a Jew
6. The name Jacob means
   (A) champion (C) cheat
   (B) covenant (D) shepherd
7. Abraham had a child by Hagar because
   (A) he liked her better than Sarah
   (B) God told him to
   (C) Sarah was childless and he wanted a son
   (D) he wanted more than one heir
8. Abraham didn't want Isaac to marry a "local" girl because
   (A) Abraham didn't trust Isaac's judgment
   (B) there were not enough "local" girls to choose from
   (C) Abraham did not want Isaac to marry an ungodly girl
   (D) Isaac said he wanted a wife from somewhere else
9. When Jacob wrestled with God, Jacob's name was changed to
   (A) Jehovah
   (B) Israel
   (C) Joseph
   (D) Ishmael
10. When an angel talked to Mary before Jesus was born, she
    (A) told everybody about it who would listen to her
    (B) refused to believe the angel
    (C) told the angel that she would not obey the message
    (D) accepted the message with humility

TRUE-FALSE (Circle T for True or F for False.)

T F 1. God wants His followers to be humble. (T)

T F 2. God still intervenes in the lives of His people today. (T)

T F 3. After God made a covenant with Abram, Abram no longer made any serious mistakes. (F)

T F 4. Lot was blessed through his association with Abraham. (T)

T F 5. God would have spared Sodom and Gomorrah if there had been six godly people in the place besides the members of Lot's family. (T)

T F 6. The conflict between Israel and the Arab nations today can be traced to the troubles between Rachel and Leah. (F)

T F 7. God wants every person to be saved, no matter how bad the person is. (T)

T F 8. Good works produce faith. (F)

T F 9. When Laban tricked Jacob, Jacob was "getting a taste of his own medicine." (T)

T F 10. God told Joseph to tell his dreams to his brothers. (F)

MATCHING (Some of the choices at the right will be used more than once; others will not be used at all.)

H	1. Abraham	A.	Was chosen by God through a servant
D	2. Abram	B.	A slave
H	3. Sarah	C.	A twin
B	4. Hagar	D.	Left home at God's command
J	5. Isaac		
A	6. Rebekah		

C 7. Esau
C 8. Jacob
K 9. Rachel
L 10. Ishmael

E. Was killed on a mountain
F. Loved Leah more than Rachel
G. Built a big tower
H. New name given to a person by God
I. Had no children
J. Was fooled by his son
K. Was married to someone who wrestled with God
L. Was born to a slave

COMPLETION (Write the word or phrase that best completes each statement in the spaces at the left.)

1. The people who built the Tower of Babel were guilty of the sin of [pride, or idolatry].

2. In building the Tower of Babel, the builders were breaking God's command to [fill the earth, or give all glory to Him].

3. Lot's top priority in life was [materialism, or Lot].

4. God blessed Abraham so that he would [be a blessing].

5. A gift should never be held in higher esteem than [the giver].

6. God changed a man's name from [Jacob] to Israel.

7. Working seven years for Laban taught Jacob [patience].

8. A predominant sin in Sodom and Gomorrah was [homosexuality].

9. Because he was afraid that Pharaoh would kill him, Abram told Pharaoh that Sarai was his [sister].

10. The wife of Jacob who had the most children was [Leah].

ESSAYS (On a separate sheet of paper, write briefly about any four of the following 10 topics. Be sure to put the number of the topic at the beginning of each essay.)

1. Describe the relationship between works and faith in the life of a Christian.

2. Describe the origin of the various languages and races in the world.

3. How do we become a child of Abraham?

4. How was the sacrifice of Isaac a symbol of the sacrifice of Jesus?

5. List similarities and differences between Isaac and Ishmael.

6. Tell how God uses hardships to refine our characters.

7. Describe the troubles Sarah and Rebekah caused when they tried to play God in carrying out His covenant.

8. What can we learn from Jacob's prayer when he faced Esau's army?

9. How can a small group of godly people be a blessing to a whole nation?

10. Tell about dreams and visions at Joseph's time and today.

Feel free to duplicate the above questions for use in testing. Please add the following credit line: Concordia Publishing House, copyright 1986. Used by permission.

Unit 4: The Covenant Family Multiplies

Joseph and Moses provide excellent models of lives of submission to God's will and timing. The awesome power of Jehovah, as it is demonstrated in this portion of Scripture, can become personally reassuring to your students when they view it in the context of the fulfillment of God's covenant and as an invitation to all of humanity to recognize and worship the true God.

PLANNING THE UNIT

Session 20: Bring some advertisements or TV listings that illustrate the immorality in today's hedonistic society.

Session 23: Bring ads and newspaper articles that illustrate some modern-day "gods" and post the materials in the classroom.

Session 24: Bring nine magazines to class and coach one or two students to assist you in the **"Introduction."** Also bring examples of trademarks or logos to class and post them.

Session 25: Invite a speaker to explain the seder meal or obtain information so you can explain it. Bring some matzos to class.

Session 26: Bring a recording or in some other way prepare for a song of praise (see **"Praise as a Form of Appreciation"**).

Session 20: Slave to Sovereign (Joseph in Egypt)

BIBLE BASIS: Gen. 39--50

CENTRAL TRUTH

God empowers us to hold unwavering trust and unquestioning obedience to Him. This trust and obedience results in a God-directed, purposeful life --not trouble free, but challenging and certain to bring undreamed of blessings.

OBJECTIVES

That the students will:

1. Identify times when they should not conform to the world around them and times when conformity is not harmful
2. Discover ways in which Joseph was a courageous nonconformist
3. Translate Joseph's experience with Potiphar's wife into today's culture, identifying with the powerful temptation it represented
4. Identify Joseph's trust in God as his source of strength during his cycles of persecution, patient obedience, and success
5. Find in God's trustworthiness the motivation to follow Joseph's example during the trying times in their lives

BACKGROUND

Peer pressure is probably most powerful in adolescence. The Judeo-Christian ethic is certainly not the norm in today's hedonistic society. This lesson seeks to answer the questions, "Just how 'different' does God expect me to be?" and "I'm not good enough; how can God possibly expect me to live up to His standards?"

In order to focus on this adolescent crisis, this lesson touches only lightly on much of the familiar material on Joseph's life. Rather, it emphasizes the infinite possibilities for personal and corporate blessings that can result from totally committing our past, present, and future to the service and lordship of God.

Self-pity and resentfulness, even in times of undeserved reversals, do not only show lack of trust in God's wisdom and love; they become Satan-serving, self-destructive roadblocks to the Christian life.

INTRODUCTION (Objective 1)

Encourage students to share their feelings and/or experiences related to Nancy's fears. **How do we "fit in" with strangers? How much can we adapt without losing our identities?** Identify areas where we dare not conform, but also stress that we should retain and share our basic personalities: friendly, fun-loving, honest--while adapting in areas of adiaphora.

JOSEPH IS DIFFERENT (Objectives 2, 3, 4, and 5)

Help students to see that Joseph, as a Hebrew, God-fearing slave and a "displaced person" in a pagan ruler's household, must have dealt a crushing blow to the ego of Potiphar's wife by his rejection of her advances. Following Adam's example, Joseph could have yielded and then blamed his sin on Potiphar's wife as his legal mistress. The students should recognize Joseph's (a) keen sense of responsibility, (b) loyalty to his master, and (c) fear of God as the items he mentioned when he was called upon to resist what must have been a very powerful temptation.

Satan often capitalizes on the poor self-image of the typical teenagers. They fear that if they respond negatively to sexual advances, they will become less popular and less desirable. Make certain that the students recognize that God blesses honest, God-inspired refusals. And this refusal may, as in Joseph's case, actually enhance the courageous person's mystique.

Joseph's story is the kind of "stuff" that so many soap operas are made of. They portray infidelity so commonly that this no longer offends much of society's sense of decency. By examining the students' responses to the questions of what advice would be given to Joseph today, lead them to see how our nation's morality is being rapidly eroded by godless media presentations. Point out that to question the "rights" of two "consenting adults" is currently considered by many to be almost as radically far right as the witch hunts of Colonial America. Ask, **If the existence of God and His sovereignty is denied, who will set the standards of morality--sexual, financial, or in any other area of life?**

Point out that Joseph's decision to avoid contact with Potiphar's wife indicates that he was determined to live morally. (Joseph's training at home must have included these high moral standards.) As a slave, Joseph could not escape this temptation by quitting his job.

Examine and discuss **Prov. 1:10; 1 Peter 2:11**; and **2 Tim. 2:22-26** to help the students recognize God's advice when they face their own temptations.

Ask, **Are the actions of Potiphar's wife toward Joseph typical of today's soap operas?** Read **Gen. 39:21-23**. Ninth-graders often resort to pouting, sullenness, and "pity parties" when they feel they have been unfairly treated. Allow free exchange of reactions to the "fairness" of Joseph's imprisonment. Help them identify bitterness as self-destructive and ungodly. Affirm the strength God provided for Joseph--and promises to provide for them--in the face of tempation.

SOME DREAMS COME TRUE (Objective 4)

Note how in **Gen. 41:16** Joseph credited God (not himself or some special formulas) for his interpretations.

If time permits, you might point out some of the fringe benefits of Joseph's new position: terrific wardrobe, late-model chariot, great authority, an aristocratic wife, and unlimited expense account, extensive travel, etc. How richly God can bless his followers!

The story of Joseph's interaction with his brothers when they came to buy food should be familiar to all students. If you notice that the story is new to some, you or one of the other students might summarize the highlights of chapters 40--44, or you could assign an extra-credit summary of these chapters to those individuals.

"CURSED" TO BE A BLESSING?
(Objective 5)

Read **Gen. 45:1-11**. Very likely the students will immediately recognize Joseph's attitude toward his brothers as a "super human" reaction, a "grace" of insight and wisdom from God, given through his close relationship with God.

If time permits, read **Ps. 37** responsively verse by verse. David underscores Joseph's philosophy of life. David's God-given attitude, developed through patient endurance and unwavering trust, mirrors that of Joseph beautifully: We should not be unduly disturbed when wicked people prosper and we suffer. God asks us to commit our ways to Him and trust Him completely, and He promises to deliver and bless us.

Rom. 12:1-2 contains Paul's classic answer to the adage, "When in Rome, do as the Romans do." The renewing of our minds through Bible study and guarding against the subtle inroads of secular humanism will result in our ability to **"test and approve what God's will is--His good, pleasing, and perfect will."**

Close by leading the class in the following prayer or by asking a capable student to compose and lead the class in an extemporaneous prayer of commitment to God.

Dear Jehovah, God of Abraham, Isaac, and Jacob--and Joseph, I commit my life to You. I ask You to take over the reins of my life and guide it wherever <u>You</u> choose. Give me patience in times of difficulty; give me the

grace to perform whatever tasks You send--large or small--willingly and faithfully; and enable me to be a blessing to others. In Jesus' name. Amen.

Suggest a book report on Lord of Life, Lord of Me by Bill Ameiss and Jane Graver (St. Louis: Concordia, 1982).

Session 21: A Family Becomes a Nation (Israel in Egypt)

BIBLE BASIS: Gen. 15:13-14; Gen. 46--50; Ex. 1

CENTRAL TRUTH

Even when things seem to be going badly, we can be sure that God is always with us. He often uses things that seem bad to us to accomplish His purposes.

OBJECTIVES

That the students will:

1. Explain how God used the time in Egypt to change the family of Jacob into the nation of Israel
2. Identify ways God showed His presence among His people
3. Describe blessings Jacob's family enjoyed in Egypt
4. Recognize a Christian's life as a pilgrimage to heaven
5. Appropriate God's promises to see them through their times of trial

BACKGROUND

"You are a chosen people, a royal priesthood, a holy nation, a people belonging to God, that you may declare the praises of Him who called you out of darkness into His wonderful light" 1 Peter 2:9.

These words from God mirror the images He used in the Old Testament. Already in **Gen. 12:2** God told Abram that He would make him into a great nation. As we have examined the lives of Abraham, Isaac, and Jacob, however, we have seen the development of a chosen family. Not until the 400 year exile in Egypt did the family become a nation.

As was pointed out in session 18, we know that God does not cause evil in the world; all evil has been caused by sin. But, remarkably, God again and again "turns to good" events caused by sin and accomplishes His purposes through them! God used the evil of Joseph's brothers and a horrible famine to solidify His chosen family into a chosen nation--a nation set apart from those around it.

God still acts in the same ways today. Because we see only such a small segment of the sweep of history, we sometimes question whether He really is acting among us. Your goal during this session should be for students to grow in their trust that God really is with them--that He really does care for them and control the events around them for their good. In response He calls for them to **"declare the praises of Him who called you out of darkness into His wonderful light."**

INTRODUCTION (Objective 1)

Open with prayer. Use the Student Book introduction to set the stage for discussion of a family becoming "contaminated" with other families. Students should be familiar with the melting-pot principle. Most ethnic groups in the United States are becoming proportionately smaller because of intermarriages. Probably some of your students can share how their families today have less of a German or Scandinavian or other background than they did in their grandparents' day. And even when the ethnic group remains strong, the families within the group tend to disappear. During the session your students will see how God prevented this from happening to Jacob's family as it became the nation of Israel.

CHOSEN FOR THIS? (Objective 2)

Have **Gen. 15:13-14** read aloud in class. Give some time for student reactions to the promise and how Abram might have reacted. Remind them of Abram's absolute trust in God's goodness even in the face of sacrificing his long-awaited son.

Ask if anyone has ever gone white-water canoeing. Examine the comparative merits of a slow-moving, uneventful ride with the more pleasure-laden, fast-moving adventure that requires a keen mind and quick physical skills. Ask, **Which gives a greater sense of accomplishment at the end?**

If the latter also results in saving lives, imagine what a sense of satisfaction that would bring.

Point out that God's chosen people are part of an infinitely greater adventure. His plan spans all of history; His stage is the universe; His purpose is to lift humanity from the clutches of Satan and hell into the ecstasy of paradise. Every believer has a part to play in that drama **(Eph. 2:10)** that will reach its climax on Judgment Day.

Starvation and loneliness **(Gen. 45:11 and 28)** motivated Jacob to move to Egypt. Now, when the time was right, God again appeared to Jacob and clearly identified Himself as the covenant God of Abraham and Isaac. He reassured Jacob of His plan to (1) make him a great nation in Egypt, (2) be with Jacob wherever he goes, (3) bring him back to the Promised Land, and (4) give him a peaceful death, with his favorite son, Joseph, attending him. Ask, **Do you think that perhaps Jacob puzzled over how God could fit all those promises into one plan (given the time factors involved in building a great nation while in Egypt and Jacob's returning to Canaan)?** After some years, Jacob has accepted the fact that his body will be returned to Canaan **(Gen. 17:30)**.

THE GOOD LIFE IN EGYPT (Objective 3)

Make certain that the class has a clear picture of the size of Jacob's family at this time: 70 direct descendants, of which 49 are through Leah and her maid, and 21 through Rachel and her maid **(Gen. 46:5-7)**. Ask, **How did Joseph know which part of Egypt was ideal for Jacob's family?** The resulting discussion should conclude that Joseph's travels in collecting grain gave him an excellent opportunity to look over all of Egypt--another "hidden blessing" designed to further God's plan for His covenant people.

Rejoice that God can turn even such unlikely sources as bigotry into blessings: Because the Egyptians despised shepherds, Jacob's family was allowed to grow and multiply in virtual isolation!

Thus Jacob's illness occasioned a special visit by Joseph, and Jacob seized the opportunity to adopt Ephraim and Manasseh, blessing them and all his sons.

If it seems helpful, point out that some have attributed Joseph's double portion to the fact that Jacob considered Rachel his "true" and chosen wife and therefore her firstborn son as the true heir to the double portion. Jacob's gratitude and Joseph's respect **(48:10-12)** are exemplary. Jacob's promise to Joseph that God will take him back to "the land of your fathers" bears witness to his firm trust in God's promises.

JACOB CROSSES THE FINISH LINE (Objective 4)

The Student Book emphasizes Jacob's calm acceptance of his death and the recognition that it is his realization that life is only a pilgrimage (a journey to a sacred place) that transforms death into the finish line of a race. Read **Heb. 11:13-16** to the class to summarize the patriarchs' attitude toward death.

You might also spend some time developing the concept that the finish line is never determined by the runner. To do so (suicide) is a violation of the rules of the race and forfeits the prize.

THE FAMILY BECOMES A NATION (Objectives 1 and 5)

The Student Book summarizes the action of God: He used the time in Egypt to change a family into a nation. As you discuss question 3, watch for attitudes of fatalism--that we can just go about our merry ways and do anything, because God will do what He wants to anyway. Certainly God will accomplish His purposes, but throughout Scripture He calls upon us to serve Him so He can accomplish them through us rather than in spite of us.

Use the last four questions to develop assurance in God's promise, **"Never will I leave you; never will I forsake you" (Heb. 13:5).**

CONCLUSION (Objective 4)

Discuss the role of suffering in the world and particularly in the lives of believers. Stress that those who seek to live within God's will are not spared suffering but are strengthened by it. By relating this to the discipline within earthly families, students may accept being disciplined as an expression of love. These future parents in the class should recognize the importance of wise and loving discipline in developing strong character in their children.

OPTIONAL ACTIVITY

Read **Mark 8:31-38** for the teachings of Jesus concerning suffering, its place in God's plan, and Satan's role in encouraging us to avoid it in **"this adulterous and sinful generation."** In **Mark 10:29-31**, Jesus assures us that our sufferings will be turned into blessings. In **Mark 10:42-45**, He identifies the role of the suffering servant with His own life.

Session 22: Retrofitting a Reject (Moses' First 80 Years)

BIBLE BASIS Ex. 2--4; Acts 7:20-35

CENTRAL TRUTH

God can mightily use His children, even in seemingly impossible circumstances. He accomplishes this as we submit to His will, making the most of every opportunity to learn and to serve.

OBJECTIVES

That the students will:

1. Recognize that frustrating circumstances and apparent "roadblocks" in their lives may become "building blocks" for an exciting ministry in the body of Christ
2. Describe Moses' training in Egypt and his rejection as a leader
3. Contrast the second 40 years of Moses' life with his first 40 and recognize his degree of submission in each segment
4. Identify--through an examination of the call of Moses, his training, his reluctant obedience, and his acceptance by Israel--some ways they may grow in their own development and covenant relationship with I AM

BACKGROUND

The first 80 years of the life of Moses are nearly the reverse of the life of Joseph. Moses was trained as a prince and found himself serving as a shepherd. Whether going from rags to riches or riches to rags, God empowers His children to adapt to the circumstances of the moment, serve Him faithfully and obediently, and trust completely in His wisdom, love, and mercy.

Probably the question most often asked of an adolescent is, "What do you want to be when you grow up?" Sometimes the pressure to choose a course of study begins even before adolescence. Through this lesson you should attempt to prepare the fortunate few who have a clear goal in mind to adapt it gracefully if the need arises; help the vacillating majority to pledge themselves to study the courses currently on their schedules, confident that God is directing their paths; and encourage all of them to catch the spirit of high adventure that rightfully accompanies total commitment to the lordship of Jesus.

The life of Moses has been the subject of so many books and films that it may be necessary to remind the class, where discrepancies in biographical details arise, that the Bible is the original source, and that dramatizations usually adapt or embellish the story to suit their own unique purposes.

INTRODUCTION (Objective 1)

After an opening prayer, use the introduction to set the stage for the students to identify with the frustrations of Moses. Both Fritz's environment and training were chosen for him, and then he seemed to fail when he attempted to do what he thought was God's will. Many college graduates today are forced to accept jobs outside their area of expertise and interest--far below their projected goals. Perhaps the students know someone who is already in this predicament--someone they can "bless" with the assurance that God really is involved in the lives of His followers.

A "BORN LEADER" IS REJECTED
(Objective 2)

Quickly review the conditions in Egypt at the time of Moses. This episode provides an excellent opportunity to tie in the currently pressing issue of the Christian's role in an abortion-obsessed society. Invariably in the Bible, babies are cherished as signs of God's love and favor. (Refer to the fervent prayers of Abraham, Isaac, Rachel, and Hannah for children.) So much pro-abortion material is flooding the media that it is important that we lay a firm, Biblical foundation for our young people who will confront the issue repeatedly among their floundering peers. One passage they have recently read in Scripture provides a powerful message: God told Rebekah that **"two nations are in your womb" (Gen. 25:23)**. God saw beyond the two prenatal baby boys to the thousands who would descend from them. This is certainly a far cry from the "ambiotic mass" that abortionists like to write off as subhuman!

Point out that Jochebed risked her life (even though she had other children to care for) to save this one endangered infant. God then provided a miraculous deliverance. Not only did she save her child's life, but she was allowed to care for him during those precious, formative years! Stress the unchangeableness of our God and the importance of focusing on Him at <u>all</u> times, but especially in times of confusing and difficult circumstances.

The first 40 years of Moses examined in the Student Book are based on **Ex. 2:1-10** and on Stephen's reference to Moses in **Acts 7:22-29.** Draw out the logical conclusion that, trained spiritually by his God-fearing parents and academically in Pharaoh's court, Moses had a realistic vision of himself as a deliverer of the Israelites. What a blow his rejection must have been--to his own ego and to his high hopes for God's people!

RETROFITTING A LEADER IN THE DESERT
(Objectives 1 and 3)

Using the Student Book exercise as a background, ask: **Did Moses show any signs of bitterness or resentment?** You might want to point out that the Midianites are descendants of Abraham through Keturah after Sarah's death (**Gen. 25:2** and **4**)--and must have been familiar with the traditions of Abraham's God. Accepted as an Egyptian, Moses became a part of Jethro's family through his marriage to Zipporah and worked for him as shepherd.

When you reach the spot where the class concludes that Moses was there for 40 years, lead a discussion of the changes in his life and character during that period. Student insights should include Moses' more rugged life-style, his expanded knowledge of the geography of the Sinai Peninsula, his mellowing as he matured, his new humility, and a deepened spirituality born in the solitude of nature's grandeur. Remind the students where Jesus went for spiritual nourishment **(Mark 1:35; 6:46; Luke 9:28)**.

THE RELUCTANT LEADER (Objective 4)

Most of the students probably know the details of how a burning bush got the attention of Moses. Bring out the drama of the situation: After 400 years of silence, God spoke directly and clearly to His chosen and meticulously trained leader. Stress key phrases in **3:2-10** such as **strange sight . . . no closer . . . holy ground . . . the God of Abraham . . . I have seen . . . I have heard . . . I am concerned . . . I have come down to rescue . . . to bring them up . . . into a good and spacious land**

. . . the home of the Canaanites . . . I am sending you to Pharaoh to bring My people out of Egypt.

Help the students to see that in 500 years some of the countries of Abram's day may have been destroyed completely, but the area described was clearly the land of the covenant. Student lists should include:

Moses' Excuses	God's Remedies
Who am I?	I will be with you.
How will I tell them who sent me?	I AM sent you. The Lord of your fathers sent you.
They won't believe me.	The elders will listen to you. Here are three miracles.
I am not eloquent.	I will help you speak.
Send someone else.	Aaron will assist you.

After going over the promises and the new name, I AM, allow students to walk in Moses' sandals as he contemplated this new life. Write on the board the questions that students think may have haunted Moses at this time, e.g., "How many Israelites have survived the last 40 years of cruelty?" "Who is in power now?" "What approach shall I use?" "What sort of guy is Aaron to work with?" "Will I have difficulty meeting with the elders of Israel?"

The circumcision confrontation is like an exploding "blood bomb" that interrupts the story. Circumcision was the outward sign of the covenant --a condition that could not be ignored! We confront puzzling circumstances in our lives, too, and we must search our actions for covenant-breaking acts or areas of neglect, confident that, in the end, God's goal is to bless--even as He blessed Moses.

Stephen's witness in **Acts 7** points up Stephen's knowledge of Scriptures and God's faithfulness. Some parallels between Moses and Jesus can be found in **Matt. 21:42-46** (rejection; threat of arrest) and **Luke 9:22-24** (self-denial).

Plan a sharing time based on the student summaries of **Rom. 8:26-39.** Encourage them to lean on God completely, especially in moments of rejection--because we know that nothing can separate us from His love! Emphasize this Gospel truth as you discuss the last question. God's love transcends not only roadblocks others set up, but also our own sinfulness!

Session 23: I AM for Everyone (Moses Confronts Pharaoh)

BIBLE BASIS: Ex. 5--11; Ps. 90

CENTRAL TRUTH

Although God chose the Israelites to be His unique people, and the Old Testament narrative deals primarily with their history, God's love knows no boundaries; He desires that all come to know and worship Him.

OBJECTIVES

That the students will:

1. Recognize in Moses a man of God blessed to be a blessing not only to Israel but to all the world
2. See, in Israel's plight, the necessity for "blind faith" even in our darkest hours
3. Recognize that God uses even the actions of the world's most powerful rulers for His eternal purposes
4. Reaffirm their belief in the universal scope of God's love and power--also in the present day
5. Be aware of the presence of the "gods" their contemporaries worship, and see them as impotent in the presence of the great I AM

BACKGROUND

Among those who know about the Bible but are not very familiar with its contents, there is often the feeling that the God of the Bible prefers Jews and sees everyone else as "second-class citizens." Pray that through this lesson students will recognize that they, as believers, are sons and daughters of God--coheirs with Christ **(Rom. 8:17)**. Because this course focuses on God's covenants, and because the Old Testament focuses primarily on the Abramic Covenant, you need to consistently remind the students of the ultimate goal of God's plan of salvation **(John 3:16, 2 Peter 3:9, Rom. 10:12)** and of His New Covenant in Christ **(Eph. 2:19-22)**.

INTRODUCTION (Objective 1)

Open with prayer, or read **Ps. 100** as the opening devotion. Have **Ps. 90** read aloud in class--perhaps in unison. Since Scripture itself ascribes this psalm to Moses, who lived 400 years before David, this may be the first of the psalms to be written. Moses' training in the court of Pharaoh probably included poetry, and we have other examples of Moses' songs in **Ex. 15** and **Deut. 32**. Rabbinic tradition also assigns **Ps. 91--100** to Moses.

Examine **Ps. 90:1-12** for any signs of exclusiveness or bigotry on Moses' part. **Ps. 100** is even more forceful: **". . . all the earth . . . He made us . . . we are His people . . . all generations."** Only after Moses praises the God of all creation and recognizes the sinfulness of all mankind does he mention his special requests and concerns **(Ps. 90:13-17)**. A good model to follow! Ask the students if they are familiar with the acronym **ACTS**. Write the letters on the board and ask them to supply the appropriate words. In **Ps. 90, verses 1-6** deal with **A**doration, **verses 7-11** with **C**onfession, **verse 12** with **T**hanksgiving, and **verses 13-17** with **S**upplication.

DARKNESS BEFORE DAWN (Objective 2)

The story of **Ex. 5--15** should be familiar to all the students. Be sure they recognize here that when Moses first contacted Pharaoh, Pharaoh claimed that he knew nothing about the God of Moses and had no intention of obeying Him. This sets the stage for the things God accomplished through the plagues.

In reestablishing His covenant, note that God first identified Himself **(6:2-3)** and then promised the Israelites the land of Canaan **(6:4)**, freedom **(6:6)**, a "special people" relationship **(6:7)**, and a safe journey **(6:8)**. Help the students to recognize that just as the Israelites let their suffering blind them to the hope that God offered, so we often let our problems prevent us from experiencing the hope, joy, and peace that are ours in Christ Jesus.

MIGHTY ACTS AND A HARDENED HEART (Objectives 3 and 4)

Develop the realization (which the Student Book materials have spawned) that God did not play random tricks, but that He carefully chose and planned plagues that exposed the impotence of the Egyptian gods and built to a mighty climax that would get the attention of the entire world and reverberate down through the centuries. The first sign of Moses, that of turning a rod into a serpent, ridiculed the Egyptian serpent-god, Nechebt. The following are the plagues and the corresponding deities at which each of them was directed:

Plague	Deity
1. Blood (from water)	The Nile (worshiped as source of fertility)
2. Frogs	Hapi (a frog-god)
3. Gnats (from dust)	Seb (the god of earth)
4. Flies	Uatchit (a fly-god)
5. Cattle Disease	Ptah (a bull-god)
6. Boils (from ashes)	Ashes of idolatrous sacrifices were said to have healing power
7. Hail	Nut (god of heaven) or Horus (sky-god)
8. Locusts	Serapis (protector-god who kept locusts away)
9. Darkness	Re (the

	sun-god)
10. Death of Firstborn	Pharaoh (his son, the heir-apparent, died)

Examine the progression of plagues to show that the impact of each plague was successively more severe. Call attention to the fact that the land of Goshen was exempted from the effects of some of the plagues, which certainly dramatized God's mighty power. (God and His people again and again used the term "mighty hand" when speaking of the way God delivered Israel from Egypt. See, for example, **Ex. 3:19-20; 13:3; 32:11; Deut. 4:34; 5:15; 6:21; 7:8; 7:19; 9:26; 11:2; 26:8;** and **2 Chron. 6:32.**)

It is important that the students recognize that God used the stubbornness of Pharaoh to achieve His stated purpose: that Pharaoh, his officials, his people, God's people (the Israelites), and all the world acknowledged God's power and authority --His ultimate sovereignty. The texts in the Student Book lead to the conclusion that God does indeed achieve His loving purpose. Conclude this section with the observation that all around the world people still marvel at the mighty works of God and praise His name!

PLAGUES FOR TODAY (Objective 5)

Ask, **If God were to use the same approach today--attacking present-day gods in the form of nationwide plagues, making them repulsive and powerless--what might the plagues be like? Think of a possible plague for money, electronic gadgetry, cars, and other modern "gods."**

Encourage the students to use their imagination. They might come up with inflation and economic recession as examples of "plagues" that reveal the basic impotence of money-gods, Orwellianism as an example of the evil inherent in the worship of computerization and electronic gadgetry, and the financial and human tolls exacted by our obsession with cars as evils resulting from excesses. Allow for free range of expression. Be prepared for some unexpected "gods" to surface as the students vent their frustrations over the hang-ups of their peers or families (drugs, alcohol, sex, professional ego, social rank, etc.).

GOD'S NEVER-CHANGING MESSAGE
(Objective 4)

This section highlights the parallels between the Old and New Testaments, showing that God's message and approach to His creatures is timeless and universal. He uses mortal, fallible humans to deliver His message. He testified to the message with **"signs, wonders and various miracles, and gifts of the Holy Spirit" (Heb. 2:4).**

1 Cor. 12 provides information about spiritual gifts. God has equipped us mortal, fallible humans --He has given us spiritual gifts. He calls upon us to use these gifts for the common good **(v. 7)**, regardless of the gift each of us has **(vv. 8-11)**. He exempts no one **(v. 27)**, He assumes that we are eager to serve **(14:12)**, and He calls upon us to use our gifts in love **(12:31--13:13)**.

Close by reading **Heb. 4:16; James 5:13-18;** and **Eph. 3:20-21** in unison and agreeing with each other to be more diligent in our service to Jesus and His body, the church.

Session 24: I AM--a Key to God's Word

BIBLE BASIS: Ex. 3:14; 9:16; John 8:58; 20:30-31

CENTRAL TRUTH

The Bible reveals Jehovah (I AM) as the only true God and proclaims faith in His Son, Jesus Christ, as the only way to have a proper personal relationship with Him.

OBJECTIVES

That the students will:

1. Recognize the communication that occurs through logos, trademarks, secret passwords, and various means of Christian identification (I AM, fish

symbol, cross, etc.)

2. Examine the innate simplicity and profound complexity of the name, I AM

3. Recognize that the God of the Exodus and Jesus (the Messiah) are one and the same

4. Tell how God acts to "protect" and glorify His name, thus investing it with greater power

5. Respond to God's great love as He continues to reveal Himself in the Word, written and incarnate

BACKGROUND

In the mushrooming arena of computer technology, possibilities for white-collar crimes and the invasion of privacy are only beginning to surface. This has led us to devise methods to protect data--such as a code word that must be entered into the computer before an individual can gain access to a given program. The 1984 movie, War Games, illustrated this technique dramatically. Cryptic phrases or symbols can also be used to "key in" the operators who have been trained to recognize them. In the marketing field people use logos as a means of instant identification, and in counterintelligence work they use code words.

In revealing to Moses His name, I AM, God was providing an access code, a symbolic logo, and an easily identifiable password for His people of both the Old and New Testaments--a common link that ties the two parts of the Bible into a single integrated unit. This lesson focuses on that unifying theme of God's power and love in both Testaments.

INTRODUCTION (Objective 1)

Intellectual knowledge about I AM does not automatically lead to a faith relationship with God. We need a trusting, personal relationship with our loving God in order to receive the peace and joy He offers.

Use the following demonstration to illustrate graphically what can happen when two parties establish a personal relationship:

Place the desks in a large open circle. Arrange nine magazines or books on the floor in the center of the circle. Before class select a student (preferably one whose "image" could use a little bolstering) and explain your code to that student. Ask him or her to leave the room, and ask the remaining students to select one of the nine magazines as the target. Then invite the selected student back into the room. Point to individual magazines at random, each time asking, "Is this the one?" When you give the predetermined sign, the student will identify the mystery magazine.

Use the following code or devise one of your own. The numbers below represent the position of the magazines:

1 2 3
4 5 6
7 8 9

When you point to a magazine other than the selected mystery magazine, touch it at a spot other than its corresponding position on the floor. For example, the magazine in the upper left part of the arrangement is No. 1 and may be touched anywhere but in the upper left corner of the magazine, and the upper right magazine in the arrangement is No. 3 and may be touched anywhere but in the upper right corner.

When you are ready to indicate the mystery magazine, touch that magazine in its appropriate spot. Thus, if you touch the magazine in position 5 (the center of the arrangement) at its center, the selected student would immediately identify it as the one the class has chosen.

Help the class to draw the conclusion that the leader-follower relationship, communication, and cooperation can accomplish seemingly impossible feats. Apply these principles to our relationship with God. An optimum relationship occurs when we recognize and trust Him as our wise leader, communicate freely with Him, and cooperate with or obey Him.

WHAT'S IN A NAME? (Objectives 2 and 3)

Use the Student Book material to lead into a brief discussion of names and their meanings, using examples like Adam (man), Eve (living), Cain (brought forth), Peleg (division), Abraham (father of many), Jacob (heel or deceiver), and Israel (he struggles with God).

Because God wants all people to believe in Him, He cares a great deal about the reputation of His name. In giving a "new" name to Moses, He revealed more about Himself to all of us. He had been known by the name, God Almighty, but now he added to this picture of power the dimension of the ultimate, infinite source of life. Jehovah means I AM, the Existing One.

Jesus underscores the eternal dimension of the name of God in **John 8:56-58** as He identifies Himself with it by pointing out His existence before the time of Abraham.

An important focus in most cosmological theories is the primal impetus that gave birth to the universe, e.g., the so-called Big Bang. Be sure the students find in **Col. 1:15-17** the eternally existing Creator, I AM, in the bodily form of Jesus--whom the New Testament reveals as our Savior.

THE POWER OF GOD'S NAME (Objective 4)

The mighty acts recorded in Scripture reveal God's power. But they also communicate the integrity of God's name. Trust in God and the power of His name gave David the courage to challenge Goliath and gave the disciples the power to heal and cast out demons. At times, however, we limit the power of God's name in our midst by our lack of faith in it **(Matt. 17:14-21)** and by our unwillingness to call upon it (**James 4:2** and **John 14:12-14**).

"I AM" REVEALED (Objectives 3 and 5)

Jesus is I AM "enfleshed." The beautiful truths that He reveals about Himself apply also to the Father, because they are one. Stimulate discussion of the inherent meanings of the familiar phrases to bring out the implications for us, which are often as profound as His name.

Read **John 20:30-31** together. In the Old Testament I AM delivered His people by His mighty hand. The New Testament I AM--Jesus--provides eternal deliverance for us ". . . **that by believing you may have life in His name."**

Close by singing or reading familiar hymns that magnify the name of Jehovah, reminding the students that "Jehovah" is the Hebrew form of I AM. The following are good examples of such hymns:

All Hail the Power of Jesus' Name (especially stanzas 1, 3, 4, 6, 7)

Jehovah, Let Me Now Adore You

Before Jehovah's Awesome Throne (especially stanzas 1, 2, 4, 5)

Guide Me Ever, Great Redeemer

We Praise You, O God, Our Redeemer Creator

Session 25: A Night to Remember--Passover

BIBLE BASIS: Ex. 11:1--13:16

CENTRAL TRUTH

Jehovah God (I AM) in His mercy provides a specific escape from slavery and from certain destruction: the blood of a sacrificial lamb (Lamb).

OBJECTIVES

That the students will:

1. Describe the setting and elements of the first Passover
2. Describe the Passover celebration as it exists in Jewish communities today
3. Recognize the paschal lamb as a type of Christ
4. Develop a deeper appreciation for the priceless gift of salvation symbolized by the Passover festivities
5. Participate frequently in the Lord's Supper, thus expressing their faith in the New Testament Paschal Lamb and at the same time growing in their faith in Him
6. Worship the Lamb of the Book of Revelation in all His splendor

BACKGROUND

The richly meaningful symbolism of the Passover develops an increasingly beautiful patina with each additional examination--much like fine tableware. God reveals fresh facets of His love with each successive walk through the Bible. And because it is a living Word, we will never exhaust the supply of blessings to be found there--or cease to marvel at the intricacies of interrelationships waiting to be discovered.

Hearing a Messianic Jew describe the traditional Passover celebration through eyes opened by faith in Jesus can bring a new depth of appreciation to the festival. It may also create a strong bond of brotherhood between us and the Messianic Jew--brotherhood strengthened through a deeper understanding of the relationship of the Old Covenant and the New.

Write to the Board for Evangelism Services, The Lutheran Church --Missouri Synod, 1333 South Kirkwood Road, St. Louis, MO 63122-7295 to receive a listing of current resources about the Seder (e.g., A Passover Haggadah for Christians) and about Christian ministry among Jewish people.

INTRODUCTION (Objective 1)

Open with prayer and **Ps. 68:19-20.**

Discuss the symbolism of the Passover meal. If all or most of the students have never attended a Seder meal or heard an explanation by a Jewish believer in Jesus, try to schedule such a speaker for an all-school assembly. Perhaps individuals or groups in your community can help you arrange or even conduct a Seder. Contact the Task Force on Witnessing to Jewish People (Board for Evangelism Services, LCMS), Jews for Jesus, American Board for Mission to the Jews, or other Jewish Christian missionary agencies.

THE FIRST PASSOVER (Objective 2)

Take a few minutes to immerse the class in the environment of **Ex. 11.** Nine plagues have had a mighty impact on the Egyptians and the Israelites alike. The fact that the land of Goshen was immune to several of the plagues only heightened the sense of awe toward the power of God. The turmoil caused by the increasingly troublesome plagues mounted steadily. The awful three-day darkness took its toll on nerves that were already strained to the breaking point. Pharaoh's officials urged him to free Israel even before the eighth plague struck **(Ex. 10:7).** Now Moses announced the final plague: every firstborn Egyptian--man and beast --will die!

Using Student Book materials, review God's purpose for the plagues: to multiply His wonders; to get people's attention; to ridicule the gods of Egypt; to reveal Himself as God to Egypt and all the world; to strengthen the faith of the Israelites; and to free Israel from slavery.

In preparation for their delivery, God told the Israelites to set aside a yearling lamb without defect, kill the lamb at twilight on the 14th day of the month (Abib), apply its blood to the top and sides of doors, roast the lamb and eat it with bitter herbs and unleavened bread, burn any leftovers, eat quickly, and wait until morning before leaving the house. The obedience of the people showed their increasing faith.

The **"many other people" (Ex. 12:38)--"mixed multitude"** in the KJV--who left Egypt may have included some Egyptians who recognized Jehovah as God and who chose to emulate the obedience of the Israelites and were consequently spared by God. This picture of God's justice and mercy is consistent with the rest of Scripture.

PASSOVER CELEBRATIONS TODAY (Objective 2)

The Student Book material is self-explanatory. Perhaps some students will be able to share personal experiences about a Seder. Show the class a matzo and let them taste it if they wish. Call their attention to its unique appearance. The stripes on it have been compared to the whiplash scars of Jesus and the holes to His pierced side, hands, and feet. And these unleavened breads are made by Jews, not by Christians! This is the same kind of bread Jesus used when He said, "This is My body."

Point out that Elijah, who is

anticipated in the Jewish ritual, has come and gone. Ask three students to read **Matt. 17:9-13; Mark 9:9-13;** and **Luke 1:17** for Scriptural affirmation that John the Baptizer was the one who filled the prophetic role.

Explain that the breaking of the matzo in the center of a stack of three matzos is believed to signify the death of Jesus, the second person of the Trinity. When the hidden piece is returned, it is restored to wholeness, just as Jesus was raised to life. This is a fitting stimulus for breaking into the wonderful Passover psalms of praise (**113--118**)!

THE SYMBOLISM OF THE SACRIFICIAL LAMB (Objectives 3 and 4)

Vicarious atonement by means of a sacrificial lamb is a golden thread that shines throughout the Bible. It provided the focus of remembrance for the Exodus, was reenacted in countless sacrifices, reached a climax in Jesus' death on the cross, and was celebrated in the majectic visions that John recorded in the Book of Revelation.

The texts listed in the Student Book help to clarify a number of parallels between the Passover lamb and the Lamb of God. Jesus, the Lamb whom John identified, was without blemish or defect, was set apart from sinners, and cleanses us from our sins. The Roman soldiers did not break any of His bones after He was sacrificed on the cross.

Isaiah 53:7 and **Acts 8:32** and **35** add the aspect of quiet submission in the face of approaching death. Other references include **Matt. 26:63; 27:12-14; Mark 14:61;** and **15:5.**

THE LAST SUPPER (Objectives 4, 5, and 6)

The students' celebration of Holy Communion should take on a new depth of meaning as they reflect on its roots in the Passover meal and the new covenant it represents. The old covenant required the annual sacrificing of many lambs, but in the new covenant the blood of the Lamb was shed once for all.

It might be helpful to point out that the first covenant rite, the rite of circumcision, was replaced by Jesus with Baptism and the second rite, the Passover, was replaced by Jesus with the Lord's Supper (or Communion).

Heb. 9:22 emphasizes the centrality of blood sacrifices in the Bible and their intrinsic importance.

The Student Book briefly introduces attendance at the Lord's Supper. Let the nature of you class determine whether you want to expand the discussion of blessing of the Lord's Supper, frequency of attendance, appropriate preparation, the witness we provide to others when we attend, etc. If students in your class recently received the privilege of receiving the Sacrament, let them share some of the feelings they experience as they prepare for and participate in it. You may need to remind them that God--not our feelings --makes the Sacrament valid for all.

Close the session by reading the passages in Revelation that are listed in the Student Book. You might also read **Ps. 116** and **117.**

Session 26: Free at Last! (The Exodus)

BIBLE BASIS: Ex. 13:17--15:21

CENTRAL TRUTH

Because of Jehovah's mighty power, Christians can entrust their lives to Him in humble obedience and can face any circumstances with the calm assurance that He will never forsake them. Jehovah always keeps His covenants.

OBJECTIVES

That the students will:

1. Identify frightening circumstances and sources of comfort in their own lives
2. Recognize the Exodus as a step in the fulfillment of God's covenant with Abraham
3. Describe the amazing impact of the pillar of cloud/fire and the horrors represented by the physical

impossibility of escape for the Israelites at the shores of the Red Sea

4. Recognize the Red Sea crossing as a harrowing, faith-building experience

5. Compare the Exodus with the deliverance from sin, death, and hell, which Christ accomplished for them

6. Appreciate the Exodus as the history-making demonstration of Jehovah's infinite power and His willingness to save His people from slavery

7. Demonstrate their appreciation of God's power by praising Him enthusiastically.

BACKGROUND

Even Cecil B. de Mille's experienced special effects crew, while making the film, The Ten Commandments, could not reproduce the awesomeness of the walls of water that Jehovah heaped up by His mighty hand as He allowed the Israelites to cross the Red Sea on dry land or the crashing of the waters over the obstinately pagan Egyptian armies. God has given us this demonstration of His sovereignty and power as a faith-building gift. And we, like the emancipated Israelites, cannot but respond with wholehearted, uninhibited, enthusiastic worship, praise, and the eager recounting of God's mighty acts to those who are still enslaved by ignorance, fear, and unbelief.

God allowed Elisha's servant to see the angelic hosts that were ready for battle in **2 Kings 6:15-17.** Sometimes, when we face the struggles around us, we wish we could have the same kinds of vision. Then, we say, we would more easily recognize the power at our disposal through the Holy Spirit who lives in us. Praise God, He does assure us of this power (e.g., **1 John 4:4**)! Accepting these realities by faith, we join the white-robed multitude of **Rev. 7:10** in proclaiming, **"Salvation belongs to our God, who sits on the throne, and to the Lamb."**

INTRODUCTION (Objective 1)

Open with prayer. Then encourage the students to explore the root causes of fear and of comfort in their lives. Unpleasant experiences and the unknown foster fear and distrust, while familiarity and experiences of justified trust and fulfilled promises nourish feelings of comfort.

THE COVENANT PROMISE FULFILLED (Objectives 2 and 3)

Help the students to recognize that the covenant promises in **Gen. 15:13-14** and **Ex. 3:18-22,** and their precise fulfillment in **Ex. 12:31-41,** are parts of a strong, faith-building pattern that God repeats again and again, for the benefit of all who will listen, throughout Scripture. This is a good time to underscore the importance of family devotions as a means of communicating faith from one generation to the next.

God's promise to Jacob of a prolific progeny in **Gen. 46:3** and its fulfillment as recorded in **Ex. 12:37** is another example of this pervading pattern. Using the figures in **Ex. 12:37-38,** build an awareness in the students of the herculean task that Moses faced as leader of this large mass (perhaps more than 75 miles long) of humanity and livestock. Then allow the students to develop the picture of the miraculous pillars of cloud and fire, together with the physical and spiritual blessings that are inherent in them as the people traveled under the hot desert sun by day and under darkness and cold at night.

MISSION IMPOSSIBLE (Objectives 4 and 5)

Most students have probably seen movies depicting the Exodus and therefore have some awareness of the drama of the situation. Some students, however, may not be aware that these dramatic events did not occur because of poor planning by Moses. God designed them so He could demonstrate His protective and destructive powers--to the end that everyone might come to worship Him.

Ask if any student is willing to share an "impossible situation" that he or she has faced and how God's deliverance from that plight came about (e.g., close calls in a car, "terminal" illnesses that have been in remission for years). Ask, **How does God's use of an "impossible" situation reflect His love?** It is sobering to realize that, in spite of the repeated hazards that were brought about by the plagues, the Egyptian army still did not turn to God, and through their stubbornness they brought about their own destruction. Help the students see that the roles are the same in difficult situations today: some leaders still refuse to turn to God for direction; some "baby" Christians still blindly follow "religious" leaders (sometimes to their destruction, as in the case of Jim Jones) rather than make the effort to form a personal, knowledgeable relationship with God through prayer and Bible study; and there still are scoffers who depend on their own intellect and skills in waging the battle of life.

PRAISE AS A FORM OF APPRECIATION
(Objective 6)

Take a few moments to discuss how we respond to greatness at an athletic event, a political rally, or a rock concert. Ask, **If your favorite quarterback runs broken-field for 80 yards to score a touchdown, do you sit quietly and discuss whether he should have shared the glory by passing the ball to a teammate--or do you cheer? How can you tell whether a friend appreciates that you saved her life? How do your parents know that you appreciate the sacrifices of time and money they make in order to feed and clothe you and send you to this school? How does anyone know that you are giving God the credit for the success and blessings in your life? Do you let God know how you feel about being saved? How do you let Him know?**

Be sure the students see that God designed the Exodus to strengthen our faith as well as that of the Israelites, and that this same powerful and loving God of the Exodus is the God we worship in our time.

How great is our God! How great is His name!

How great is our God--forever the same!

He rolled back the waters of the mighty Red Sea

And He said, "I'll never leave you; put your trust in Me."

--Anonymous

Just as the people of David's and Isaiah's day praised God for His deliverance of the Israelites centuries after the event had taken place, so we should join in that praise today. But even more than that, let the students recognize (1) their own deliverance from slavery to Satan and from the oppression of guilt over mistakes--both of omission and commission, and (2) the power that is theirs as God's children.

This is an excellent opportunity to make use of spirited songs of praise in the classroom. The Song of Moses has been repeatedly set to music--often with accompanying clapping and shouting. (Look for an appropriate song in a youth hymnal in your school library.) Perhaps some members of the class play guitars and would be willing to lead the class in several rousing songs of praise. Or, appropriate recordings can be used to end the session with a lively celebration in honor of the God who always keeps His covenants. (Check the public library for recordings of Hebrew songs of praise.)

Suggested answers for this section:

1. So that succeeding generations will remember God's statutes, will put their trust in God, and keep His commands.
2. Remember that God delivered us before and He will do so again.
3. Rulers, authorities, powers of this dark world, and the spiritual forces of evil in heavenly realms.
4. God's power.
5. By avoiding human philosophies and following Jesus.
6. As children of God, nothing can prevent our victory.
7. Those who are victorious--the believers; the song of Moses and the Lamb.
8. Because His mighty acts have been revealed.

Session 27: Concluding Activities for Unit 4

Use the following questions as a review, a test, or in another way that seems appropriate to you.

MULTIPLE CHOICE

Write the letter of the best answer in the blanks.

1. Joseph was thrown into prison because
   (A) he interpreted Pharaoh's dreams incorrectly
   (B) he lied to Potiphar's wife
   (C) Potiphar's wife lied to her husband
   (D) Potiphar lied to Joseph
2. An important reason for the prosperity of Egypt at the time of Joseph was
   (A) the frequent change of climate
   (B) the annual flooding of the Nile
   (C) the heavy rainfall
   (D) the location of Egypt in the Fertile Crescent
3. When God appeared to Moses in the wilderness, He spoke to Moses from
   (A) a bush (C) a mountain
   (B) the sky (D) the wind
4. When it says in the **Book of Revelation** that Jesus is "the Alpha and Omega," it means that He
   (A) fulfilled all the prophecies in the Bible
   (B) will come again at the end of the world
   (C) has power over death
   (D) is everlasting
5. In the Passover, the lamb is a symbol of
   (A) the suffering of the Israelites in Egypt
   (B) the plagues that were sent to the Egyptians
   (C) Jesus, the Messiah
   (D) the sins of the people
6. To prevent the angel of death from killing their firstborn during the first Passover, the Israelites had to
   (A) put blood from the sacrificial lamb on the doorposts
   (B) borrow jewelry from the Egyptians
   (C) sing a song that was taught to them by Moses
   (D) leave their homes before sundown
7. When the Israelites left Egypt, Pharaoh
   (A) gave them presents of gold and silver
   (B) decided to worship Jehovah
   (C) sent his army after them
   (D) sent a messenger to Moses to tell them to come back
8. The Red Sea parted for the fleeing Israelites because
   (A) Moses struck the water with his staff
   (B) God wanted to show His power and love for His people
   (C) a strong wind dried up the water
   (D) there was a drought in the land at the time
9. The best way to respond to the blessings that we receive from God is to
   (A) boast about them to other people
   (B) be a blessing to others
   (C) make a list of the blessings
   (D) enjoy the blessings as much as possible
10. Jesus came to seal our covenant relationship with God because
   (A) we believe everything that God told us
   (B) we have kept our part of the covenant
   (C) the Old Testament covenant did not work
   (D) He loves us

TRUE-FALSE

Circle T for True and F for False.

T F 1. Joseph sinned when Potiphar's wife tempted him. (F)

T F 2. When Joseph's brothers came to Egypt, Joseph disguised himself from them in order to get even with them for selling him into slavery. (F)

T F 3. In order to stop the increasing population of the Israelites, Pharaoh commanded that all their newborn male infants should be killed. (T)

T F 4. When Moses told the Israelites that he would lead them out of Egypt, they immediately accepted his leadership. (F)

T F 5. The plagues that were sent to the Egyptians ridiculed their false gods. (T)

T F 6. At first, the plagues in Egypt made things even worse than better for the Israelites. (T)

T F 7. Jesus and the I AM who led the Israelites out of Egypt were one and the same. (T)

T F 8. When Moses had a son, he circumcised him immediately. (F)

T F 9. The Exodus was a step in the fulfillment of God's covenant with Abraham. (T)

T F 10. God chose Moses to lead the Israelites out of Egypt because he was a good speaker. (F)

MATCHING

Write the letters of the correct answers in the blanks. Some answers will not be used.

F 1. Joseph	A. Complained that he could not speak well
E 2. Potiphar	B. Son of Moses
J 3. Pharaoh at the time of Joseph	C. Jacob's oldest son
	D. Told the Israelites to leave Egypt
D 4. Pharaoh at the time of Moses	E. Joseph's first boss in Egypt
	F. Jacob's favorite son
C 5. Reuben	G. Father-in-law of Moses
I 6. Benjamin	H. Son of Pharaoh
A 7. Moses	I. Jacob's youngest son
K 8. Aaron	J. invited the Israelites to Egypt
G 9. Jethro	K. Brother of Moses
N 10. Jochebed	L. Jacob's second oldest son
	M. Son of Joseph
	N. Mother of Moses

COMPLETION

Write the word or phrase that best completes each statement.

1. The part of Egypt that was inhabited by the Israelites was called [Goshen].

2. The Israelites were in Egypt for [430, or 400] years.

3. Moses was [80] years old when God called him to lead the Israelites out of Egypt.

4. Another way of writing the name of God, I AM, is [Jehovah, or Yahweh].

5. The part of the Lord's Prayer in which we ask God to help us to respect Him properly is the [First] Petition.

6. The name by which Abraham, Isaac, and Jacob knew God is [God Almighty].

7. In the Seder, an empty chair is saved for [Elijah].

8. The total number of people who left Egypt in the Exodus is about [2,000,000].

9. The unleavened bread used in a modern-day Passover meal is called [matzo].

10. To show the Israelites where to go when they were traveling in the wilderness at night, God used [a pillar of fire].

ESSAYS

On a separate sheet of paper, write briefly about any four of the following topics. Be sure to put the number of the topic at the beginning of each essay.

1. When and how should we conform to the world around us? When should we not conform?

2. How can God turn curses into blessings? Give examples from the life of Joseph.

3. Tell about the importance of patience in the life of a Christian. Give examples from the life of Moses.

4. Describe the "gods" that many people worship today instead of the true God.

5. How can you use the term ACTS as a guide in praying?

6. Give the meaning of the name, I AM, by which God calls Himself in the Bible.

7. Identify ways the Bible tells us to treat God's name.

8. List the similarities and differences between the Passover and the Lord's Supper.

9. Tell how the crossing of the Red Sea was a faith-building experience for the Israelites. How is it also a faith-building experience for us?

10. Describe ways to show appreciation to God for His love and for His mighty acts. Give examples from the story of the Exodus.

Feel free to duplicate the above questions for use in testing. Please add the following credit line: Concordia Publishing House, copyright 1986. Used by permission.

Unit 5: The Covenant Nation Is Nursed and Nurtured

The mass of humanity that left Egypt was made up of more than 2,000,000 Israelite slaves who had lived entire lives of dependency and servitude. This unit deals with the one year of intensive training God provided to mold them into a purposeful nation. Thus God prepared them to assume their role as His chosen people who were dedicated to keeping His laws. They were destined for worldwide prominence, ongoing dominion based on justice and truth, and promulgation of the worship of the mighty Jehovah.

PLANNING THE UNIT

Session 28: Have maps available for locating the Red Sea and other areas involved. A photo of a recent large gathering (for the bulletin board) might help students to visualize the number of people that Moses was responsible for. If hymnals are not readily available, you might want to duplicate the words of "Savior, I Follow On" to use as a closing hymn.

Session 29: Choose a portion of C. S. Lewis' Screwtape Letters to read in class to illustrate Satan's special approach to believers. Check with the librarian to make sure the book is available for student reports. Also check for the availability of material related to full-time church work careers.

Session 30: Illustrations and diagrams of the tabernacle are appropriate for the bulletin board for this lesson.

Session 32: Pictures of contemporary "counterfeit tickets" to heaven, such as flowers placed before a statue of Buddah, would be good bulletin board material for this session as well as for Session 33.

Session 33: Provide copies of the words to the folk hymn, "Pass It On" (p. 103 in this guide.)

Session 28: Infant Israel Begins to Walk

BIBLE BASIS: Ex. 15:22--18:27

CENTRAL TRUTH

We can trust God completely to provide for all our needs.

OBJECTIVES

That the students will:

1. Conclude that actions of an individual or a nation can help or hinder their maturation process
2. Recognize that God used Israel's vulnerability to show His love, increase their faith, and establish an atmosphere conducive to learning how to live as His children.
3. Discover that God requires certain things of those to whom He makes His promises
4. Recognize the enormity of the problem of keeping the new Israelite nation supplied with food and water
5. Identify themselves with God's chosen people, trusting and praising God daily for all their needs
6. Trust God as their source of protection in the face of all odds
7. Analyze Moses' attitude toward constructive criticism and seek to emulate it
8. Pray for a joyfully submissive spirit in their relationship with God

BACKGROUND

God used the "womb" of Goshen to provide for all of Israel's needs until they were strong enough to emerge as a nation. The Red Sea experience "birthed" Israel by faith, and now they had to learn to walk by faith. In their "infancy," God their Father lovingly provided for all their wants: warmth, shelter, protection and guidance (in the form of a pillar of cloud and fire), clothing (via the Egyptians), water, and food. God was preparing them for their role as His covenant people--a nation whose successes and failures serve as a lesson to all the world throughout history. This session deals with "infant" Israel.

INTRODUCTION (Objective 1)

The unit introduction in the Student Book is designed to lead the students to "back off" for a wider view of this period of Israel's history, personifying the nation and comparing its development to that of a child from conception through gestation and infancy to its first faltering steps. As you help the class to recognize the necessity for this period of maturation, lead right into the introduction to Session 28. Encourage the students to share their own experiences and insights, both from the point of view of the child and of the "caretaker." Draw out such maturation factors as:

1. Protection is good, while overprotection is bad.
2. Some provision is helpful, while too much is harmful.
3. Mutual love and trust create a good learning atmosphere.
4. Rebellion and refusal to listen (on the child's part) can slow down the learning process and necessitate the pain of discipline or natural cause-and-effect suffering.
5. Trial and error is an effective learning technique that can become less painless when a person seeks and accepts leadership and advice.

ISRAEL IS TAUGHT HOW TO WALK WITH GOD (Objectives 2 and 3)

Use the classroom map to help students recall the Israelite's environment. Point out that the Israelites, like most people, were very "teachable" during times of difficulty. Help the class conclude that God continues to call upon His people to "live" their faith in much the same way as He called upon Israel to follow His rule in **Ex. 15:26.** Some New Testament verses to illustrate this are **Luke 6:46; Matt. 7:21; 2 Tim. 3:16.** Use passages like these to remind students of the responsibilities God gives to them. Just as the new freedom of the Israelites brought new responsibilities, so our freedom in Christ brings responsibilities today. Freedom is always a two-sided coin made up of privilege and responsibility.

Obviously, this teaching of cause and effect must not be carried to extremes, as Jesus indicates in **John 9:1-3**, but it is still valid. See **1 Cor. 11:29-30** and **James 2:14-19.**

JEHOVAH PROVIDES (Objectives 4 and 5)

Go over the work done by the students in their books, dwelling for a few moments on the impossibility of Israel surviving without God's miraculous intervention. Discuss the lack of trust displayed by the Israelites and their tendency to grumble. Pose the question: **Are we any more trusting today? Do we spend more time praising or asking for more things to keep us happy?**

JEHOVAH PROTECTS (Objective 6)

Note: Jewish tradition suggests that Hur was Miriam's husband and the grandfather of Bezalel, the builder of the tabernacle (**Ex. 31:2**).

Use the Student Book materials to emphasize God's mighty power to save--then and <u>now</u>. Ask, **Is God more powerful than nuclear warheads?** Develop the concept that God can overcome in <u>all</u> situations. Many young people fear nuclear war. Point out that working to avoid such a war is a Christian obligation. Worrying about it, however, does not show trust in God as our Protector.

GOOD ADVICE (Objective 7)

Build on the Student Book material to instill an awareness of student reactions to advice from parents, teachers, and peers. Stress the value of listening to and offering constructive criticism with humility and love.

THE JOY OF BEING AT GOD'S MERCY (Objective 8)

Read **Matt. 6:25-34** aloud in class. Take time to bask in the warmth of God's love as it is expressed by Jesus in these verses.

If you feel it will be helpful to the class, reflect on the message in **1 Thess. 4:11-12** and **2 Thess. 3:10**, bringing the class to the realization that although worry is not godly, work is.

You might close with the hymn, "Savior, I Follow On," which is based on the stories of the Exodus (especially stanzas 2 and 3).

ADDITIONAL ACTIVITY

In response to **Ex. 17:15**, read the beautiful blessing by King David in **Ps. 20:1-5** and encourage one or more members of the class to design and assemble a banner reflecting their gratitude to God for His deliverance from their enemies. Display the banner in the classroom or hallway.

Session 29: Schooling at Sinai

BIBLE BASIS: Ex. 19--24; Deut. 4--6

CENTRAL TRUTH

What, then, was the purpose of the Law? . . . The Law was put in charge to lead us to Christ that we might be justified by faith (**Gal. 3:19** and **24**).

OBJECTIVES

That the students will:

1. Compare an eagle's care for its young with God's care for them
2. Recognize that all nations are God's, but that He chose Israel as His special nation
3. Recognize that God's law shows them their sins and their need for a Savior
4. Rely on Jesus--not on following a set of rules--for salvation
5. Describe the laws God gave for governing the nation under a theocracy
6. Describe the relationship between God and His covenant people
7. Recognize that God nourishes them and develops their faith and faith life
8. Commit themselves to a richer life with God

BACKGROUND

God continued to build the awe and respect of the Israelites for His name with the dramatic happenings at Mount Sinai. He had "carried [them] on eagles' wings" **(Ex. 19:4)** and brought them to Himself. Now He was about to provide His law--a vehicle through which He would continue to bring them to Himself.

The Ten Commandments (the Moral Law) protected the people from coarse outbreaks of sin, showed them their sin and their need for a Savior, and gave direction for living lives that demonstrated their response to God's love; the commandments led them to Christ, the promised Savior would come at the proper time--unconditionally. The civil and ceremonial laws **(Ex. 21--40; Lev. 1--27)** provided means through which the people could realize that God was among them and through which they, then, could demonstrate their love to Him.

In **Ex. 19:5** God said that the level of Israel's obedience would affect the way He would deal with them--a fact demonstrated again and again through the rest of the Old Testament. As you discuss this verse, emphasize that God here was not talking about an end of His love to the people. God always loved them, just as He always loves us. The people of Israel were saved by grace alone, just as we are saved by grace alone. Only our refusal to accept God's gift in Christ can keep us out of God's kingdom, here and in heaven.

INTRODUCTION (Objective 1)

If some students are familiar with the activity of a mother eagle as she "forces" an eaglet to fly--but at the same time offers her strong wings as a safe place of refuge--invite them to describe this process for the class.

Then lead a discussion in which you compare this scene with God schooling and protecting us.

NOW WHAT? (Objective 2)

Emphasize that before God gave the Ten Commandments, He reviewed His relationship with the people. Certainly the Red Sea and wilderness experiences had led them to recognize the power and certainty of God's care. Knowledge that God chose them as "My treasured possession" and "a kingdom of priests and a holy nation" would motivate them to want to serve God--which, in **Ex. 19:8** they promised to do.

Emphasize that the Ten Commandments are for all people. They were pronounced by God for all to hear. Other names for the Ten Commandments are the Decalog, the Moral Law, the Tables of Testimony. Point out that not every religious organization numbers the Ten Commandments in the same way, but the contents are the same. Jesus summarized both tables of the Law beautifully in **Mark 12:28-31.**

OF WHAT VALUE IS THE LAW?
(Objectives 3 and 4)

The Law shows us how inadequate we are in God's sight. The more we recognize our trespasses, the more we realize that we need to rely on God's grace, which He gave in Jesus, who died as a ransom to save us.

Gal. 3:15-25 points out that the Law did not set aside the covenant or impart life. Life comes through Jesus, the Seed of the promise. Thus, the Law was not the promise, but God gave it to lead us to this Seed--Christ--**"that we might be justified by faith" (v. 24).**

In **1 Cor. 15:56-57** Paul calls the Law the power of sin and assures us of victory through Christ.

NEW GROUND RULES (Objective 5)

Spend some time reflecting on the confusion that must have reigned among these millions of people. The need for regulations and guidelines became obvious. Help the students differentiate between the universal precepts in the Moral Law and the temporary, adaptable ordinances of the civil and social laws. Develop the concept of the theocratic form of government as it was instituted for the Israelites.

Take time to examine the rules listed in the Student Book (and more if a student has a further observation) so the class becomes aware of the self-discipline and sense of responsibility that God expects of His children.

A COVENANT IS RATIFIED (Objective 6)

God required His covenant people to obey Him, to worship Him only, not to make covenants with anyone else, and not to let idolators live in the land. As long as they would do these things, God promised to guard them, guide them, fight for them, take away all sickness and barrenness, give them long life, and establish them in their land.

Emphasize that the Israelites solemnly agreed to keep God's covenant not just once but at least three different times **(Ex. 19:8; 24:3; 24:7).** After their promise, Moses wrote God's words in the Book of the Covenant and offered burnt offerings to the Lord.

Heb. 9:11-14 connects the Old Testament sacrifices--like the one of Moses here--to the sacrifice of Jesus, as He offered His blood on the cross. As you make the reference to the blood of Christ in the Lord's Supper, you might point out how **Ex. 24:8** foreshadowed this sacrament.

Gal. 5:4-6 stresses the danger of work-righteousness **(v. 4)** and points out the natural outcome of faith **(v. 6)**, which expresses itself in love. "Working through love" leads the Christian to a life of commitment to God and service to others.

CLOSER TO GOD (Objectives 7 and 8)

Note the way God keeps the two-sided coin of privilege and responsibility in balance. He still gives us everything we need to do His work. By the same token, if we are not willing to work, we will not be drawn as close to Him or experience Him as clearly as those whose willingness exposes them to greater risks and needs--and, therefore, greater evidences of God's love and power. God's love for His people is not greater in one case than it is in another, but the needs of the people vary and, therefore, so do their experiences.

Ask students to share their experiences in increasing their commitment to God. Ask, **Have any of you had the experience of making a new commitment and then having everything in your life seem to go wrong?** Recall Joseph's problems after his commitment to avoid adultery. Discuss the logic of Satan's attacks on those who are the most effective workers--the leaders. Aaron's part in the golden calf incident indicates that Satan must have pressured him pretty hard to make him act so irresponsibly. Read a selection from The Screwtape Letters, by C. S. Lewis, and encourage interested students to read the entire book for an extra-credit project.

Help the students to see the Christian walk as a monumental spiritual adventure in which Satan and his workers try to infiltrate the ranks in various guises and lead the believers astray. Quote the powerful encouragement from **1 John 4:4: "You, dear children, are from God and have overcome them, because the One who is in you is greater than the one who is in the world."**

This would be an excellent opportunity to encourage students to consider full-time church work or to decide to train for other professions at a Christian college. (Strong Christian leaders can develop and encourage Christian young people to live committed lives in every field of endeavor.)

Session 30: New Relationships Are Formed (Ceremonial Laws)

BIBLE BASIS: Ex. 25--31

CENTRAL TRUTH

God assures us of His abiding presence and tells us how to express and acknowledge our relationship with Him in rituals and forms of worship.

OBJECTIVES

That the students will:

1. Recognize that God "cuts and shapes" people to make them His "precious gems"
2. Describe pre-Sinai worship
3. Examine the components of the God-designed sanctuary
4. Describe how God used the tabernacle, priests, sacred rites, and Tables of Testimony to make and keep the Israelites aware of His covenant with them
5. Identify ways God assures them of His abiding presence among them
6. Identify ways they express and acknowledge their relationship with God
7. Worship God meaningfully

BACKGROUND

In **Ex. 19--24** God tells how He made a covenant with the descendants of Abraham. He set forth its terms and the people accepted them.

Then Moses again ascended Mt. Sinai **(24:15-17)** to receive additional covenant promises and stipulations. God prescribed ways in which (1) He would assure His chosen people of His abiding presence and (2) they were to express and acknowledge their covenant relationship with Him in rituals and forms of worship.

The people were to acknowledge their communion with God by erecting the tabernacle **(chapters 25--27)**, designating certain people as priests **(chapter 28)**, instituting sacred rites **(29:1--31:17)**, and accepting the Tables of the Testimony **(31:18)**. The tabernacle was a visible pledge of God's invisible presence in the midst of the people of Israel; the service of the priests reminded the people daily of the ongoing need of intermediaries between a sinful people and the "comsuming fire" **(24:17)** of a holy God; the sacred rites symbolized the people's dependence on the mercy of God if their covenant relationship with Him was to be maintained; and the Tables of the Testimony were the permanent record of the covenant.

In this session you will only be able to "scratch the surface" of worship. You will have an opportunity to build on this section during Sessions 62--66 (in connection with the building and dedication of the temple).

See "A New Setting" for a possible student project to be completed in advance.

INTRODUCTION (Objective 1)

This account emphasizes the importance of knowledge and practice in dealing with precious and sophisticated commodities. God presented us with the precious jewel of a perfect relationship with Him; we lost it; only He knows how to restore it. Help the students conclude that God has brought them, too, into a covenant relationship with Him, and that He works in them to increase their trust in Him and His covenant. Still today, worship is a key means through which God works in His people.

PRE-SINAI WORSHIP (Objective 2)

The texts selected show the gradual development of worship over the centuries before the Exodus. The Bible references show the offering of firstfruits; spoken or sung prayer and praise; specific animals designated as "clean"; bowing down as an expression of worship; not bowing down to anyone or anything but God; altars built of undressed stone; Moses setting up a "tent of meeting," a pillar of cloud descending at the entrance while Moses spoke to God inside, and the people worshiping.

A NEW SETTING (Objectives 3 and 4)

Call attention to the fact that God devotes more than a dozen chapters of **Exodus (Ex. 25--31, 35--40)** and the whole **Book of Leviticus** to the description of the worship life of the Israelites and the duties of the priests. Ask, **Why do you suppose God spends so much time on these matters?** The students should conclude that it is important, and that we should study it for a deeper understanding of our own worship life.

Be sure the students have a clear picture of the tabernacle and its furnishings. If possible, have a volunteer prepare a large sketch before class as an extra credit project. Then ask that student to explain the parts of the sketch during class. If that is not possible, provide your own sketch on a chalkboard or poster. Call attention to the fact that this sanctuary showed God's presence among the people **(Ex. 25:8)** and that God began with the ark of the covenant (or ark of testimony) and the mercy seat, where He would meet with Moses and Aaron, and proceeded to "build" around it. True religion begins with God! Save any sketches for use again in unit 9.

A NEW ORDER (Objective 4)

Stress the fact that God established the priests as intermediaries between the holy God and sinful people. The intermediaries, too, were sinners, and the prospect of appearing before the holy God would seem awesome to them. Therefore God provided a complicated seven-day ordination or rite during which atonement was made for the priests and the altar. Only then could they perform the rituals of atonement for the people.

Reaffirm the fact that only God can devise a system that will properly prepares a person to meet Him. Point out that even the artists who created all these items for worship were prepared by God for their tasks. Those students who have artistic ability and inclination should be encouraged by the discovery that God provides for and blesses these areas of Christian endeavor in such a special way. Ask, **Have you asked God to prepare you for whatever tasks He has planned for you? Does He have**

tasks planned for everyone? Read **Eph. 2:10** and take a few moments to reflect on the wonder of this text, encouraging the class to recognize the high adventure it represents as they seek to discover their specific callings.

Following are suggested answers to the questions in this section:

1. To give the priests dignity and honor; to serve as a continuing memorial to the Lord; to make decisions
2. Seven days
3. Two lambs, with flour, oil, and wine (one each morning and evening)
4. To burn incense twice a day and tend the lamps
5. By the half-shekel atonement offering that each man paid
6. The altar for burnt offerings and the basin for washing
7. God gave them wisdom
8. The Sabbath
9. They showed the people that God dwelt among them, and that He was the Lord their God

THE FOCUS OF ISRAEL'S WORSHIP (Objectives 4, 5, 6, and 7)

Develop the concept of the ark and the mercy seat as a focal point of the Israelite community. Remind the students that God designed the tabernacle to remind the people of His presence and to provide a setting for them to glorify Him through the worship services conducted there.

Bring out the fact that while the ark housed the conditions of the covenant (the Ten Commandments, or the Law), the mercy seat, by its very name, represented the forgiveness available through repentance. This sin-consciousness, reaching out in gratitude to accept God's free grace, illustrates the purest form of worship. Today we worship through Jesus, the New Testament intermediary, who has made us priests.

WORSHIP IN OUR TIME (Objectives 5, 6, and 7)

Col. 2:16-17 makes clear the temporary value of the Old Testament rituals described in this lesson and the permanence of Christ's sacrifice. Conclude the lesson by reading **Col. 3:1-17** aloud and leading the students to verbalize their concept of what God expects of us today--what constitutes worship.

OPTIONAL ACTIVITY

Invite small groups or individuals from your class to report on selected items and ceremonies from **Ex. 25--31.** The reports should describe the item or ceremony and explain its significance. If they wish, they could also show sketches or models of the sacred items.

Session 31: Rebellion and Recommitment (Israel's Adolescence)

BIBLE BASIS: Ex. 32--40

CENTRAL TRUTH

We Christians sometimes backslide in our faith life. When we do, God graciously empowers us to repent and ask for forgiveness. God uses these means to right the wrongs and reestablish our relationship with Him.

OBJECTIVES

That the students will:

1. Find comfort in the fact that confusion and frustration are normal feelings during the adolescent and teen years
2. Sympathize with Israel's good intentions and poor performance
3. Recognize the leadership traits God gave to Moses
4. Describe the courage and loyalty of the Levites
5. Desire the leadership traits of humility, compassion, and intercession
6. Thrill to the realization of the awe-inspiring truth that the same God whose glory filled the tabernacle now dwells in each believer

BACKGROUND

Sometimes the teacher of religious truth becomes so intent on differentiating between good and evil that the student with a poor self-image despairs of ever being considered a righteous child of God. In this lesson, we hope to show in Israel's rebellion, God's condemnation, Moses' intercession, Israel's repentance, God's mercy, and Israel's recommitment a pattern with which everyone can identify. Every student should realize anew that God saves them to love them--in spite of their sin, not because they are so "good."

INTRODUCTION (Objective 1)

Most students will readily identify with Maria's good intentions, failure to follow through, and ambivalent feelings toward parental counseling. But since most teenagers are self-conscious, they often assume they are the only ones struggling with frustration.

You might have students roleplay to help them view common teen-parent confrontations through the parents' eyes. Attempt thereby to promote greater understanding and awareness of the dynamics involved. Sample situations are:

1. Maria and her mother. (What would they advise, as Maria's mother?)
2. Vance wants a car. His after-school job is interfering with his grades and his opportunity for extracurricular activities. He goes to his father for advice (not money).

Other "hypothetical" situations suggested by the students could be even more productive.

Encourage the students to recognize that their frustrations are often due to being allowed to make their own decisions and discovering that there are often no easy answers. Help them to see that the process of growing us is a mixture of new freedoms and new responsibilities. In accepting the exhilarating prospect of increased independence, we sometimes revert to the childlike position of expecting our parents to solve our problems and remove our frustrations; and then we rebel when they make mature suggestions.

REBELLION (Objectives 2, 3, and 4)

Help the students to find parallels between adolescence and Israel's developmental period. Point out that Israel was trying to "grow up." She had accepted God's proposed covenant that provided her with new freedoms, and she had accepted specific responsibilities, including the restriction of worship to Jehovah only. During this time she experienced major changes and frightening circumstances--lightning, thunder, Moses' disappearance into the cloud-covered mountaintop. As an emerging theocracy, Israel failed miserably in her promise to remain faithful to her God. She deserved to lose her position as a covenant nation.

Ask, **Have you ever failed someone who deserved your loyalty and because of that you yourself deserved to be "written off" as his or herfriend? If so, and if someone "went to bat" for you, you know what a blessing it is to have an intercessor. Have you ever interceded for someone else? Sometimes it's not easy to do--right?**

Whether God really wanted to abandon the rebellious Israelites or was just helping Moses to reaffirm His loyalty to them at this point is an academic point. We can learn much about the selflessness of a true leader by studying Moses' example. Point out that Moses could not have acted this way on His own; God gave him to power and faith that led him to act as he did. Allow sufficient time for the class to react to Moses' intercession on behalf of these grumbling, fickle people of which he is in charge. Emphasize the contrast between Moses' attitude and that of the egocentric philosophy promulgated by today's society.

Call attention to the drama and pathos of **32:26-28** and the resulting status of the Levites. As you work through the remaining portion of this section, call attention to the role of the faithful intercessor as played by Moses here and identify the source of his persistence (**33:16**) as his recognition of the fact that it was the unique position of those "chosen by God" that set them apart from the rest of humanity.

Following are suggested answers for this section:

1. God said that if they obeyed His covenant, they would be His holy nation; Israel was afraid and asked Moses to speak to God and then tell them what He said; Moses disappeared into a cloud of fire and smoke.

2. He wanted to destroy them and start all over again, making a nation of Moses' descendants.

3. For His name's sake, so the Egyptians and others would not mock God; because of His covenant with Abraham, Isaac, and Jacob.

4. He broke the tablets of the Law; he burned the calf, ground it, and sprinkled the dust on the drinking water.

5. God's chosen people became a laughingstock to their enemies.

6. Tell whether or not they were for the Lord.

7. The Levites.

8. "You have been set aside to the Lord today."

9. He offered to be blotted out of God's book in their place.

10. His action foreshadowed a similar kind of action in Christ.

11. A plague struck them.

12. If you won't go with us, don't send us at all.

13. Without God, they were not unique.

14. "I will do the very thing you have asked."

MERCY AND RECOMMITMENT (Objectives 5 and 6)

After referring briefly to the Israelites' actions and attitudes up to this point, ask **Do God's dealings with Israel reflect the attributes listed in Ex. 34:6-7?** Take a moment to reflect on the comfort that we can take from these verses. If students question the last part of **verse 7,** be prepared to lead a brief discussion on ways we can jeopardize our immediate descendants through such sins as alcoholism, laziness, greed, and dishonesty.

Call attention to the fact that Moses did not exclude himself when he acknowledged the sinfulness of Israel **(34:9).**

GOD'S HOUSE VALIDATED (Objective 6)

Read **Ex. 40:34-38** aloud in class. Reflect on the awesomeness of this spectacle and then develop that theme as the class examines the implications found in **1 Cor. 6:19-20:** God lives in our bodies; we are God's temples.

ADDITIONAL ACTIVITIES OR SPECIAL REPORTS

1) Who intercedes for God's people today? Do we have a mediator? Refer to **Rom. 8:26-27** and **Heb. 9:15.**

2) How do our covenant and worship regulations compare with those of the Israelites? Refer to **Heb. 9.**

Session 32: Atonement/Justification

BIBLE BASIS: Lev. 1--7; 16

CENTRAL TRUTH

We, as sinners, cannot possibly become reconciled with the holy God apart from the atonement provided by the blood of Jesus Christ, His Son; this alone justifies all those who trust Him as Savior and Lord.

OBJECTIVES

That the students will:

1. Consider what constitutes a valid admission ticket (as compared with a counterfeit one)

2. Accept the premise that a holy God cannot live with sin

3. Acknowledge the hopelessness of their sinful condition

4. Contemplate God's agape love as demonstrated in His dealings with the Israelites

5. Gratefully accept, through the power of the Holy Spirit, the atonement provided by God through Christ

6. Recognize that, just as rejection is the consequence of relying on counterfeits, justification is the inevitable result of trusting in Christ's atonement

7. Grow in their realization that heaven is their sure inheritance in Christ

BACKGROUND

The concepts of atonement and justification are often distorted in the minds of believers. This lesson presents the keystone in the arch of Biblical principles. If we can clearly communicate (1) God's sovereign authority to decide what constitutes valid atonement, (2) the universality of sin, and (3) the foolishness of refusing God's free gift of salvation through Jesus, we will render immeasurable service to our students. To God alone be the glory!

INTRODUCTION (Objective 1)

The illustration and introduction establish the basic comparison that is used throughout this lesson. Allow the students to "get into" the counterfeit-ticket situation, guiding them to the logical conclusion that the producer of a show, not a patron, determines what constitutes a valid ticket.

VALID TICKETS VS. COUNTERFEITS
(Objectives 1, 2, and 3)

Stress the fact that only the Bible, among all the religious writings in the world, suggests a plan for removing guilt by the action of God rather than of people.

Proceed to illustrate the impossibility of our cleansing ourselves by asking the students to picture the following scene:

A king builds a fabulous castle of white marble, with beautifully landscaped grounds and a gigantic swimming pool. He prepares a sumptuous feast for all his subjects to enjoy after they have taken a dip in the pool. A sadistic prankster pollutes the water in the pool with a greasy substance that clings to everyone in the water. The people do not dare to leave the pool to attend the feast unless they are clean. Yet the more they try to rub off the offensive substance, the more tenaciously it sticks to them.

Explain to the students that this is a picture of our own natural spiritual condition **(Is. 64:6)**. Born in sin, we are powerless to cleanse ourselves; only God Himself can help us.

ATONEMENT IN THE OLD TESTAMENT
(Objectives 2, 3, and 4)

Using the materials in the Student Book, take class time to reestablish the concept of sin as a universal condition. Session 6 (Saved--by the Grace of God) discusses our plight in terms of being spiritual corpses. You might refer back to that lesson at this point if further illustration is necessary.

Briefly review the role of blood as the acceptable means of atonement --the valid ticket, if you will--that God established. Point out that in **Leviticus** God describes acceptable worship for the children of Israel.

If you occasionally assign extra credit activities, you might ask volunteers to report on the various offerings of **Lev. 1--7**. If possible, read **Lev. 16** during class.

Help the class visualize the cloud of God's presence over the tabernacle and the column of smoke from the daily burnt offerings in the center of the community. Suggest that, for Israel, the Day of Atonement was comparable to our Christmas and Good Friday and Easter combined!

Following are suggested answers:

1. It also gets dirty.
2. We were conceived and born in sin.
3. No.
4. Our righteous acts are like filthy rags.
5. A lamb had to be sacrificed.
6. A bull and two rams.
7. A bull.
8. The Day of Atonement.

ATONEMENT IN THE NEW TESTAMENT
(Objective 5)

Calling attention to the prophetic visual lessons of blood sacrifices in the Old Testament, lead the class into a fresh look at Jesus as the reality that these sacrifices foreshadowed **(Col. 2:16-17)**. The section in session 25 on the symbolism of the sacrificial lamb laid the foundation for this concept and should be reviewed here. Jesus, our sacrificial

Lamb, atoned for all our sins. Pertinent texts include **1 John 1:8; Heb. 9:19-28**; and **1 John 1:7**.

JUSTIFICATION (Objectives 6 and 7)

The material in this section is designed to lead the students to the realization that, although our atonement is complete and valid in Christ, our personal justification depends on our individual recognition and acceptance of that fact. As you teach, do not emphasize the terms objective and subjective justification. Rather, focus on the completeness of Christ's sacrifice for everyone and on the need for faith in His sacrifice in order to be saved.

Because the concept of righteousness by works is so common, emphasize the futility of this idea or of any other "ticket to heaven" that people might devise in the name of religion. Be sure to pick up on the Student Book accent that "accepting" Christ's atonement also is not something we can do on our own. God deserves all the credit both for the atonement and for our justification!

Lest the students fall into the trap of viewing Christian liberty as license, be sure that they find in **Gal. 3:24** the role of the Law as a means of reminding us of our sinful condition. The role of obedience in the Kingdom will be dealt with in the next session.

For the students who are haunted by the fear that their sins are too devastating for God to erase, apply the comfort that we receive in **Is. 1:18** and **Ps. 103:11-12**. Close the session on a triumphant note by reading **Rom. 8:31-39** in unison, followed by a hymn of praise, such as "How Great Is Our God," "Amazing Grace," or "Just as I Am."

Following are suggested answers for this section:

1. It won't work.
2. Faith in Jesus.
3. Yes.
4. They point to our sin and our need for a Savior.
5. Peace with God; safety from His wrath.
6. It's as though our sins are changed from scarlet to snow-white, from crimson to wool.

Sessions 33: Firstfruits--Grateful Response to God's Grace

BIBLE BASIS: Lev. 7--8; Num. 18; Deut. 14; 26; 2 Cor. 8--9

CENTRAL TRUTH

God's free gift of salvation moves His people to gratefully seek to serve Him.

OBJECTIVES

That the students will:

1. Describe Israel's practices of bringing firstfruits and tithes to God
2. Identify reasons why the people brought their firstfruits and tithes to God
3. Identify God's love as the reason for our responses of love in return
4. Describe appropriate responses to God's love
5. Make a commitment to God

BACKGROUND

God's plan of salvation has been accomplished. When we become members of God's family, we are removed from the domination of Satan. We are new creatures, spiriutually alive under the lordship of Jesus Christ. In this session you will examine one aspect of this new life: the way we respond to God's love to us.

High-school students receive strong pressure to "do your own thing," "look out for yourself--no one else will," etc. You will have the opportunity to help them see that God has richly blessed them, and that He empowers them to respond in love to Him and for Him. As they respond, they not only glorify God among the people around them, but they also receive assurance of God's continued blessings. Then to "do your own thing" changes. It no longer remains pressure to conform to the peers; rather, it becomes the freedom to show love to God and to look out for others. If students sense this at the end of this session, you will have observed a rich blessing from the Holy Spirit!

FIRSTFRUITS AND TITHES FROM ISRAEL (Objectives 1 and 2)

God required firstfruit and tithe offerings from the Israelites. This would have been enough of a reason for them to bring these offerings to Him. (And that may have been the only reason some of them brought their gifts.) Bring out this reason, but also be sure to accent the willingness to give and the blessings God gave the people through their offerings.

Following are notes on the Student Book material:

1. God indicates that at times the fellowship offerings were an expression of thankfulness, the result of a vow, or a freewill offering.

2. Instead of asking each Israelite family to give Him their firstborn son, God had set apart an entire tribe (Levi) for service to Him. They would not receive a portion of the Promised Land for an inheritance. Rather, each person was to bring the tithe to support them. Note that tithes and firstfruits also supported the poor and provided food and drink for the festival celebrations.

3. Instead of bringing produce, people who lived far away could sell the produce, bring the money to the place where God "collected" the tithe, and buy the equivalent of their tithe there to present to God. Note the festive atmosphere connected with the giving of the tithe **(Deut. 14:26)**.

4. The commands in **Deut. 26:1-15** show that the giving of firstfruits and tithes should be more than a dead ceremony. God here provided an opportunity for the people to be brought closer to Him. The people acknowledged that He had fulfilled His promise **(v. 3)**; they recalled His miraculous delivery from Egypt **(v. 8)** and the wonder of the land He had given them **(v. 9)**; and they called upon God to keep His promises to them **(v. 15)**.

5. Students may recall God's command, the thankful hearts of the people, the provisions God made for the Levites and the poor, the evidences of God's goodness and faithfulness that the people recalled when they brought their offerings, and the opportunity to claim God's promises as the people brought the offerings.

6. This incident is a rare example of freewill giving--so great that the people were bringing too much and Moses had to tell them to stop!

OFFERINGS TODAY (Objectives 3, 4, and 5)

Much of this section focuses on elements of intensive stewardship efforts, such as "His Love--Our Response," in many Districts of the LCMS. These efforts stress managing rather than merely giving--managing all things to advance the kingdom of God.

1 and 2. Use the **2 Cor. 5:15** passage to focus your discussion. God reached down to us with His forgiveness, acceptance, and promise of eternal life. He fills our empty hands with His grace and continues to place many and varied resources into our hands so we can respond to His love.

3 and 4. Discuss how we respond in love when we manage our bodies by eating, excercising, and resting properly; by avoiding abuse with alcohol and drugs; etc. Ask students to suggest ways they can manage their time and abilities to the glory of God.

5. Allow time for students to respond on their own to this question. If you need to provide discussion starters, talk about the witness we give to others when we abstain from alcohol and drugs, when we make a banner for our school or church, when we show that our family is important to us, etc.

6. The widow gave all she had --total commitment--while the wealthy people, who gave much more, gave only a part of their wealth. Jesus praised sacrificial, freewill giving.

7. Paul suggests regular and proportionate (percentage) giving in **1 Cor. 16:2**.

8--10. The Macedonian Christians gave out of joy that led to generosity, they gave as much as they were able--and more, and they considered it a privilege to give. Note that **"they gave themselves first to the Lord" (2 Cor. 8:5)**.

11. As you examine Paul's words in **2 Cor. 9**, be sure to place them into the context of his words in **5:15**. Otherwise we risk giving a Law emphasis to words that center on the Gospel. God promises to bless generous givers **(9:6)**. God wants willing, cheerful gifts **(v. 7)**. God's grace empowers us to do good works **(v. 8)**. God promises both physical and spiritual blessings **(v. 10)**. Generosity in unselfish giving to others will result in thanksgiving to God **(v. 11)**. People will praise God for our generosity, and will pray for us **(vv. 13-14)**. God's indescribable Gift--our redemption --undergirds our giving.

12. Allow at least three minutes of quiet time for students to complete the final activity. (Do it yourself, too!) Then lead the class in prayer. Ask God to send His Holy Spirit to all of you, for without this Gift none of you will be able to keep the commitment you have made.

Talk about this activity at least once a week for several weeks. Invite students to share their successes and failures. Then pray, asking for forgiveness for any shortcomings and renewed strength to keep the commitment in the future.

Session 34: Roots: Final Instructions at Sinai

BIBLE BASIS: Num. 1--10

CENTRAL TRUTH

God provides means through which He helps us remember all that He has done for us, thus building us up in our faith.

OBJECTIVES

That the students will:

1. Share experiences that are meaningful to them because the experiences remind them of things God has done for them
2. Explain how the census strengthened Israel's roots
3. Compare the **Numbers** census with the **Luke 2** census
4. Describe the way God used orderliness to help the Israelites along the way
5. Recognize the importance of Israel's remembering her origins and the source of her new freedom and blessings--and then apply that ongoing need to themselves
6. Reaffirm that the Sinai experience was a means to an end--a preparation for active service as God's people
7. Rejoice in the blessings God promises them

BACKGROUND

In **Ex. 19:1-2** we read that in the third month after the Israelites left Egypt, they encamped at Sinai. All the remaining events of **Exodus**, and all the events of **Leviticus**, occurred there. Finally, almost a year later (on the 20th day of the second month of the second year--**Num. 10:11**), the Israelites moved on.

The first 10 chapters of **Numbers** contain God's final instructions and the final events at Sinai. In this session you will focus on the "roots" aspect of these chapters. The people's tribal roots became the organizing basis for the census ("numbering") and the camp arrangement; the people's roots in Jehovah assured them of God's blessing; and the offerings, tabernacle dedication, and Passover celebration reminded them of these roots.

INTRODUCTION (Objective 1)

Ask, **How were Margaret's roots important to her? Who helped Margaret establish her roots? As Margaret grew older, how could she help others establish, develop, and remember their roots?**

Then ask if anyone has read Alex Haley's book, Roots, or has seen the TV movie based on this book. **Why are our roots important--especially our Christian roots?** Talk about events in the past that helped them grow in their Christian faith, events in the present that help them remember what God has done for them, people who helped them establish their roots in Christ, etc. If you wish, also discuss ways students can help others grow in their relationships with God.

This discussion could become significant for students. If so, allow it to continue for much of the class period. If necessary, check the homework after class.

ISRAEL'S ROOTS (Objectives 2 and 3)

God's instructions provided an opportunity for Israel to look back to the past (to their tribal beginnings) and look forward to the future (to times when they would need to go into battle). They also provided future generations with another opportunity to look back and remember what God had done for His people--their ancestors.

Following are suggested answers to the Student Book questions:

1. To find out how many men were able to serve in Israel's army.
2. 603,550
3. Joseph.
4. Levi.
5. They were not to serve in the army because they were in charge of the tablernacle. (Note that God had selected the Levites instead of the firstborn from each family--**3:39-41**.)
6. Each time the people organized for battle, they remembered their tribal ancestor. This remembering also called to mind the whole history related to the entry into Egypt, the time there, and the Exodus.
7. The **Numbers** census prepared Israel for their journey. It foreshadowed the **Luke** census, which provided the context for the beginning of Jesus' "journey" on earth. Later Israel would look back on God's mercy with His nation; today we look back on God's mercy in sending a Savior.

ORDERLINESS (Objective 4)

Use local examples to help students visualize one million people (e.g., ten thousand times as many people as were at the big game). Then ask, **If all these people were going to go to the same place at the same time, what would happen? What do you think the leaders of your community would do to avoid chaos when they wanted the people to move? How could they again prevent chaos when the people arrive at their destination?**

After this discussion, look at God's system for orderliness in travel and camping while Israel traveled in the wilderness. Students should have placed the tribes of Judah, Issachar, and Zebulun (in that order) to the east; they traveled under the banner of Judah. Reuben, Simeon, and Gad camped to the south; they traveled under the banner of Reuben. Ephraim, Manasseh, and Benjamin camped to the west; they traveled under the banner of Ephraim. Dan, Asher, and Naphtali camped to the north; they traveled under the banner of Dan.

The Levites camped in the center, around the tabernacle. The clan of Gershon camped to the west, the clan of Kohath to the south, and the clan of Merari to the east. The families of Moses and Aaron camped to the east, in front of the tabernacle.

Do a quick book check and note which students have completed their work. Choose someone to sketch the plan on the board for others to use as a check for their own work. Leave the sketch on the board so you can add numbers later.

REDEDICATION AND REMEMBRANCE (Objective 5)

Help the students to visualize the solemnity of the tabernacle dedication that is reflected in the precise repetition of offerings by each individual tribe in **Num. 7**. This was followed by the first anniversary celebration of their liberation from slavery--the Passover festival. Show the students that God designed all this to keep Israel focused on Him so that Satan would not lead them astray.

Tie this concept into the reason for our worship today. We have been freed from the bondage of sin. For many, this occured when they were baptized; others received the benefit of Christ's atonement when they came to faith prior to their baptism. Many of the elements of worship bring to mind the work God has done to save us.

It is not uncommon for young people to accept a peer's rationalization: I don't need to attend church to be a Christian; I can worship God in my own time, place, and way. Help the students to examine the need for regular group worship--as a spiritual "support system"--a reminder, if you will, of who we were, who we are now, and to whom we owe our freedom from Satan's tyranny.

TIME TO MOVE ON (Objective 6)

Read **Num. 9:15--10:7** aloud in unison. Help the students to visualize the dynamics of this system of theocracy--the complete dependence on and immediate obedience to God's day-by-day direction for their lives. The cloud lifted; the silver trumpets were sounded; and then what? Chaos? Hardly! The ark led the way **(10:33)** and all Israel followed. Beginning at **Num. 10:11**, have one student read the grand plan aloud as another numbers the groups on the blackboard in proper sequence (1--Moses and Aaron; 2, 3, 4--Judah, Issachar, Zebulun; 5, 6--Gershon, Merari; 7, 8, 9--Reuben, Simeon, Gad; 10--Kohath; 11, 12, 13--Ephraim, Manasseh; Benjamin; 14, 15, 16--Dan, Asher, Naphtali).

A BLESSING FROM GOD (Objective 7)

End the session with a discussion of the blessings God has promised and we receive. Note the Trinitarian nature of the Aaronic blessing, and discuss the significance of the fact that we still use this blessing in our services today.

Close by singing "Blest the Children of Our God" ("Blessed Are the Sons of God" in The Lutheran Hymnal).

Session 35: Concluding Activities for Unit 5

Use the following questions as a review, a test, or in another way that seems appropriate to you.

MULTIPLE CHOICE

Write the letter of the best answer on each blank.

1. The number of people who left Egypt at the time of the Exodus was about
   (A) 500,000 (C) 2,000,000
   (B) 1,000,000 (D) 4,000,000
2. The passing of the Israelites through the Red Sea can be compared to
   (A) the birth process
   (B) maturation
   (C) adolescence
   (D) confirmation
3. The two men who held up the hands of Moses during the battle with the Amalekites were
   (A) Aaron and Jethro
   (B) Jethro and Hur
   (C) Aaron and Hur
   (D) Jethro and Joshua
4. The Bible teaches that one who refuses to work, that should
   (A) be forced to work
   (B) pay more taxes
   (C) go hungry
   (D) give to the poor
5. The form of government under which the Israelites lived in the wilderness is called
   (A) democracy (C) socialism
   (B) communism (D) theocracy
6. The high priest made atonement for the sins of the people by
   (A) collecting tithes from them
   (B) offering a sacrificial lamb for them
   (C) reading the Commandments to them
   (D) praying to God for them
7. The holiest day of the year in the life of the Israelites was
   (A) Passover
   (B) The Day of Atonement
   (C) New Year
   (D) The Day of Feasts
8. The most important thing about a gift is the
   (A) wishes of the giver
   (B) nature of the gift
   (C) needs of the recipient
   (D) reason for the gift
9. The best way to determine the will of God is to
   (A) study the Bible
   (B) study the universe

(C) talk to people
(D) tithe

10. The purpose of the census in the wilderness was to
(A) see how many people there were
(B) determine the ratio of men and women
<u>(C) establish a basis for tithing</u>
(D) find out how many men could serve in the army

TRUE-FALSE

Circle T for True and F for False.

T F 1. At one point in the wilderness, Moses used a piece of wood to purify water miraculously. (T)

T F 2. God told the Israelites to keep several days' worth of manna on hand in the wilderness at all times. (F)

T F 3. When God invites us to be His children, we have the power to refuse the invitation. (T)

T F 4. When God invites us to be His children, we have the power--on our own--to accept the invitation. (F)

T F 5. When the Ten Commandments are listed in the Bible, each commandment has a specific number ascribed to it. (F)

T F 6. All the laws of the Old Testament were abolished when Jesus came. (F)

T F 7. When the Israelites built and worshiped a golden calf, Moses became so angry that he asked God to destroy the whole nation. (F)

T F 8. When Moses asked for donations for the building of the tabernacle, the people gave so much that Moses had to ask them to stop. (T)

T F 9. The teachings of Jesus support the idea of giving a proportionate amount of one's earnings to the Lord. (T)

T F 10. The reason that the Levites did not have to serve in the army was that there were enough soldiers without them. (F)

MATCHING

Write the letter of the best answer on the blanks. Some of the choices will not be used.

D 1. The tabernacle
I 2. Ark of the covenant
H 3. The courtyard
F 4. Desert of Shur
M 5. Pillar of cloud and fire
B 6. Mount Sinai
N 7. The golden calf
A 8. The Mercy Seat
K 9. The Most Holy Place
G 10. The Promised Land

A. Sculpture that signified God's forgiveness

B. Place where Moses obtained the Ten Commandments

C. Another name for the Sinai Peninsula

D. Contained the courtyard, Holy Place, and Most Holy Place

E. The place where Moses sat when he judged the people

F. Place where Moses purified the drinking water

G. Place that Moses saw but was not allowed to enter

H. Place in the tabernacle where the priests offered sacrifices

I. Contained only the Ten Commandments, Aaron's rod, and manna

J. Place where Moses made water come out of a rock

K. Contained only the Ark of the Covenant

L. Place that Moses was allowed to enter after he repented

M. Covered the Tabernacle as a sign of God's presence

N. Was ground up and sprinkled in the drinking water

COMPLETION

Write the word or phrase that best completes each statement in the blank.

1. The name of the food that God miraculously provided every morning for the Israelites in the wilderness was [manna].

2. [Jethro] told Moses to appoint elders to help rule the people.

3. Another name for the Ten Commandments is [Decalog, or Moral Law].

4. The book of the Bible that is primarily devoted to the description of the worship life of the Israelites in the wilderness is [Leviticus].

5. The most important symbol in the worship of the Israelites was [sacrificial blood].

6. Proportionate giving is similar to [tithing].

7. The laws that God prescribed for His people in the Old Testament were designed to benefit [the people].

8. The tribe of the Israelites that was responsible for the tabernacle and worship services was the tribe of [Levi].

9. The census in Numbers foreshadowed the census at the time of [Jesus' birth].

10. The detailed rules about the way in which the Israelites were to set up camp around the tabernacle taught them the importance of [organization, or obedience].

ESSAYS

On a separate sheet of paper, write briefly about any four of the following topics. Be sure to put the number of the topic at the beginning of each essay.

1. How can overprotection can be harmful as a person matures? Give examples from the story of the Israelites in the wilderness.

2. Describe the privileges and responsibilities that make up the life of freedom in Christ.

3. What's the difference between moral laws and civil laws? How was each important at the time of Moses? Describe the role these laws play in the story of salvation.

4. Compare the worship of God in the tabernacle with the worship of God in churches today.

5. Distinguish between atonement and justification in the life of a believer. What is the role of good works?

6. Compare Jesus and the sacrificial lamb in the worship of the Israelites.

7. What does the Bible teach about tithing?

8. Draw a sketch of the sections of the tabernacle. Label the sections and the contents of each section.

9. What is the difference between objective and subjective justification?

10. Describe the importance of rules and organization in the spiritual and secular life of a person.

Unit 6: The Covenant Nation Begins to Function

After the spiritual and military preparation God had provided at Mount Sinai, He was now ready to lead the Israelites into the Promised Land, where they would reign in righteousness and justice--a people set apart by their unique covenanted relationship with the Creator. Through them all the nations of the earth were to be blessed.

This unit examines the painful aftermath of doubt and rebellion that eliminated an entire generation and passed the torch of hope and the challenge of obedience to the next generation, a nation tempered by trials, tribulations, and a solemn warning by both Moses and Joshua to heed their covenant responsibilities.

PLANNING THE UNIT

Session 36: Find examples of "good guys" getting "bad breaks" in recent newspaper or magazine articles to stimulate opening discussion.

Session 37: Alert the librarian to the need for books about the life of Joni Eareckson. Have classroom maps ready.

Session 38: Articles about religious charlatans could aid in the classroom discussion.

Session 39: The medical profession's symbol is mentioned in this session. A picture of it could be helpful. Have classroom map ready to point out the trans-Jordan region already under Israel's control.

Session 40: Ask a social studies teacher for examples of legislation that are a direct outgrowth of Israel's laws.

Session 43: A group might want to prepare a dramatization of the Gibeonite deception for a class presentation or chapel illustration.

Session 44: A current article about some young person who had a fine reputation, but ruined his or her life in a single brash moment, would be appropriate here. Have a classroom map available to locate tribal allocations and cities of refuge.

Session 36: Equipped for Action (Israel Moves North)

BIBLE BASIS: Num. 11--12

CENTRAL TRUTH

God's people experience hardships, but He always provides for their needs.

OBJECTIVES

That the students will:

1. Describe how the acceptance of Christ as Savior and Lord affects day-to-day living (negating any "God owes me something"attitudes)
2. Find, in Israel's experiences, evidences of God's attitude toward grumbling: it is lamentable and evidence of spiritual weakness
3. Acknowledge that God keeps His promises--even when they seem impossible of fulfillment
4. Recognize jealousy and pride as prime causes of trouble among believers
5. Recognize the fact that God does not take presumptuous criticism of His leaders lightly

BACKGROUND

Grumbling and backbiting are familiar habits in all too many congregations. Teenagers are sometimes the worst offenders. This lesson will help them take a "God's-eye view" of these activities and recognize them for what they are: dangerous and sinful. As we struggle to overcome our own weakness in these areas, God's promise to "make all things new" is our only hope. Living by the Spirit, we can grow to full spiritual maturity in Christ. As Luther admonished, we must daily drown the Old Adam within us and allow Christ to reign.

INTRODUCTION (Objective 1)

Begin the unit with a brief summary of Israel's national life thus far. You could use the first paragraph from the Teacher's Guide Unit Overview for this purpose. Point out that God now considered Israel ready to carry out His purposes in the land that He promised centuries before to Abraham.

The introductory poem, "What God Hath Promised," may be familiar to some of the students. Before looking at the texts, draw the students into a discussion to bring out family attitudes toward hardship. Ask, **Have you ever heard someone say something like, 'Why should this happen to me? I'm a good churchgoer?"** Stimulate the discussion with references to recent news items in which "good guys" get a bad break. Was God sleeping? After various views have been aired, proceed to look at Jesus' teachings as listed in the Student Book. Help them to conclude that God does not promise to shelter them from every hardship, but He does promise to strengthen them in the midst of hardships.

ISRAEL GRUMBLES (Objective 2)

Ask for the student assessments of what the lives of the Israelites were like at this point. Would they like to change places with them? Why? Why not? (Disadvantages and hardships of camping in the desert, for example should be readily apparent.) The Israelites did experience hardships! Does God see that this justified grumbling? Lead into an examination of how we react to frustrations, or how our families and friends react. Ask, **Do you know anyone with very few problems who complains a lot? Anyone with many problems who manages to remain cheerful? Who is happier?**

Develop the concept that God promised the Israelites a very exciting future and provided adequate provisions for the present. If they had spent more time thinking about their purpose in life and less about their pleasures, what could have resulted? Remind the students that the same truths apply today.

Attitudes make all the difference. And since God does not change, we can be sure that He still frowns on complaints. Be sure students recognize that God first addressed the cause of complaints--spiritual lack--but He also promised to deal with the complaints, in spite of seemingly insurmountable odds.

GOD DELIVERS (Objectives 3 and 4)

Have **Num. 11:24-30** read in class. Look briefly at the responses of Joshua and Moses to Eldad's and Medad's prophecying. Point out that Moses welcomed it while Joshua, Moses' aid and heir apparent, felt threatened by it. Observe that sometimes weaker Christians are upset when a fellow Christian is spiritually blessed, but those who are spiritually more mature usually welcome spiritual growth in others (as well as in themselves).

Encourage the students to try to visualize the almost incomprehensible number of quail the Lord "rained" on the Israelites, considering that no one gathered <u>less</u> than 60 bushels! Ask, **Do you ever get sick from eating too much candy or too many cookies?** Greed often makes us ill.

RACIAL PRIDE AND PREJUDICE (Objective 5)

Suggest that perhaps Aaron and Miriam felt less important now that there were 70 more spiritual leaders in the camp. Maybe they blamed Moses for what they saw as loss of prestige. At any rate, they resented him and looked for an excuse for their resentment. Moses' wife became the scapegoat. They used her race as their excuse to undercut Moses' authority.

Call attention to the amazing fact that Moses, in spite of his astonishing success and international fame, is still described as "more humble than anyone else on the face of the earth." To underscore the concept of God blessing the humble, have someone read **1 Peter 5:5-6.** Help the class see that Moses did not worry about defending his image. Lead the class to make present-day applications of the concept described in **Rom. 12:17-21.**

Lest students get the impression that they should tolerate false teachings and support their proponents, devote the remaining class time to an examination of the texts listed in the Student Book to determine our duties and responsibilities toward maintaining true doctrine and practice today. **John 13:14-17, 20,** and **Eph. 5:1-21** are two more sections of Scripture that examine this topic.

Session 37: God's Plan and Israel's Rebellion

BIBLE BASIS: Num. 13--14 (Deut. 1:19-46; 9:23)

CENTRAL TRUTH

Focusing on the negatives of life (Satan and his works) results in defeat. But when we look to God in faith and obedience, He assures us of victory.

OBJECTIVES

That the students will:

1. Express their attitudes about the way people react to tragedy and success
2. Recognize Caleb and Joshua's faith, courage, and frustration
3. Describe the effect that negative thinking had on Israel's ability to function properly
4. Identify God's promises as the key to claiming His mercy and forgiveness
5. Realize that God wants them to deal with feelings (which sometimes are not sinful in and of themselves) in ways that please Him
6. Identify faith in God and obedience to His "Kadesh Barnea marching orders" as the means through which God accomplishes His will for us

BACKGROUND

We have been born again, nurtured, taught, and empowered by God. Now He frequently puts us in a position to do His work. How often we refuse to move and act because we focus on our own natural lack of ability and on the obstacles we see, rather than on God's power and promises! (We call this shortcoming a "rationalization.") God asks us to move out in faith today: to witness, to start home Bible groups, to form prayer cells, to pray for miraculous healings, to feed the hungry, clothe the naked . . . and all too often we look to ourselves and feel like "grasshoppers."

Emphasize in this lesson the importance of positive attitudes born of faith in and obedience to God. Pray that through the spiritual insights in this lesson at least your students will view their limited cups of life as "half full" rather than "half empty."

INTRODUCTION (Objective 1)

Joni Eareckson's story illustrates the strength available to each one of us through faith in God. Encourage students to share what they know of her struggles and triumphs (or other examples from their own lives) and to pray for God's strength when they face their own disappointments in life.

When you discuss chronic complainers, remind students not to give the names of the people they describe. Help the students recognize the ever-present danger of allowing Satan to draw our attention away from God's work (our blessings) and toward Satan's work (our problems) and thus rob us of the joy that is ours in Christ--even in the most difficult circumstances.

ISRAEL'S GREAT OPPORTUNITY (Objective 2)

Refer to the parable of the wedding banquet in **Matt. 22:1-14.** Have someone read the king's invitation in **verse 4.** Propose the same situation today. Ask, **What if your father planned a grand wedding reception and all the guests refused to come?**

Explain that God was now inviting His chosen nation into the land that He was eager to give them. After the scouts explored the land, they would be able to tell the people what a marvelous gift God was giving them. Point out that Moses' instructions to the 12 scouts sound like they came from someone who was considering a property he wanted to occupy rather than from a general who was planning a military campaign.

Use classroom maps to show the class how comprehensive the 40-day trip of the scouts was. Point out that Kadesh Barnea is in the Wilderness of Zin on the southern border of Palestine and Lebo Hamath is about 100 miles north of the Sea of Chinnereth (Galilee).

In comparing the reports of Joshua and Caleb with that of the other 10 scouts, bring out the fact that the circumstances were the same for both groups, but the attitudes were affected by the focus of the individuals involved--on God or on self.

ISRAEL'S TRAGIC MISTAKE (Objective 3)

Briefly review the miraculous events of Israel's past two years to underscore the foolishness of their decision to listen to the ten rather than the two. Ask, **What happens to the "majority rules" concept in a situation like this? Should the majority always rule?** Some students may quote a slogan such as, "God and any other individual makes a majority." This poses the question, "How do we know whose side God is on in a dispute?" Point out the importance of listening to God and what He says (the Bible). The Israelites listened to ten men who focused on Satan's negatives rather than two men who focused on God's promises.

MOSES INTERCEDES AGAIN (Objective 4)

Have someone read **Num. 14:13-19** as the students watch for the reasons Moses gave for asking God to forgive the Israelites rather than destroy them. Be sure they recognize that Moses did not claim that Israel deserved to be forgiven, but that God's name would be upheld by preserving His people. Refer to **verse 18** and ask whether Moses was saying that forgiveness should exclude all punishment. Compare Moses' intercession (especially **v. 19**) with Jesus' intercession for the thief **(Luke 23:32)** and for us **(Heb. 7:25)**.

CONSEQUENCES OF ISRAEL'S MISTAKE
(Objective 5)

Have students read about the consequences of Israel's rebellion in **Num. 14:20-45.** Talk about the difference between (a) involuntary feelings (anger, lust, resentment, greed) and (b) prolonged indulging in these thought patterns, which is often accompanied by voluntary (usually sinful) acts. Emphasize that some feelings may not be sinful (e.g., Jesus became angry when he drove the money changers from the temple--**Matt. 21:12-13**), and even when Satan brings negative, sinful thoughts into our consciousness, we can, with the help of God's Holy Spirit, apply God's Word to the situation; thus God will change our thought patterns before they destroy us. As Luther once said, quoting an ancient church father, "I can't prevent the birds from flying over my head, but I can keep them from building nests in my hair." (From Luther's Works, Erlangen Edition, vol. 43, p.111.)

Ask, **Does the 40-year wandering, during which all those over 20 would die, and the death of the 10 cowardly scouts mean that all these people were eternally damned?** Lead into an examination of the relationships between sin and forgiveness as compared with sin and its consequences. Ask for examples that illustrate this principle. For example, it is a sin to be wasteful, and even if that sin is confessed and forgiven, we can expect the consequences--a condition of lesser affluence--to follow. Perhaps the students will add other examples, such as the forgiveness of a "sexually active" person who must still deal with the reality of the resulting child. Or, even though lack of diligence in school is forgivable, the lack of preparedness and its aftereffect will remain.

DO GOD'S WILL--IN HIS TIME
(Objective 6)

We tend to ask God to do things in our way and at the time that seems best to us--especially when we feel sure that we're asking for something that we know is according to His will. Have someone read **Ex. 23:27-30.** Clearly it was God's will to occupy the Holy Land, but the timing was under His jurisdiction. Sometimes we try to force God's hand, or we wait for Him to push us into doing His work. Point out that, faced with the prospect of 40 years of wandering and death, the Israelites decided to attack. They tried --unsuccessfully--to carry out God's plans on their own, and not through faith in and obedience to Him.

Use the remainder of the class period to examine God's wonderful plans for His people today. He calls us to repent (now); let our light shine (now); be reconciled to our brother (first); stop swearing (now); not hoard earthly things (never); not judge one another (never); obey His teachings (now); watch for Jesus to return (always); and help the needy and strangers (always).

Help the students see the Great Commission as our "mandate to occupy." In this "promised land" He promises to give us **the fruit of the Spirit . . . love, joy, peace, patience, kindness, goodness, faithfulness, gentleness, and self-control (Gal. 5:22).** Through faith and obedience we are to "occupy," today, as **Heb. 3** and **4** clearly admonishes us.

Close with a prayer for greater faith, prompt obedience, and eager anticipation for the many unexpected blessings God has in store for us, ending the prayer with **Eph. 3:20.** God grant it for Jesus' sake. Amen.

Session 38: Follow the Leaders God Gives You

BIBLE BASIS: Num. 15:1--20:13

CENTRAL TRUTH

God sets up leaders and uses them to accomplish His will on earth. He expects us to obey these leaders.

OBJECTIVES

That the students will

1. Identify consequences that sometimes occur when people challenge or ignore their leaders
2. Discover how generously Moses shared his leadership with others
3. Recognize that power and prestige can easily make people think too highly of themselves
4. Agree that God is eager to build faith and explain His will
5. Recognize the consequences of spiritual carelessness
6. Identify both God's judgment and grace in His dealings with the people of Israel

BACKGROUND

Authority. Many teenagers rebel at it. But God has established it. He places people (including you, the teacher) into leadership positions. He expects you to carry out His will faithfully, and He expects your students to follow--not to rebel against--your leadership.

But what happens when followers rebel? Sometimes, nothing that's very obvious; in His love God permits people to live "normal, happy" lives. Sometimes, rebellious followers experience consequences that don't seem too severe; for example, a student may get a "D" on a test because she refused to study. Sometimes, followers who rebel suffer very severe consequences; for example, a student may become a drug addict because he chose to ignore his teacher's and parents' warnings about drug abuse. Always, God is ready to forgive the rebellious sinner who repents.

The episodes in today's session provide examples of severe judgment by God, but we also find examples of His mercy. And again we find frequent intercessions by Moses, their leader.

INTRODUCTION (Objective 1)

Some students will probably disagree with the action of the coach in the Student Book story. Without getting into an argument of whether he was right or wrong, point out the reasons for not lifting the suspension: Twice Chuck had challenged his leadership openly (on the field and in the locker room) and secretly once (by breaking training rules). The coach felt that more challenges to his leadership would have hurt the team, and lifting the suspension would have encouraged others to make those challenges.

This incident might stimulate discussion on the role of student leaders--both on and off duty. Ask, **Is it right to expect more of leaders than of other students--even off duty? Why?** The discussion should bring out some of the outstanding characteristics that identify leadership material (a mature outlook, dependability, strength, charisma, talent, skill, etc.) and the added advantage that this gives for making wise decisions.

You might also address the topic of hero worship. Help the students recognize that a follower's mistakes may affect only one person, whereas a leader almost always influences the lives of followers. You may want to refer to **James 3:1** and **Luke 12:48b.**

LEADERSHIP IN ISRAEL (Objectives 2 and 3)

Use the Student Book materials to bring out the facts that (1) the present leaders of Israel (except, at this point, Moses, Aaron, Joshua, and Caleb) were are all doomed to die during the wilderness wanderings--a fact that was very upsetting to them, and (2) Moses, far from being defensive about his leadership position, was very generous in delegating power and eager to develop leadership capabilities in others.

Go on to examine how these additional leaders handled this new power--especially when they realized what their rebellion at Kadesh Barnea has brought upon them. Be sure the students recognize that these were not outcasts or underprivileged people who challenged Moses and Aaron--they were leaders who were hungry for more power.

Notes on the Student Book questions:

1--2. God clearly had chosen Moses and Aaron.

3--4. Moses had first appointed officials to help judge the people, and later God gave His Spirit to 70 elders.

5--7. Korah, Dathan, Abiram, and On led the rebellion of 250 community leaders.

8--9. God, not Moses and Aaron, had given them their leadership positions.

10. Some rebels were swallowed up by the earth; others were destroyed by fire.

11--12. After the people grumbled about this incident, God killed 14,700 of them in a plague. Ask, **What was the root cause of all this unrest?** Lead the students to see that we all tend to refuse to accept the undesirable aftereffects of our sins. Apparently the Israelites realized that Moses and Aaron had obediently accepted God's pronouncement of 40 years of desert wandering, so they wanted to follow the leaders who suggested that they could somehow override God's decision if only they could get rid of Moses and Aaron.

A LASTING REMINDER (Objective 4)

Have **Num. 17** read aloud in class. Point out that when the people finally became submissive, God provided a permanent object lesson for them. Note also that, in His eagerness to teach, God delivered even more than He had promised. Ask, **Do you think that perhaps Aaron, having inside information, could have "fixed" the outcome by selecting an almond branch that was about to sprout?** Develop this thought to the conclusion that, just in case the people might have suspected this, God arranged for buds, blossoms, and almonds to grow --something that was clearly impossible overnight by natural means!

WATER FROM A ROCK--AGAIN!
(Objective 5)

Today's society encourages us to "do our own thing." We need to impress upon our classes that God requires us to "do His thing." Moses' words in **Num. 20:10** (which may have been spoken in anger) pointed the people to himself--rather than to God --as the one who would provide the water, and striking the rock--rather than just speaking to it--obviously demonstrated a lack of trust in God **(v. 12)**.

"GOD OF GRACE AND GOD OF GLORY"
(Objective 6)

As students look at God's harsh judgment upon the people, they may lose sight of the evidences of His grace that we find in these chapters (separating the masses from the rebellious leaders so they would not also be killed; stopping the plague when Aaron stood in the midst of the people with the incense; providing water in spite of Moses' disobedience). Be sure to remind your class of the grace they receive each day as a result of Christ's atonement for them.

ADDITIONAL ACTIVITY

Have students calculate approximately how many Israelites have already died since their arrival at Kadesh Barnea.

Session 39: Marking Time (Trials, Tribulations, and Types)

BIBLE BASIS: Num. 20:14--33:49 (Deut. 2--3)

CENTRAL TRUTH

Even during the 40 years of marking time in the wilderness, God continued to teach, warn, encourage, and train the rising generation for the faith and obedience they would need as His covenant nation.

OBJECTIVES

That the students will

1. Acknowledge that we learn much of what we need to know from life experiences

2. Discover that God tailored the Israelites' experiences in the desert to fit their needs--sometimes discipline, sometimes encouragement --but the covenant continued uninterruptedly

3. Compare God's use of a bronze snake to rescue Israel with our rescue from sin through Jesus' death on the cross

4. Reflect on the irony of Israel's impervious position--being vulnerable only from within--and apply this principle to today's church

5. Describe the thrill they experience when they recognize divine providence in the circumstances that affect their lives

BACKGROUND

Often, particularly in the teen years when schooling is mandatory, students have the frustrating feeling that they are only "marking time," and that nothing really worthwhile is happening. Many Bible-oriented people refer to these periods as "desert experiences"--perhaps because so many people in the Bible went through such times of frustration while in desert settings: Moses in Midian, the Israelites in their wilderness wanderings, and Jesus in the wilderness after His baptism. In this session you will have the opportunity to instill in the students a sense of adventure and anticipation as they review the wilderness years of the Israelites and witness God's careful preparation of His people for the challenges that lay ahead.

INTRODUCTION (Objective 1)

The Student Book presents the familiar--but hardly universal--example of the traditional homemaker who finds joy in her chosen profession and inspires others to imitate her. Magazines and other branches of the media are probably applying pressures on the girls in the class to refuse to be trapped in the "drudgery" of being a traditional homemaker. Such pressures imply that we should use the income produced by an individual to measure their value to their families and/or society in general. You may need to point out that we do not necessarily guarantee increased happiness when the number of women in the job market increases or when a person's income increases.

Ask, **What if every member of your basketball team insisted on playing center and trained specifically for that position? How well would the team do?** Emphasize the exciting concept of the uniqueness of the individual. Assure the class that God has an excellent "track record" for training and preparing specific individuals for specific tasks. He has not changed over the years.

Help the students see that we should center our life's adventure on discovering God's purpose for our lives. Our comfort lies in the conviction that even the hairs on our heads are all numbered and that nothing escapes His all-seeing eye. Assure them that the "abundant life" that Jesus came to secure for us **(John 10:10)** is ours no matter into which vocation He leads us.

ISRAEL'S GOAL: OCCUPATION OF THE PROMISED LAND (Objective 2)

Draw parallels between God preparing an individual for a specific task (by training and experience) and His preparation of the new generation of Israelites. Help the class to recognize that God's goal for us can be attained in many ways and that when we do not resist His teaching, His ways seem simpler and more palatable to us.

You might want to use the story of the farmer who hit his donkey over the head with a club. When a passerby asked why he was doing such a seemingly inappropriate thing, the farmer replied, "It's the only way that I can get his attention!" Stress the advantage of listening when God speaks so that He doesn't have to hit us over the head to get our attention!

Point out that God expressly protected the Edomites and Moabites because He had given Edom specifically to the descendants of Esau, and had given Moab to Lot's descendants **(Deut. 2:1-9)**. God also protected the Ammonites because they, too, were Lot's descendants **(Deut. 2:16-19)**.

IMPATIENCE IN THE DESERT (Objective 3)

1. Encourage the class to address this Student Book question. Every Christian experiences impatience. Teenagers have grown up surrounded by "instant" solutions to every need: 24-hour-a-day banking; instant coffee and tea; sleeping pills; microwave cooking, etc. Patience is developed by experiencing delay, so perhaps we feel we have an historical "right" to feel impatient when our desires are not quickly satisfied. Warn the students of the root cause of impatience: a feeling of superiority, frequently born of a lack of knowledge. You might use the following example:

Mother is baking bread. The children become impatient with the time-consuming kneading, rising, and baking, and they would like to rush the process. If the mother listens to the pleas of the children to bake the dough immediately, and at a higher-than-specified temperature, what will happen? (The result will be a decidedly inferior product--probably more fit to play catch with than to eat!)

Use this or a similar story to illustrate that when we try to tell God exactly how and when to answer our prayers, we are courting disaster by implying that our knowledge and insight are superior to His.

2. As you discuss **Num. 21:4-9**, emphasize the "ridiculousness" of God's solution--to save people who look at a bronze snake on a pole! Note that this salvation required an act of faith--looking at the snake.

3. Seek comparisons such as: poison of snakes and poison of sin; a bronze snake and Jesus; temporal death for those who refused to look to the bronze snake for healing and eternal death for those who refuse to look to Jesus for salvation (emphasize the element of prideful stubbornness in each case).

PROTECTED FROM WITHOUT; INFECTED FROM WITHIN (Objective 4)

Use a classroom map to show the large area already occupied by the Israelites even before they entered the Promised Land (from the Arnon River north to the Sea of Kinnereth, or Galilee).

Reflect on the fact that while God protected Israel from a great military tragedy **(Num. 22--24)** without their even being aware of it, their self-centeredness caused the deaths of tens of thousands of people. Contrast Phinehas' violent reaction to immorality **(25:8)** with today's laissez-faire attitude toward many sexual aberrations in the movies, on TV, and the like. Ask, **What does God expect of us? What if Phinehas had just shrugged his shoulders and said, "Who am I to judge? Live and let live!" Or, worse yet, what if he had asked Zimri to introduce him to that gorgeous prostitute's sister!?**

COUNTING OFF AND GETTING SET (Objective 5)

An old proverb says, "God's mill of justice grinds very slowly, but it grinds exceedingly fine!" The second census of Moses illustrates this concept well. Use the examination of Joshua's careful preparation through "coincidental" circumstances and specifically prescribed activities as a springboard for stimulating faith and anticipation as the students apply these concepts to themselves.

ADDITIONAL ACTIVITIES

Examine **Num. 27:1-11** for evidence of God's pro-woman stance even in the Old Testament.

Compare current methods of selecting and commissioning religious leaders with those used for Joshua, Barnabas, and Saul.

Session 40: Final Words from Moses (Part 1)

BIBLE BASIS: Selections from Deuteronomy

CENTRAL TRUTH

Through Moses, who was well aware of Israel's short memory and his own impending death, God reminded the people of all that had taken place under Moses' leadership and reassured them that God's covenant still stood. God is our Refuge and Strength.

OBJECTIVES

That the students will

1. Identify the value Moses' instructions could provide to the Israelites as they prepared to enter the Promised Land
2. Recognize the importance of parents sharing their religious experiences and insights with their children (and grandchildren)
3. List truths they receive for their own lives as they "read between the lines" of Moses' historical review
4. Recall the many blessings God promises to those who obey His commandments
5. Discover in Moses' instructions the core of a unique, compassionate national constitution
6. Discuss the system of justice represented by cities of refuge and compare it with our own judicial system
7. Turn to Jesus as their very own "City of refuge" when the destroyer threatens, because Satan has no power there

BACKGROUND

As teachers, we can readily identify with Moses' dreams and frustrations at this point in his life. God had revealed enough to him so that he experienced, through God's Spirit, an all-consuming zeal to encourage the Israelites to be all that God had planned for them--to realize their full potential as God's chosen people. Moses had caught the vision. He was enthusiastic. He used every means at his disposal to convey this spirit of anticipation and adventure to his "pupils." He began by laying a foundation of facts. He pointed out cause-and-effect relationships. He chided. He encouraged. He prodded and he pleaded.

Moses' overriding theme is as applicable today as it was then: God has laid down the terms of His covenant. He has always kept His end of the bargain. History reveals what happens to those who accept and obey His covenant--and to those who do not.

INTRODUCTION (Objective 1)

The introduction sets a classroom scene for the children of Israel at this point. Discussion of the opening question will illustrate that there are many ways to prepare for a test. (Perhaps some "one-track-mind" students in the class will be inspired by this discussion to consider trying new methods for studying for their next tests and thereby improve their grades!)

Point out that Israel's next test will be a real "biggie." All the preceding four centuries of exile in Egypt, slavery, and wandering in the desert had been preparing them for this moment. Ask, **What could Moses, as their teacher, say at this point to help them pass the test?**

REMEMBER GOD'S MIGHTY WORKS
(Objectives 2 and 3)

If the people were to succeed in their attempt to conquer the Promised Land, they would need to trust God, not themselves. It's no wonder that Moses began his "teaching" or preparation by reviewing facts that show how invincible the Israelites were--not apart from God but under His lordship.

Say, **Some people have observed that Christianity is never more than one generation removed from the possibility of extinction.** Use this sobering truth to compare the need for those born in the wilderness years to hear of God's plan, promises, and powerful acts with the need for today's youth to hear about sin, salvation, and God's activity in their parents' lives.

Suggest the following scenario:

Suppose that enemy tanks are bearing down on you as you near the shores of a large lake. Suddenly a dense fog holds the enemy back while the waters of the lake form two walls that allow you and half of your state's population to walk through on dry land. Then the fog lifts and, as the enemy rapidly closes the gap provided by the delay, the water closes over the onrushing attackers and all is quiet. Do you think you would remember that incident 40 years from now?

Help the class to recall that thousands of Israelites were in their teens as they passed through the Red Sea, and they were now mature adults ready to occupy the Promised Land. Moses simply "prodded their memories."

Following are the Column 2 answers for the Student Book activity, followed by possible Column 3 answers in parentheses. Answers will naturally vary, but this adds to the value of the lesson. The most important outcome is the application of each "message" to our own circumstances so that we are prepared for any tests we face.

Judges were appointed (people should not expect Joshua to answer every question or dispute that arose); the spies gave their report (the land is good); Israel refused to occupy land (when God says to go, obey); Israel attacked on their own (when God says to stay, obey); God watched and provided for them (don't worry about safety or material needs); they experienced 40 years of wandering and death (God always does what He says He will do); they passed by Edom, Moab, and the Ammonites (God will tell you whom not to attack); they conquered Sihon and Og (God will give victory over those whom He tells you to attack); cities that were destroyed had high walls (don't fear fortified cities); Og's bed measured 13' x 6' (don't fear giant-sized people); God gave trans-Jordon land to Gad, Reuben, and Manasseh (the land west of the Jordon will go to the other tribes); Moses told Gad, Reuben, and Manasseh they must fight (you must stick together until everyone has their land); people committed idolatry and adultery at Baal Peor (God will not tolerate idolatry); God gave the Law at Sinai (you must obey God); God delivered with plagues and the Exodus (God performs great miracles for His people); God delivered them (God will continue to honor His covenant with Israel's forefathers).

REMEMBER TO OBEY (Objective 4)

The mighty acts of God are undeniable. He keeps His covenant. He promises blessings to His people. He asks only that they accept and obey its conditions. This they promised to do at Mt. Sinai against the dramatic backdrop of lightning, thunder, and smoke.

Again, as the students identify all the blessings God promised to those who obey, emphasize the validity of God's unchangeable promises for all time and the ultimate beneficiaries of obedience--the people, not God.

Following are the blessings listed in the Student Book passages:

Respect of others; long life; prosperity; victory over enemies; God's love and blessings on all you own; children; freedom from disease; strength; favorable weather; land; superiority over enemies; freedom from poverty.

ABOUT FALSE PROPHETS, IDOLATERS, ETC. (Objective 6)

If you're running short on time, just check student answers to this section. Be sure to allow time for the last section. Following are suggested answers to these questions:

1. Kill them.
2. Kill them.
3. Destroy it.
4. Don't do it.
5. Eat only those animals called "clean" by God.
6. Bring a tithe to the tabernacle.
7. Cancel all debts of Israelites every seven years.
8. Free them every seventh year.
9. Be openhanded, not tightfisted.
10. Appoint tribal judges; seek justice.

11. Go to the priests for a verdict.

12. Choose the Israelite whom God points out.

13. Do not practice it or allow it.

CITIES OF REFUGE (Objectives 5, 6, and 7)

Alert the students to the fact that the laws listed here are the basis of much of our own judiciary system. They are designed to protect the innocent and punish the rebellious.

Allow sufficient time for the Gospel-oriented comparison between God's Old Testament cities of refuge and Jesus as our Refuge from Satan, who is eager to destroy us.

Close by singing or praying together the hymn stanzas printed in the Student Book (or another appropriate selection).

Session 41: Final Words from Moses (Part 2)

BIBLE BASIS: Selections from Deuteronomy

CENTRAL TRUTH

God led Moses to bid farewell to his precious people with divinely inspired words of teaching, revelation, admonition, encouragement, and prophecy.

OBJECTIVES

That the students will:

1. Identify with the excitement and anticipation that immediately precedes any major, long-rehearsed production
2. Recognize the interdependence of everyone involved in a major undertaking in order to bring it to a successful conclusion
3. Describe Moses' complete personal dedication and his lack of confidence in the character and dedication of the people
4. Thrill to Moses' witness to the unshakable faithfulness and power of Israel's God
5. Identify the moral corruption of the Canaanites as the reason for the directives to destroy that nation completely
6. Describe some prophecies that the Israelites will later see fulfilled in minute detail
7. Recognize Moses as a man of God--one to whom God spoke face-to-face

BACKGROUND

Moses literally "pulls out all the stops" in his ardent plea to Israel to faithfully keep their covenant with God. Moses yearned overwhelmingly for the Israelites to realize their great potential. This is a "type" or shadow of God's unceasing yearning also for each of us to realize our own God-given potential. We, like Israel, stand poised at the door to unimaginable power and blessing, while Satan strives with all his might to topple us into disbelief and all the horrors of his domain.

INTRODUCTION (Objectives 1 and 2)

Use the opening section of the Student Book to instill in the students an inkling of the electricity in the Israelite camp--something akin to the moments preceding the firing of the starting gun for an important race. Encourage students to share their own similar experiences in order to create the proper atmosphere. Carry this tone over into the next section.

MOSES FEELS THE TENSION (Objective 3)

This is the climax of Moses' long life. Will all the participants in the coming drama "follow through"? None of the people he is addressing, except for Joshua and Caleb, have invested half as much time as he has, since the oldest among them is only 60. Moses knows the dangers the people will face. What can he do to strengthen them? Has it all been for naught?

Take a moment to briefly review Moses' life, emphasizing the incredible chain of events that prepared this spiritual giant for this special task. Point out that, as he was about to lose his role as a leader, he agonized over the weaknesses of his flock and tried to caution them without discouraging them. Allow more than one student to read their paraphrases in order to bring out various facets of each example. (Keep the covenant, or you will be punished by exile; don't become proud--it is God who will conquer; if you worship Canaan's gods, you will lose the land, as they did; you do not deserve the land, you are getting it because of the covenant, you are stiff-necked and rebellious; God wanted to destroy you, but He spared you when I interceded.)

Ask, **Do you sometimes feel weak? How and when can weakness be a blessing?** Refer to **2 Cor. 12:9-10.**

MOSES IS SURE OF GOD'S MERCY
(Objective 4)

Comment that Moses also knows of the availability and boundlessness of God's power and mercy in the face of human weakness, and he enthusiastically calls Israel's attention to all the "pluses" they have going for them. Again, allow more than one student to read their paraphrases, encouraging discussion when it seems productive. (The land is large, with flourishing and well-furnished cities, wells, vineyards, and olive groves; God is faithful; God will love you, bless you, and increase your numbers and crops; God will keep you free from disease; God will fight for you; the land has ample water, various crops and mineral resources; God will quickly destroy even the giants before you; God has chosen <u>you</u>; you will be successful wherever you go.)

DIVINE STRATEGY (Objective 5)

Point out that conquest means war, and winning a war requires a strategy. As you work through the Student Book materials, it will become abundantly clear that for this battle by a theocracy, God used strategies that were far from traditional!

Because the merciless destruction of everything that breathes is often an offensive concept to idealistic teenagers, emphasize the all-pervasive evil of the Canaanites. Archaeologists and historians indicate that, encouraged by cultic orgies, sexual perversions (including homosexuality and bestiality, which are mentioned in **Lev. 18:23; Rom. 1:26-27;** and **Deut. 27:21**) were so rampant that the cattle as well as the populace were infested with venereal diseases.

PREDICTION OF THINGS TO COME
(Objective 6)

Take this opportunity to observe with the students that foretelling the future is clearly a minor part of the role and life of a prophet. At least this is the case when it comes to the amount of time and Biblical space that is devoted to this activity of prophets (though prophetic utterance certainly are very important). Much of Deuteronomy sets forth firm cause-and-effect relationships, but very little in that book delineates what will actually take place as clearly as do **Deut. 31:16-18** and most of the Song of Moses' **(32:15-43).**

FINAL FAREWELL (Objective 7)

If time permits, ask the girls in class to read **28:1-14** in unison and the boys **28:15-37.** Perhaps nowhere in all of Scripture are the blessings of obedience more clearly set forth. Point out the relationship between Law and Gospel here. Unless we recognize what sin is, we feel no need for a Savior. So Moses uses the truths of **chapter 28** to set the stage for the renewal of the covenant: He is our God, we are His children--and heirs of salvation and all that this implies.

After referring to Moses' final official acts of encouraging Joshua and the Levites, the blessing of all of Israel, and Moses' death, take some time to examine the Song of Moses **(32:1-43)** with the students. Ask, **What is the tone as the song begins?** Lead them to recognize how tender and loving the first two verses are. Then identify the next two verses as proclaiming God's greatness and justice.

Ask, **What is the tone of verses 5--35?** Observe that the Israelites must wonder to whom the song is referring--like the disciples of Jesus when they asked Him at the Last Supper, "Lord, is it I?" The closing section **(v. 36-43)** restores hope as God again comes to the aid of His beloved people.

Point out God's infinite patience --and His unchangeableness. Ask the students to recognize that God inspires Moses' earnest plea in **Deut. 30:11-20**, and it is His plea to us today. Have the class read it aloud in unison. Conclude by considering the fact that God's great plans for His people today are just as full of promise and power as they were on the shores of the Jordan nearly 2,500 years ago.

Session 42: Israel Enters the Promised Land

BIBLE BASIS: Joshua 1:1--5:12

CENTRAL TRUTH

Generations come and go; civilizations rise and fall; individuals accept or reject God's covenants; but the almighty God remains faithful--unchanged and unchangeable--forever!

OBJECTIVES

That the students will:

1. Consider the pivotal role of the pastor in a congregation and the effect of congregational attitudes on his effectiveness
2. Describe the the assurance Joshua received that God would be present as the ongoing source of "strength and courage" for <u>all</u> His people
3. Identify the evidences of God's universal love in Rahab's story
4. Describe similarities and differences between the miraculous crossings of the Red Sea and the Jordan River
5. See the resuming of the covenant rite of circumcision, the celebration of Passover, and the cessation of manna as signaling the end of the Israelites' wandering
6. Recognize the Lord's Supper as our present-day bread from heaven that sustains and strengthens us spiritually and physically

BACKGROUND

In this rapidly changing world we all desperately need an anchor--a reference point around which we can orient our lives. Israel's God, and ours, provides for that need through His Word and Sacraments. The Messianic covenant has remained valid and constant from its inception before the world began. Succeeding generations have been given various rites and other reminders to undergird and clarify this covenant, but its golden thread reflects the light of His love throughout history. Each generation in turn has been invited to respond in grateful reverence and obedience. It is our privilege as teachers to nurture those entrusted to us in the awe-filled faith that appropriates the blessings of that covenant. This session is eminently suited to that purpose.

INTRODUCTION (Objective 1)

You might ask two students to roleplay a pastor and a congregational officer. They should both voice some of their concerns as the pastor begins his new ministry. Lead the students, through this exercise and the examination of Israel's transition from Moses to Joshua, to recognize the importance of faith in God's ongoing love and concern during a transition (as well as at all other times).

GOD'S LEADER IS DEAD! LONG LIVE GOD'S LEADER (Objective 2)

Be sure the students notice that after God made His initial promise to Joshua, He called upon Joshua to be strong, courageous, and obedient, and to meditate constantly on God's Word.

Joshua's prompt military action and administrative "savvy" got everything off to a fine start. The people also had a good attitude. Remind the class that this land has been promised for more than 400 years. The time graph begun in session 7 should have the following (after creation) dates entered in it:

	Birth	Death
Abraham	1946	2121
Isaac	2046	2226
Jacob	2104	2353
Joseph	2197	2307
Moses	2662	
Exodus		2742
Joshua appointed leader		2781

Following are suggested answers for this section:

1. "I will give you every place where you set your foot."
2. Strong and courageous.
3. "Obey My Law; meditate daily upon the Book of the Law."
4. God promised to be with him wherever he went.
5. The officers of the people.
6. Tell the people to get supplies ready.
7. In three days they would cross the Jordan to take possession of the Promised Land.
8. Abraham; Isaac; Jacob; the Israelites.
9. "We will respect and obey you as we respected and obeyed Moses. Only be strong and courageous."

A RECONNAISSANCE MISSION
(Objective 3)

Ask, **Did any of you notice the alternate translation of the word prostitute in Joshua 2:1?** Point out that irreligious women did not consider prostitution particularly evil. Satan delights in every form of debasement, such as "using" the female body to satisfy the sinful lusts of the male with no respect for the woman's personhood (or vice versa). Rahab, however, was "born again" when she accepted Jehovah (**2:9-13;** especially **11b**) and as a renewed child of God adopted a new life-style, married into the tribe of Judah and became an ancestor of the Messiah. Surely Rahab, like the thief on the cross, is a clear witness that no one who comes to God will be turned away **(John 6:37)**.

GOD'S POWER AND PRESENCE REAFFIRMED
(Objective 4)

Have someone locate the position of the Israelites on the east side of the Jordan, just north of the Dead Sea. Then have them point out Zarethan. (Zondervan's Bible Atlas shows it just north of the mouth of the Jabbok River.) Note that topographical markings indicate more rugged land here that could "contain" the heaped up water more readily than the flatter land just north of the Dead Sea.

A photograph in Zondervan's Pictorial Bible Dictionary (Grand Rapids: Zondervan, 1969) shows the flow of the Jordan River temporarily blocked by earthquake-caused landslides in 1927. We don't know if God used similar events in Joshua's days, but this is the same area that is referred to in **Joshua 3:16.** Students should be able to relate the circumstances of the two miraculous crossings (of the Red Sea and the Jordan). Each event:

--Firmly established a relatively new leader as God-sent and God-empowered

--Showed the unique role of the ark of the covenant and the priestly office.

--Became the source of internationally expressed awe and respect for the God of Israel.

Following are suggested answers for this section:

1. The ark of the covenant.
2. The Jordan River.
3. There was no wall of water nor an approaching enemy.
4. One large stone.
5. As soon as the priests left the riverbed.
6. The river was at flood stage.
7. The people revered him as they had revered Moses.
8. To remind them of the miracle.
9. So all the world would know God's power and fear Him.
10. They lost their courage to fight.

SACRED RITES RESUMED (Objective 5)

The Passover (before Gilgal) was celebrated shortly before God's planned conquest of Canaan. Forty years earlier God had instituted the Passover feast just before the Exodus. God carefully reminded His people of His power and presence before major events in their history!

Ask, **Why did God stop the manna?** Develop the concept that God does not perform miracles for our amusement or convenience, but in response to our needs and our faith, as God perceives them. Israel was now "home."

OUR BREAD FROM HEAVEN (Objective 6)

Use the Student Book materials to lead into a discussion of Communion practices and attitudes today and how they relate to and fulfill Old Testament prophecies and evidences of God's love.

Following are suggested answers for this section:

1. For free food
2. Providing manna
3. Bread from heaven
4. The Bread of life
5. Through faith, via the means of grace
6. Passover
7. New covenant

If time permits, sing or read in unison the hymn stanzas that are printed at the close of the Student Book material.

Session 43: Conquest: No Contest!

BIBLE BASIS: Joshua 5:13--12:24

CENTRAL TRUTH

Only divine guidance, implemented by a faithful and obedient army, could bring about such a far-reaching and rapid conquest of the well-fortified and militarily superior country of Canaan.

OBJECTIVES

That the students will:

1. Identify the unseen power that exerts itself at God's command on behalf of believers
2. Recognize, in the military strategy at Jericho, another invitation to all the world to believe in the one true God
3. Describe community responsibility concerning sin
4. Differentiate between temporal punishment and eternal damnation
5. Discover that after a covenant breaker had been dealt with and the covenant dramatically renewed, Joshua suffered no further military defeats
6. Recognize God's willingness and ability to use even our mistakes for His purposes
7. Discover that God honors bold requests when the motivation for them is to glorify His name
8. Develop skill in refuting fatalism

BACKGROUND

Joshua's military triumphs in spite of a relatively inexperienced army, inferior weapons, and the absence of allies bears clarion witness to his contemporaries and to all who read about the Israelite conquest that God intervened on their behalf. His covenant stands --irrevocable. The sins of the Canaanites, foreseen more than a thousand years before, have come to an intolerable crescendo--much the same as did the misdeeds in Sodom and Gomorrah in Abraham's day. The beautiful land these people had been allowed to occupy had brought about an attitude of blasphemous hedonism rather than humble gratitude. Now the land would cradle God's chosen people --chosen to illustrate God's power to bless.

Use this session to impress on the students the absolute dependability of God's promises and the responsibility we share as his current name-bearers.

ISRAEL'S NOT-SO-SECRET WEAPON (Objective 1)

Point out that God's army is invisible, invincible, and ready to act whenever God gives the word. Not only did Joshua <u>not</u> order God's army around, he was reminded to maintain a reverent and submissive attitude **(Joshua 5:14-15)**. You might mention that the "army" is not just used for military purposes--it also announced Jesus' birth to the shepherds and will gather the elect at the end of the world. Even nuclear weapons are no match for God's army!

JERICHO--A "PUSHOVER" (Objective 2)

Because the Jericho story is so familiar, it is only briefly referred to here. If any students seem unfamiliar with it, recommend **Joshua 6** for some exciting, faith-building reading. Spend a few moments reflecting on the obedience of the Israelites in the destruction of all the people and livestock except for Rahab's family.

Use the Student Book material to point up Joshua's role as a prophet and the accuracy of his prophecy. Ask, **If Hiel had been a student of and a believer in Scripture, do you think he would have attempted to rebuild Jericho?** It pays to know your Bible!

THE IMPORTANCE OF COMMUNITY RIGHTEOUSNESS (Objectives 3 and 4)

Make sure the students are aware of the fact that the Israelites were given clear warning concerning "devoted things" and the specific punishment for disobedience. Help them to empathize with Joshua (in his euphoria after the amazing Jericho conquest) as he overlooked the need to confer with God before undertaking even a small battle. Even the defeat of the Israelites didn't lead them to recall God's words (**Joshua 6:18-19**). We can be comforted by the fact that when Joshua approached the mercy seat out of concern for the reputation of Israel's army and their God, the Lord didn't "play games" but gave Joshua a straightforward answer (that a covenant community is responsible for the actions of its members) and directed him to a surefire solution--punishment by death.

Ask, **How does this concept of community responsibility apply to God's people today?** If a clear understanding of the role of church discipline is lacking, read **1 Cor. 5** in class, noting particularly the phrases **"not at all meaning the people of this world" in verse 10** and **"anyone who calls himself a brother" in verse 11-13**. Point out that any church discipline is intended to purify the body of Christ and warn the offending persons so they can repent and be saved. Other appropriate readings are **1 Tim. 5:20; Matt. 18:15-17; Gal. 6:1;** and **James 5:19-20**. "Live and let live" is not a Biblical direction for God's covenant people. He tells us that we <u>are</u> our brothers' keepers.

Play up the drama of the successively narrowing selection of tribe, clan, family, and individual. In the discussion of whether or not Achan and his family went to hell, it will be important to emphasize the sure and certain promise of forgiveness to all who confess (repent) in **1 John 1:9**. Some student may point out the Achan had little choice but to confess. However, "I have sinned" and "I coveted" indicate a recognition of wrong. Help the class to conclude that, in the final analysis, <u>God</u> knows if Achan repented and, if he (or any member of his family) did, each was thereby cleansed. Emphasize that capital punishment does not condemn anyone to hell. It simply serves as a deterrent by making a strong, public statement that certain crimes will not be tolerated.

COVENANT REVIEWED AND RENEWED (Objective 5)

The time had come for the dramatic event described by Moses in **Deut. 27**. Help the students visualize the scene. They might be interested to know that visitors to Israel have stationed groups facing each other on the mountains of Gerizim and Ebal and have read the Ten Commandments to each other. They report that the acoustics allow each group to be heard by the other without difficulty.

The Gibeonite deception receives little attention here because of time pressures. It would make an interesting dramatization for a chapel presentation or similar gathering.

JOSHUA'S MILITARY STRATEGY (Objectives 6 and 7)

Relate God's use of Israel's treaty with the Gibeonites (an error on Israel's part) to the New Testament teaching of **Rom. 8:28**. In connection with the sun standing still, ask, **How big a miracle is _your_ God capable of?**

Have one student read **John 14:13-14**, noting the motivation for the miracle--to bring glory to the Father.

Have another student read **John 15:16**, noting the prerequisite of bearing fruit (a characteristic of a properly motivated child of God).

Another good passage is **John 15:7-8**, noting the emphasis on _abiding_ in Jesus and the phrase "to my Father's glory." Other appropriate texts are **John 16:23-24; Eph. 3:20-21**; and **James 1:5-6**.

CONQUEST COMPLETED (Objective 8)

In the discussion of fatalism in the Student Book, encourage full participation. Many people today like to chalk our futures up to the whims of fate. Use present-day examples of simple foreknowledge, such as, "If you don't study, you will fail the test." The teacher's prediction does not cause the failure. A mother, seeing her toddler, moves quickly to take the forbidden item away. The pain caused by the needle prick is not caused by the mother just because she predicted it! Dwell on the wonderful mercy and love of a God who assures us that He will _always_ provide a way for us to overcome temptation.

Encourage some students to share their original "minipsalms" with the class.

Session 44: Every Promise Fulfilled

BIBLE BASIS: Joshua 13--24

CENTRAL TRUTH

God had fulfilled one covenant promise He had made to Abraham: the nation of Abraham's descendants occupied Canaan; and plans for the other covenant promise--the Savior --moved inexorably forward. Only deliberate disobedience could keep Israel from receiving worldwide recognition and other blessings as God's chosen people.

OBJECTIVES

That the students will:

1. Express an awareness of Satan's deceptive tricks to try to rob them of things they hold dear
2. Describe the way God fulfilled His promises to Caleb, Joshua, and the trans-Jordan tribes
3. Express an appreciation of the just and fair methods used to assign the remaining land
4. Take comfort in the fact that God keeps all His promises
5. Describe the importance of the elderly sharing words of wisdom with the young

BACKGROUND

This session treats a watershed in Old Testament history. The inspiring words of **Joshua 21:45, "Not one of all the Lord's good promises to the house of Israel failed; every one was fulfilled,"** which he repeats even more emphatically in **23:14**, are the capstone of all that Scripture has recorded up to this point. That statement of fact is almost as important to the Old Testament as Christ's resurrection is to the New Testament. God's promises are sure; His power is limitless; His love is so great that nothing short of our willful rejection of Him can nullify its effects.

God had been eminently faithful in carrying out all of His long-standing covenant with Abraham. His mighty hand accomplished all that was necessary to set the stage for the fulfillment of His plan of salvation. Through this action the Holy Spirit thrills our spirits, undergirds our faith, and empowers us for service.

INTRODUCTION (Objective 1)

Stimulate an awareness of Satan's subtle but unchanging approach to spoiling all that is good: undermining serious commitment to God through attractive temptations to follow worldly ways. Caution the students that if we do not trust God and remain watchful and alert, Satan can ruin the results of years of hard work in virtually no time at all--as when people experiment with drugs, drive after drinking, shoplift, become sexually promiscuous, etc.

ISRAEL'S CONQUEST IS COMPLETED (Objective 2)

Sometimes students need help to find any logic in the order of events in the Bible. Judah's and Joseph's allotments being assigned, while the other allotments were made by the casting of lots, is one of those instances. Obviously God does not limit Himself to our system of logic, but when students do find examples where His actions fit our logic, they may feel more confident as they approach God in prayer and anticipate possible answers.

Following are suggested answers for this section:

1. Divide the land.
2. God Himself would drive them out.
3. Reuben, Gad, and half of Manasseh.
4. The Anakites.
5. Strong and tall.
6. With the Lord's help he would drive them out.
7. Joseph's.
8. They said there wasn't enough land for them because the plains were occupied by people with iron chariots.
9. You can drive them out; also clear the forests.

DIVIDING THE REMAINING LAND (Objective 3)

Read **Joshua 18:1-10.** Then summarize the remainder of **chapters 18--21.** Try to impress the students with the genius of Joshua's method of allotting land to the remaining tribes. If students question the casting of lots, remind them that the Urim and Thummim were part of the priestly vestments **(Ex. 28:29-30)** and were provided for the express purpose of making serious decisions "before the Lord."

Ask a student to locate the three cities of refuge west of the Jordan, calling attention to the fact that they were selected to allow refugees ready access from anywhere in the country. Help the class to recognize God's loving concern in scattering the priestly Levite tribe among all the other tribes. Assign an essay on possible advantages of having the Levites distributed in this way, or lead a discussion of this topic. Suggest that the Levites were a constant reminder of God's presence among the people and also sources of wisdom and learning, since they were responsible for the teaching and enforcing of the laws **(Deut. 17:8-13, 18; 31:9, 24-26).**

MISSION ACCOMPLISHED (Objective 4)

Take some time to bask in the wonder of **Joshua 21:45.** Promises made nearly 1,000 years earlier had been completely and meticulously kept. In addition to that, this was all faithfully recorded and carefully preserved over the centuries for our benefit. How gracious is our God!

Draw parallels between the near civil war in Israel and present-day problems that grow from poor communication or, worse yet, complete lack of communication--especially in marriages. Point out how helpful it would have been if the trans-Jordan tribes had sent word of their intentions rather than assuming that the others could read their minds; or, on the other hand, if the Israelites had asked about the meaning of the altar rather than assuming the worst and leveling accusations. Ask, **Have you ever experienced conflicts within your church groups because of poor communication?** Share ways to improve communication.

JOSHUA'S FAREWELL (Objective 5)

Ask the students what similarities they see in Moses and Joshua as they face death. Suggestions should include: absence of fear, eagerness to speak to all Israel once more, review of Israel's history, promise of blessings for the obedient, warnings of the devastating effects of idolatry, encouragement to continue commitment to their unique covenant with Jehovah.

Ask, **Who will take Joshua's place**

after his death? National leadership changed, now that the Israelites were settled in the promised land. Since each tribe was encouraged to drive out foreign occupants in their assigned territory whenever more land was needed, these battles were tribal decisions that required only tribal action (although tribes sometimes formed alliances).

The resulting government was similar to that which existed among the American colonies before the adoption of the Constitution. The Israelites were unified by their loyalty to Jehovah, which was evidenced by the Levitical towns throughout the land and by the religious festivals in Shiloh. With God as their ultimate authority, Israel had now begun to function as an identifiable theocracy.

Remind the class that an important era of Israel's history has now ended and that a new one was about to begin. In recognition of the end of Israel's wandering, you might close by reading or singing "Guide Me Ever, Great Redeemer" (Lutheran Worship 220; "Guide Me, O Thou Great Jehovah" in The Lutheran Hymnal 54).

If time permits, reflect on the parallels drawn by the hymn writer between Israel and today's believer. Examples: the crossing of the Jordan and death as the end of our wandering on earth, and the Promised Land as a symbol of heaven.

Following are suggested answers for this section:

1. Answers will vary.
2. God would continue to fight for them.
3. Be strong, careful to obey, and hold fast to God.
4. Don't intermarry with the remaining nations.
5. God keeps all His promises.
6. They would lose their land.
7. Choose idols or Jehovah.
8. "We will serve the Lord."
9. They would serve the Lord.
10. They must be very serious about their commitment or it won't work; he wanted a second promise.
11. Some Israelites had foreign gods.

Session 45: Concluding Activities for Unit 6

Use the following questions as a review, a test, or in another way that seems appropriate to you.

MULTIPLE CHOICE

Write the letter of the best answers in the blanks.

1. Aaron and Miriam criticized Moses for marrying an African because
   (A) she was black
   (B) she did not believe in the true God
   (C) they resented the leadership of Moses
   (D) it was wrong for him to have more than one wife
2. The Bible says that we should recognize false prophets by
   (A) the results of their preaching
   (B) their appearance
   (C) the number of people who follow them
   (D) how well they are able to speak
3. The 10 scouts who said that the Israelites should not try to enter the Promised Land
   (A) were swallowed alive by the earth
   (B) changed their minds later
   (C) got leprosy
   (D) died of a plague
4. The priesthood among the Israelites was restricted to
   (A) the Levites
   (B) the tribe of Judah
   (C) the tribe of Reuben
   (D) Aaron and his sons
5. The Israelites who were bitten by poisonous snakes could avoid death by
   (A) repenting of their sins
   (B) looking at a bronze snake
   (C) bringing a sacrifice to the tabernacle
   (D) asking Moses for help
6. When Moses was about to die, his main concern was that
   (A) he would not enter the Promised Land
   (B) the people should stop their

grumbling against God
(C) the Israelites should have a good leader to succeed him
(D) there was not enough food and water for the people

7. The fate of the Canaanites was first predicted by
(A) Noah (C) Jacob
(B) Abraham (D) Moses

8. When the Israelites read the Ten Commandments to each other from two mountains in Canaan, they were carrying out the instructions of
(A) Abraham (C) Moses
(B) Jacob (D) Aaron

9. The tribe of Israel that did not receive an allotment of land in Canaan were the
(A) Reubenites (C) Ephraimites
(B) Levites (D) Danites

10. In his farewell address, Joshua said that he and his family would
(A) establish cities of refuge
(B) defeat the remaining Canaanites
(C) serve as priests in the Promised Land
(D) serve the Lord

TRUE-FALSE

Circle T for True and F for False.

T F 1. As a reward for carrying out the duties that God assigns to a prophet, God keeps hardships out of the prophet's life. (F)

T F 2. We should obey religious leaders even when they tell us to do something that is contrary to God's Word. (F)

T F 3. Most of the scouts sent by Moses to investigate the Promised Land gave an accurate report about that land. (T)

T F 4. When the Israelites rebelled against Moses, God told Moses that He was willing to kill them all. (T)

T F 5. God gives greater gifts to some people than to others, and He expects more from these people. (T)

T F 6. The Levites did not have to tithe because they were already receiving tithes from the other Israelites. (F)

T F 7. If a person performs miracles, it is a proof that he or she is a true follower of Jesus. (F)

T F 8. The stopping of manna was a sign that the wanderings of the Israelites had come to an end. (T)

T F 9. Once they entered the Promised Land, the Israelites were successful in all their military campaigns. (F)

T F 10. When the Israelites conquered Jericho, they let some of the inhabitants remain alive. (T)

MATCHING

Write the letter of the best answer at the right. Not all answers will be used.

C	1. Miriam	A.	African wife of Moses
E	2. Korah	B.	Was executed because of his greed
G	3. Joshua	C.	Was punished with leprosy for criticizing Moses
L	4. Rahab	D.	Lost two sons in the rebuilding of Jericho
H	5. Eleazar	E.	Was swallowed alive by the earth for criticizing Moses
J	6. Caleb		
B	7. Achan		
D	8. Hiel	F.	Punished a man for committing public sexual immorality
F	9. Phinehas	G.	Successor of Moses as leader of the Israelites
I	10. Aaron	H.	High priest after Aaron
		I.	His leadership was confirmed by a sprouting staff
		J.	Agreed with Joshua that the Promised Land could be conquered
		K.	Committed public sexual immorality with a Moabite woman
		L.	An ancestor of Jesus

COMPLETION

Write the word or phrase that best completes each statement.

1. Manna tasted like [honey and olive oil].

2. God provided meat for the

Israelites in the wilderness in the form of [quail].

3. To show how good the Promised Land was, the 12 scouts brought back [large bunches of grapes, pomegranates, and figs].

4. The Bible teaches that God strengthens our faith through [His Word and the Sacraments].

5. The Israelites did not destroy the Edomites because the Edomites were descendants of [Esau].

6. The bronze snake in the wilderness foreshadowed [Jesus].

7. Jesus instituted the Lord's Supper during the festival of [Passover].

8. The part of Canaan that Joshua attacked first was the [center].

9. The false teaching that our lives are determined in advance and that there is nothing that we can do to change things is called [fatalism].

10. The center of worship of the Israelites at the time of Joshua was in the city of [Shiloh].

ESSAYS

On a separate sheet of paper, write briefly about any four of the following topics. Be sure to put the number of the topic at the beginning of each essay.)

1. How does God feel about grumbling? Include examples from the lives of the Israelites in the wilderness.

2. Describe the characteristics of a good religious leader and the God-pleasing attitude of the people toward such a leader.

3. Tell about promises that God has kept--in the Bible and in your life.

4. What is the difference between obeying God willingly and obeying Him by force? Give examples from the story of the Israelites and from the life of a Christian today.

5. What is the difference between weakness of faith and disobedience to God's will? Emphasize how God views these two characteristics.

6. What actions of Moses resulted in his being prevented from entering the Promised Land?

7. List some reminders of God's goodness that Moses gave to the people in his farewell message.

8. Compare manna and the Lord's Supper.

9. Compare the crossing of the Red Sea and the crossing of the Jordan River.

10. Compare the dangers the Canaanites posed for the Israelites and the influences of the world on God's people today.

Unit 7: The Period of the Judges

This unit focuses on Deborah, Gideon, and Samson as representatives of the judges. The thread of similarity is found in the disobedience of Israel and the constant love and help from God. God helps His people in various ways.

PLANNING THE UNIT

For each session: Assign readings and student book activities far enough in advance so that students will have them completed on the day the story is discussed in class.

Session 47: In connection with the story of Deborah you will find the TRAFFIC JAM activity which will help students see how leadership can come from people when least expected. Practice the game with friends prior to class.

Session 48: Obtain a piece of real or synthetic sheepskin to demonstrate the sign with the fleece that Gideon requested from God. An inexpensive polishing bonnet available in most hardware stores or a piece of sheepskin fabric from a fabric store should serve the purpose. The fleece holds so much water that there could be no mistaking God's sign to Gideon.

BIBLIOGRAPHY

Atlas of the Bible Lands.

Maplewood, NJ: C. S. Hammond 1959.

Halley, Henry H. Halley's Bible Handbook. Grand Rapids: Zondervan, 1976.

Hunter, John E. Judges and a Permissive Society. Grand Rapids: Zondervan, 1975.

Josephus: Complete Works. Translated by William Whiston. Grand Rapids: Kregel, 1978.

Kiel, C. F. and F. Delitzsch. Biblical Commentary on the Old Testament: Joshua, Judges, Ruth. Translated by James Martin. Grand Rapids: William B. Eerdmans, 1950.

Roehrs, Walter R. and Martin H. Franzmann. Concordia Self-Study Commentary. St. Louis: Concordia, 1979.

Rohnke, Karl. Cowstails and Cobras. Hamilton, MA: Project Adventure, 1977.

Unger, Merrill F. Unger's Concise Bible Dictionary. Chicago: Moody Press, 1982.

Session 46: Introducing the Judges

BIBLE BASIS: Judg. 1:1--3:6

CENTRAL TRUTH

Our loving God remains faithful to His promises in spite of our disobedience. Though He must deal with our sin, He continues to love us **(Judg. 2:1b, Rom. 5:8)**

OBJECTIVES

That the students will:

1. Follow the history of Israel from the conquest of Canaan under Joshua to the settlement during the time of the judges
2. Conclude from a study of **Judg. 2:10** that the careful study of God's Word is a necessary part of the Christian's life
3. Turn to Jesus Christ for deliverance from sin and power to overcome temptation
4. Find reassurance for their own lives in the examples of God's faithful support of Israel during the time of the Judges

BACKGROUND

The conquest of Canaan was incomplete at the time of Joshua's death. Leadership for the "mopping-up" operations had to come from the various tribes, who quickly tired of war and forgot about the Lord. Some heathen nations and their idols remained in Canaan. As the Israelites settled in Canaan, they were attracted to the idolatrous practices of the remaining people.

The new generation was completely ignorant of the Lord God or of what He had done for Israel **(Judg. 2:10)**. While this seems difficult to believe, it reminds us to teach our children the Word of God and to testify to His activity in our lives.

It became common practice for the Israelites to set their own standards of behavior **(Jud. 17:6 and 18:1)**. Israel's disobedience angered the Lord, and He allowed them to be oppressed by the very nations whose idols they worshiped. When Israel cried to the Lord for deliverance, God raised up leaders called judges, who would usually lead them in war against their enemies. God made them victorious, and the land was at peace again.

It appears that God had a dual purpose for leaving some of the heathen nations behind in Canaan. First, He could test Israel's faithfulness **(Judg. 2:22)**. Second, He could give the inexperienced the training necessary for warfare **(Judg. 3:1, 2, and 4)**.

Judges is an incredible love story. God continued to love His people in spite of their rejection of Him.

STUDYING THE SCRIPTURE (Objective 1)

Before this session the students should have read **Judg. 1:1-3:6** and completed the Student Book activities.

Begin with a prayer. Pray for people who hurt, suffer hardships, rebel against family and government, and shut themselves out from their friends and neighbors.

As you study this account in

Judges, explain to the students that the period of **Judges** followed the general conquest of Canaan under Joshua.

GOD HELPED TROUBLED ISRAEL
(Objectives 1 and 2)

Discuss questions and answers under this heading in the Student Book. Share comments on possible reasons for God's anger over Israel's failure to drive the heathen from the land.

Ask, **According to Judg. 2:20-22 and 3:1-2, what were the two reasons God did not drive the heathen people out of Canaan?** (God would use Israel's enemies as a test to see whether the Israelites would remain faithful to God; he would give warfare experience to the Israelite descendants who had not fought yet.)

What did God expect from Israel? (He expected the people keep faithful to Him.)

GOD HELPS ME, TOO (Objectives 3 and 4)

Share ideas the students have written to answer questions in this section. Then discuss what it might be like for us if we did not have God's Word and His love to share with others.

Read aloud **Judg. 2:1-3** and **11-23**. Ask, **What other ways might God have used to deliver Israel from oppression? Would the ways you have suggested result in a robotlike obedience to God? Or would those ways result in a response of love from His people?**

Continue, **Tell about a "thorn in your side." Did you remember to ask God to help overcome that thorn and the temptations accompanying it?**

God wants us to ask Him for help when we are in trouble. He promises to always be ready to love, protect, and care for us.

Talk about answers students have written in their books. Don't force students to share. If they're reluctant, you might begin by sharing some of your own experiences. Keep an atmosphere of love and openness.

After some responses to question 4, talk about God's impossible-to-understand love. Students need to know that it's real--not just something they talk about in religion class.

I KNOW I CAN DEPEND ON GOD
(Objective 4)

Ask the students to share what they have written to answer the questions in this section in their books. Emphasize again that God continues to love us and gave us Jesus as our Savior. We know that sinful though we are, God is our loving, forgiving Father on whom we can depend.

The folk song, "Pass It On" reinforces the theme that we can depend on God, no matter where we are and what we are doing. You might use the song to sing or say as a meditative time before ending this session.

It only takes a spark to get a fire going,
And soon all those around can warm up in its glowing.
That's how it is with God's love: Once you've experienced it,
You spread His love to everyone; You want to pass it on.
I wish for you my friend, This happiness that I've found.
You can depend on Him, It matters not where you're bound.
I'll shout it from the mountaintop; I want my world to know:
The Lord of love has come to me; I want to pass it on.

PASS IT ON by Kurt Kaiser

Session 47: Who's in Charge? (Deborah and Barak)

BIBLE BASIS: Judg. 4--5

CENTRAL TRUTH

God chooses whom He will for His

service and equips them for their tasks. God prepares and supports those whom He chooses to serve Him.

OBJECTIVES

That the students will:

1. Recognize that God could not allow the disobedience of Israel to continue, since it would destroy Israel morally and spiritually
2. Understand that God will choose people to serve Him according to His own plan, and in so doing He will bless His people and bring glory to Himself
3. Appreciate each other on the basis of who we are in Christ as opposed to our physical attributes and social position
4. Celebrate God's victories in our own lives through prayers of praise and thanksgiving, songs, poetry, and relational games

BACKGROUND

Today's story begins with the reason for Israel experiencing difficulties at the time of Deborah. Israel worshiped Baal, a god of the harvest, and Ashtoreth, a fertility goddess. The worship of these false gods was not only idolatry but also involved licentious rituals including sacred prostitution.

The Canaanite king, Jabin, ordered Sisera, his commander, to oppress Israel. Sisera was very cruel and used 900 chariots to wage a mechanized war against Israel. In response to Israel's appeal for help, God spoke to Deborah, a prophetess. He ordered her to direct Barak to lead an army against Sisera. Barak agreed to do so with the understanding that Deborah would accompany him.

The staging area for Barak's 10,000 troops was Mt. Tabor. Deborah urged Barak into battle asking him if the Lord was not already preceding him **(Judg. 4:14)**.

The Jewish historian, Josephus, in his Antiquities of the Jews, states that "there came down from heaven a great storm, with a vast quantity of rain and hail, and the wind blew the rain in the face of the Canaanites, and so darkened their eyes, that their arrows and slings were of no advantage to them"

Deborah's song, in **Judg. 5**, described the way in which the rain-swollen river Kishon swept away Sisera's chariots, enabling the advancing army of Israel to conquer otherwise superior forces.

Deborah's song is a poetic description of the Lord's victory over the Canaanites. Deborah gives credit to God, Barak, and Jael, but does not claim any honor for herself. Though she played a major role in the story, she is not named with Barak as one of Israel's heroes in **Heb. 11**. God used the leader Deborah, through faith, to save His people Israel.

STUDYING THE SCRIPTURES (Objective 1)

Before this session, the students should have read **Judg. 4--5**and completed the Student Book activities.

Begin with prayer. Pray for leaders of the world, your country, state, and local governments. Include in your prayer specific leaders in your school. Ask God to bless and guide each person, as well as you and your students, so He may prepare you to better serve Him.

GOD HELPS DYNAMIC DEBORAH AND GOD HELPS ME DAILY (Objectives 2 and 3)

Discuss the questions and answers the students have in their books. If necessary, review the events of the story briefly.

If you had assigned students to research the gods of the Canaanites with particular attention to Baal and Ashtoreth, you might use this time to have them share their findings with the objective of understanding how the worship of false gods could destroy Israel.

TRAFFIC JAM ACTIVITY (Objective 4)

Object: To have two groups of at least four students each exchange places on a line of squares that has one more place than the number of students in both groups. All students to the left of center must end up on the right.

Purpose: Sometimes people have difficulty accepting the leadership of a person who does not fit the leader stereotype. (What would have happened if Barak would have ignored Deborah's message from God simply because she was a woman?) **TRAFFIC JAM** can help students recognize that sometimes leadership emerges from people whom we least suspect to have leadership ability. This certainly happens in combat situations just as it did in Israel during the time of the judges.

Setting up: In a straight line, mark off one more place than there are students in the class. Places can be marked with chalk or masking tape. They should be placed in an easy step from each other. Divide the class into smaller groups of four to seven.

Rules: To begin, one group stands on the places to the left of the middle square, the other group stands to the right. Both groups face the middle unoccupied square.

Using the following moves, students on the left side must end up in the places on the right side.

Legal Moves:

1. A person may move into an empty space in front of him or her.
2. A person may move around a person who is facing him or her into an empty space.

Thus, in illustration A 1 or 2 may move into the empty space.

In illustration B 1 may move into the empty space.

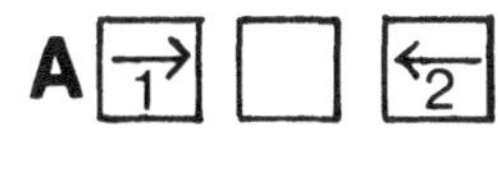

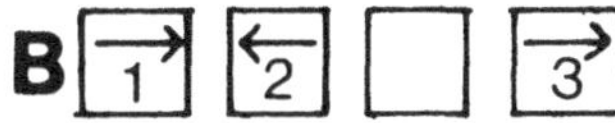

Illegal Moves

1. Any move backwards.
2. Any move around someone facing the same way you are.
3. Any move that involves two persons moving at once.

Note: This is often a difficult problem. Thus, it's not recommended for younger children.

After a solution to the problem is discovered (or chanced upon) and the group discovers that one person giving the commands is the most efficient way to solve the "traffic jam," ask the individual and the group if they can quickly solve the problem again. The leader will ordinarily stumble a bit in the repeat attempt, but the solution will eventually be reached more efficiently.

"Traffic Jam" by Karl Rohnke, taken from Cows' Tails & Cobras, published by Project Adventure, Inc., Hamilton, MA. Copyright 1977. Used by permission.

Evaluation: Ask, **What did this activity show us about leaders and followers? When is God "the Leader"? When are you?**

AM I A GOOD LEADER? AM I A GOOD FOLLOWER? (Objective 5)

Talk about the Student Book discussion questions.

Personalize this lesson for your students by relating to them times when you or a family member had a problem (sickness, an accident, a conflict). Share with them how you depended on God for help and how He cared for you.

Ask the students to write down at least one thing for which they can praise God. Use what they have written for a quiet meditative praise time.

Or, you might use the words of the Doxology (LW 461) to praise God--thank Him by speaking or singing the words as you think of all His blessings for you.

Session 48: MISSION: IMPOSSIBLE? (The Story of Gideon)

BIBLE BASIS: Judg. 6--8

CENTRAL TRUTH

God demonstrates His love for us when He disciplines us as well as when He frees us from our sins and helps us deal with problems.

God disciplines us for our good, that we may share in His holiness.

Heb. 12:10

My grace is sufficient for you, for My power is made perfect in weakness. 2 Cor. 12:9

OBJECTIVES

That the student will:

1. Describe how God loved and guided His people of Israel despite their sinful ways
2. Recognize Gideon as one of the leaders God chose and empowered to help Israel
3. Confess their sins specifically and trust God's promise of love, forgiveness, and presence for their own lives
4. Pray that God will constantly be present in their daily lives and give them power and confidence to live and share God's love

BACKGROUND

The story of Gideon covers 95 years. By now the opening words, "Again the Israelites did evil in the sight of the Lord," have become familiar to your students. The Israelites continued to worship the idols Baal and Asherah. God allowed the Midianites to oppress Israel in order to bring them back to Himself as their only God.

The seven-year oppression was so severe that the Israelites lived in caves and ravines in the surrounding mountains. At the time of each harvest the Midianites attacked Israel and destroyed their crops and animals. In frustration the Israelites cried out to the Lord for deliverance.

God responded by preparing Gideon to lead Israel. God assured Gideon that He would deliver Israel and prepared Gideon for a decisive battle with Midian. Again God vindicated Himself and freed Israel from oppression.

Finally, God demonstrated His power and love through His defeat of the Midianites. Emphasize that God's plan and power alone brought about the victory. The interpretation of the dream that Gideon overheard when he entered the Midianite camp on the night of the battle demonstrated God's planned victory.

Encourage students to pray for God to direct their own lives and trust Him to accomplish His will through them.

READING THE SCRIPTURES (Objective 1)

Before this session the students should have read **Judg. 6--8** and completed the Student Book activities.

You might ask a student to lead an opening prayer.

GOD CALLS GIDEON AND HELPS ISRAEL
(Objectives 1 and 2)

Discuss the answers students have given in this section of their books. Ask, **Why did God not allow the Midianites to destroy the Israelites for their repeated idolatry?** (While answers might include God's love, His forgiving attitude, and His promise to never destroy the whole human race, help the students conclude that God faithfully followed His plan for Jesus' birth, death, and resurrection.)

Emphasize that God, through the angel's message, promised He would be with Gideon and give His strength through Gideon. God guaranteed Gideon victory over the Midianites.

GOD HELPS ME
AND CALLS ME TO HELP OTHERS
(Objectives 3 and 4)

Share comments from the students' books.

Then demonstrate "fleecing." You need a piece of woolen or synthetic fleece, and empty bowl, and a bowl of water. Ask a student to read **Judg. 6:36-40**. Dip the fleece in water. Then wring it into the empty bowl to show the volume of water it held. Conclude that Gideon could not mistake the certainty of God's sign!

People today sometimes "fleece God"--they ask Him to provide a a specific sign to confirm His will for their lives. Ask, **Do you think Christians should ask this from God?** (**Deut. 4:29** tells the importance of sincerely seeking the Lord.)

We should carefully study God's Word, pray, and obey His commandments. God wants us to ask Him for guidance in our lives and trust

Him to provide it for us.

Discuss things that bother the students. Listen carefully as the students tell about the problems they personally face or the problems they are aware others face. Ask a student to read **Rom. 6--7.** Encourage them to confess their sins and ask God to forgive them for specific sins. Remind them that doing this will enable them to be happy--to be free to be themselves--and to claim God's promise for deliverance from sin's power. When we Christians are confessing, feeling God's forgiving power, and free then to go and be ourselves, then we are able to love and share the Lord with others. God gave Gideon that power to go and be His leader. God gives us His power, too. How is He using us?

Encourage the students to "counsel" each other, using the story of Gideon as an example of God's love, forgiveness, and power for living. You might use examples from the Student Book and take class time to roleplay situations in which one student counsels another (a friend counsels a friend who has been put on probation for drug possession; a girl counsels a girl who has run away from home; a boy counsels a shoplifting friend; create other situations of your own). Remember in this practice to include confession, forgiveness, and rejoicing!

WITH GOD ALL THINGS ARE POSSIBLE
(Objectives 3 and 4)

Conclude this session with the thought that God gave Gideon both direction and power and that He will do the same for us in our lives.

Pray together the prayer in the Student Book: Dear Lord God, thank You for Your love and presence in Jesus Christ, my Lord and Savior. Amen.

Or, pray or sing stanzas 1 and 4 of "If You But Trust in God To Guide You" (Lutheran Worship 420).

Session 49: Going God's Way? (The Story of Samson)

BIBLE BASIS: Judg. 13--16

CENTRAL TRUTH

God chose Samson to lead Israel and provided him with His Spirit and power. God directs and empowers us today to do His work as we rejoice in His love and grace.

OBJECTIVES

That the students will:

1. Tell how God used Samson, in spite of his weaknesses, to disrupt Israel's enemies
2. Recognize that God's Spirit worked in Samson to result in his strength and power
3. Evaluate the degree and effect of God's presence in their lives
4. Dedicate themselves to serve God and others

BACKGROUND

The unique story of Samson contains adventure, humor, and tragedy. Your students might compare it with a modern novel with a few minor changes in names and customs.

Samson is special. God caused Samson to be born to a once-sterile woman and specified that he be raised a Nazirite, set apart for service to God. (**Num. 6:1-21** details the requirements for the Nazirite vow. This vow could be taken for a specific time period, but Samson was to adhere to the vow for life [**Judg. 13:5**]. Point out to your students that the Nazirite vow is to be viewed as a positive decision to set oneself apart to the Lord as opposed to denying self, the pleasures of life, foods, and alcohol. This vow focuses on a person responding joyfully to the Lord rather than sacrificing earthly goods.)

In spite of the solemnity of his vow, Samson seemed to view life as a game. Endowed by God with unusual strength, Samson appeared to enjoy toying with his enemies, the Philistines. While our humane societies would object to the abuse of the foxes Samson used to set Philistine fields on fire, one can imagine that Samson may have found considerable humor in destroying

Philistine crops in this way.

Samson also appeared to be accustomed to having his own way. His demand for a wife from among the Philistines **(Judg. 14:1-3)** disturbed Samson's father but in the end it served God's purpose.

Samson's violent behavior caused significant difficulty for the Philistines, who responded with increased efforts to subdue him. Finally, they bribed Delilah to find the secret of his strength. Samson pushed the Lord to the limit of His patience by violating the Nazirite vow. The Lord left him, he was captured by the Philistines, and his eyes were put out.

Eventually, Samson cried to the Lord for help, very much like Israel cried out when oppressed. The Lord strengthened him again, and he pushed over the supporting pillars in the temple of the Philistine god, Dagon, where he and 3,000 Philistines died.

Through the story of Samson we learn that God sometimes uses people who have tremendous personal weaknesses to accomplish His purpose. During this session you and your students will evaluate God's power in your lives and discuss how He empowers you with His Holy Spirit.

READING THE SCRIPTURES (Objectives 1 and 2)

The students should have read the Biblical account in **Judg. 3-16** and completed their Student Books activities before this session.

Pray, asking God to help you be aware of how He used Samson as one of His leaders and to help you learn how He uses us today to lead and witness for Him. Personalize your prayer. Include sentences of thanks for anyone who has returned to class after an illness. Encourage students to offer short sentence prayers for anyone they might know who needs the class' prayerful support.

GOD GIVES HIS SPIRIT AND POWER TO SAMSON (Objectives 1 and 2)

Ask the students to tell the main events of this story. You might list these on the chalkboard for a quick review.

Discuss questions from this section of the Student Book. Comment on Samson's attitudes toward God, toward his parents, toward women, and toward his friends and people around him. Speculate what he might have said to these people. How might he have treated them?

Read **Judg. 16:28**. Ask the students if they find it unusual that Samson does not confess his sin before he asks God to give his strength back.

Develop a short character sketch by discussing Samson. Ask the students how Samson differs from Deborah and Gideon. (Samson worked alone, he did not use conventional warfare of that time, his personal life lacked high moral values, he played "games" with his enemies, he did not praise God for his success and victory.)

Listen to the students explain why they would--or would not--like to have Samson for a classmate.

Ask, **Why do you think God chose Samson for a leader?** (We cannot discover God's motives. God chooses those He wants to use to accomplish His purposes. Each person differs in personality traits, abilities, and faith growth. God alone knows His plan for us.)

GOD GIVES HIS SPIRIT AND POWER TO ME (Objectives 3 and 4)

Ask a student to read **Judg. 14:6** and **19. How did the Holy Spirit come to select persons in these Old Testament times?**

Discuss the answers the students gave to this section of questions. In the New Testament Pentecost, the Holy Spirit came to <u>all</u> who belong to God through faith in Jesus Christ. We can ask God for His Spirit and expect our lives to change, our faith to grow, and our relationship with God and others to be loving, caring, and sharing. A folk song, "They'll Know We Are Christians by Our Love" reminds us in its phrases that "we are one in the Spirit, we are one in the Lord" and that we give "praise to the Spirit who makes us one." You might refer to this song and sing it with your students.

Read **Gal. 5:22-23.** List the fruit of the Spirit in a Christian's life as described by Paul. Share comments students have for question 3 related to this Bible reference.

I DEDICATE MYSELF TO SERVE GOD
(Objectives 3 and 4)

Sing or say the stanzas of "Take My Life, O Lord, Renew" (LW 404). Ask, **How does knowing that God accepts you as His volunteer make you feel? Why is it important that we allow God to use us as He plans?**

Ask a student to close this session by praying the prayer that he or she wrote as requested in the Student Book.

Session 50: Concluding Activities for Unit 7

USING THIS REVIEW AND EVALUATING SESSION

Each class schedule varies. You might want to assign the students to complete the unit review in their books independently. Students could check one another's answers in pairs or in small groups. Or, you could discuss Student Book answers with the whole class. Reinforcement of the Bible accounts' main events and their applications for our lives is an important part of learning not to be bypassed. During the unit review, special needs and questions might also arise that could require your extra time and attention.

Use the following suggested evaluation questions to best help your students.

Notice that "Part I: Short Answer Definitions" concentrates on the students recalling facts from the judges' stories, while "Part II: Short Essays" requires the students to elaborate on their factual knowledge and the stories' meaning for their lives.

Part I--Short Answer Definitions

Directions: Write a brief phrase or sentence to define or explain each word or name:

1.	judge	7.	Midianites
2.	Baal	8.	Philistines
3.	Sisera	9.	Samson
4.	Gideon	10.	Barak
5.	Deborah	11.	fleece
6.	Jael	12.	Nazirite

Part II--Short Essays

1. Write a short paragraph describing the period of the Judges.

2. A common phrase in the **Book of Judges** is **"again the Israelites did evil in the sight of the Lord."** Write a few sentences describing the "evil."

3. What is the relationship between the conquest of Canaan under Joshua and the period of the Judges?

4. **Judg. 2:10** states that **another generation grew up, who knew neither the Lord nor what He had done for Israel.** How does this statement serve as a warning for our generation?

5. Select one of the judges you studied. Identify the person you are describing. Write a brief paragraph describing his/her life.

6. How did God prove to Israel that it was He alone who rescued them from the Midianites? (Gideon was the judge at the time.)

7. Why did God allow heathen people to oppress Israel?

8. How did God's activities with Israel during the period of the Judges help to preserve them as His people?

9. How is the oppression we experience when we live in sin like that experienced by Israel under the heathen people?

10. The Book of Judges is an incredible story about God's love. Tell how this was true for Israel. Tell how it is a love story for us today.

Feel free to duplicate the above questions for use in testing. Please add the following credit line: **Concordia Publishing House, copyright 1986. Used by permission.**

Unit 8: The Monarchy--A United Kingdom

During this unit, you will be helping your students understand how God expects His people to be obedient to Him, how He enables us, through grace, to lead lives that please Him, and how He fills us with power through the Holy Spirit to confess our sins and lead Christ-filled lives. Just as God gave purpose and power to the leaders of Israel when the monarchy began, He also gives us direction for our lives and equips us to serve Him. By reading about some of Israel's leaders, your students will realize that devotion and commitment to the Lord contribute to success in life as in the story of king David. While sin causes trouble in our lives, confessing that sin and accepting God's forgiveness results in our joy and happiness.

Samuel was the last of Israel's great judges. Samuel proved to be a faithful servant of God from the time his mother presented him to the Lord until the time of his death during the reign of Saul.

Saul was the first king of Israel. He faced the challenge of developing the military forces of Israel in the face of discouraging odds. God blessed his efforts and made him a mighty warrior. Unfortunately, Saul deliberately disobeyed the Lord and lost his position as king.

Scripture gives more information about David's early life than it does for either Saul or Solomon. David was truly a man of God. Even though David sinned he demonstrated sincere repentance. He was the strongest and most consistent king of Israel.

Solomon enjoyed a peaceful reign over the territory and people conquered by his father, David. God granted his request for wisdom and added wealth and fame. Solomon was highly respected for his wisdom but made serious mistakes in his multiple political marriages and acceptance of his wives' idolatry.

PLANNING THE UNIT

Session 52--Students write a letter to Samuel. Career search may involve a guidance counselor.

Session 53--Be prepared to discuss Saul's leadership qualities.

Session 54--Set up a courtroom scenario to try Saul for his sins. Prepare role assignments in advance.

Session 56--Be prepared to discuss the doctrine of Sanctification. What does it mean for us?

Session 57--The topic is David's sin with Bathsheba and the consequences. Be prepared to discuss marriage, adultery, and Christian ethics.

Session 59--Students will have to compare the measurements of Solomon's temple with their own churches. Also ask them to compute the value of gold provided by David for the temple at today's prices.

Session 60--Students will have to research the idols Chemosh and Molech. Adapt the group activity, "Setting the World Right," for your students. Discuss the consequences of our mistakes and the personal promise God gives each of us in **John 3:16.**

Session 61--Evaluation session. Use sample questions for a test or review as you consider the needs of your students.

Session 51: Israel's Tribes Unite--the Monarchy Begins

BIBLE BASIS: 1 Sam. 4--7

CENTRAL TRUTH

Just as God loved His people Israel and stayed with them during the final days of the judges, He loves and watches over us during troubled times. We can trust God's unchanging love for us.

OBJECTIVES

That the students will:

1. Recognize that God used the establishment of a monarchy in Israel to establish His people securely in a land of their own

2. Be able to relate the period of the monarchy in Israel to the same period for other cultures

3. Identify instances when God demonstrated His love for and tolerance of His people

4. Identify specific times when God showed His love and forgiveness for them

BACKGROUND

A series of political events in the world around Israel worked to Israel's advantage as the tribes became united under the reign of King David.

Egypt was in a state of decline, and the Assyrians had reached the limit of their influence. David blocked a serious threat from the Philistines. The Canaanites concentrated on developing commercial ventures by sea, and Hiram, king of Tyre, became David's friend, which was to be of mutual benefit to the two men. Saul and David conquered or otherwise controlled the Edomites, Amelekites, Moabites, and Ammonites.

Israel was very disorganized during the judges. Leadership was sporadic before Samuel, conditions improved under Saul, and finally, God helped Israel achieve real power under David's leadership.

Saul lost the monarchy through deliberate disobedience. David truly loved God but was always a warrior. Solomon enjoyed the peace and prosperity won for him by his predecessors.

The period of the monarchy in the united kingdom lasted approximately 1050--931 B.C. and each king ruled for about 40 years.

READING THE SCRIPTURES (Objective 1)

Assign students to read **1 Samuel 4:1-10** and complete the Student Book activities. Begin your session with a prayer asking God's continued blessings on your study of His people in the Old Testament.

The first part of this session may be used to review the test that concluded the previous unit.

Then introduce the new unit by giving a brief overview of the monarchy during the period when the tribes were united.

GOD ALLOWS BATTLES BETWEEN ENEMIES
(Objectives 1 and 2)

Discuss Student Book questions and answers.

Your students should sense the disunity and devastating influence of idolatry during the period of the judges. Remind them of the problems Israel faced in order to help them understand why the Israelites wanted a king. God did not approve of a monarchy for Israel because it was apparent that the people were looking for a human solution to what was a spiritual problem. But God did use the monarchy to firmly establish His people. Research together with your students the nations of Egypt, Assyria, and Philistia during this time (about 1050 B.C.). Share and compare your findings.

GOD HELPS ME FIGHT MY ENEMIES
(Objectives 3 and 4)

The history of God's people is really an incredible love story--the story of God's love for humanity. Review times when God patiently demonstrated His love to His people. Ask your students to look for times during this unit when God demonstrated His love for His people again. God disciplined His people out of His love for them and His determination to protect them from the evil that would destroy them.

God is with us. He helps us when we are in trouble. He also disciplines us as a living, wise father disciplines His children.

Discuss the Student Book questions and answers. Emphasize that God continues to use many people to lead His people. In **Rev. 3:19-20**, God promises discipline out of love for us. We are full of joy and eagerness to serve the Lord when He gives us His work. We can depend on Him to bless our service.

Session 52: Samuel: God's Spokesman

BIBLE BASIS: 1 Sam. 1--7

CENTRAL TRUTH

God continued to care for His people Israel. He answered Hannah's prayer by blessing her with Samuel, His chosen future leader for Israel.

God wants us to trust Him to guide our lives. He lovingly answers our prayers and blesses our lives when we trust in His will for us.

OBJECTIVES

That the students will:

1. Recognize that God blessed Israel by answering the fervent prayer of Samuel's mother, Hannah, and by preparing Samuel as their leader
2. Describe God's involvement in Samuel's life as He protected Samuel from the evil influence of Eli's sons.
3. Identify different church-related areas of ministry and view full-time ministry as an opportunity to serve God and people around them
4. Ask God's guidance in choosing a career, considering perhaps full-time ministry.

BACKGROUND

Before Israel became a monarchy, God raised up one more judge--the prophet Samuel--to lead Israel back to Himself. Your students may notice some similarity in the circumstances of the births of Samuel and an earlier judge, Samson. Both boys' mothers were childless until God intervened. God chose both boys for His service. At this point, however, their lives lose their similarity. Samson's life included questionable behavior for one of God's servants. Samuel's life was filled with service and devotion to God. God responded to humble Hannah's prayer for a child. She presented her son to God after He was weaned (probably about age 3), keeping her promise to God. Though the separation had potential for sorrow, Hannah demonstrated her love for God in a prayer **(1 Sam. 2:1-10)** remarkably similar to the **Magnificat (Luke 1:46-55)**. We can join Hannah in praise to God who used these unique circumstances to bring a great blessing to His people.

Samuel grew up in Eli's household with Eli's evil sons, Hophni and Phinehas. It is remarkable that Samuel grew up to be pure before the Lord **(1 Sam. 2:35)**. We can expect that God will protect and empower those who He sets apart for His service.

Studies of Samuel's life often focus on the circumstances of his birth **(1 Sam. 1)** or on his unique call by God **(1 Sam. 3:1-21)**. But the close relationship between God and Samuel is important and encouraging for us. God cared for and protected Samuel **(1 Sam. 3:19)** as He prepared Samuel to be **"a faithful priest, who will do according to what is in My heart and mind" (1 Sam. 2:35)."**

Samuel effectively led Israel for the Lord throughout his life **(1 Sam. 7:6 and 12:1-5)**.

READING THE SCRIPTURES (Objectives 1 and 2)

Assign the students to read **1 Sam. 1--7** and complete the Student Book section before class.

Begin your session with prayer. Thank God for all the guidance He has given you in the past and ask Him to continue to lead and bless you in the ways He has chosen for each of you.

Ask the students to identify important points from the first three chapters of Samuel. (Answers will vary. You can expect students to focus on Hannah's prayer, God's call to Samuel, Eli's sons and their wicked abuse of their priestly office.)

Discuss how God responded to Hannah's fervent prayer. Relate that she was an obscure woman who suffered ridicule because she was not able to have children. Emphasize that God used this situation to bring a great leader to His people Israel.

GOD CHOOSES SAMUEL TO LEAD ISRAEL (Objectives 1 and 2)

Ask, **Who remembers a TV show called "Let's Make a Deal"? Does**

Hannah's prayer (1 Sam. 1:11) sound as though she were trying to make a deal with God? How do we sometimes make promises to God in exchange for His favors? A common example might be, "Lord, get me out of this predicament and I'll never do this again!" Explain that Hannah was dealing with a real problem in her life. God loved her and responded with His blessings. She kept her promises selflessly.

Discuss the first two questions from the Student Book in this section. Then help your students identify with the intense situation surrounding Samuel's birth and consecration to the Lord. Ask, **What emotions do parents experience when their children leave home?** Ask your students to write a letter, pretending they are mother Hannah, to her little boy Samuel. In the letter, tell how you felt when you left Samuel with Eli. (Remember Samuel may have been about three years old.) Ask volunteers to read their letters in class. Then read aloud Hannah's prayer in **1 Sam. 2:1-10**. How do your letters compare with Hannah's prayer?

List with your students the different roles Samuel had in Israel. He was prophet **(1 Sam. 3:20)**, priest **(1 Sam. 7:9-10)**, and judge **(1 Sam. 7:15)**. God used Samuel to lead Israel mightily. Finish discussing the remainder of the questions in this section of the Student Book.

GOD CHOOSES ME FOR SPECIAL JOBS
(Objective 3)

Ask the students to suggest different roles they have in their lives now. (Some roles might be student, brother, sister, aunt or uncle, cousin, friend, helper at home, baby-sitter, ball-team captain or member, choir member, etc.) God certainly uses us in many different ways, doesn't He? Then discuss the questions in this section of the Student Book.

Help the students find meaningful Bible verses that assure them that God is always with them (**Ps. 16:8; 40:17; 46:1; 124:8** and **Heb. 4:16** all remind us God will help us, too.)

Remind the students that Hannah presented Samuel to God for full-time service. Ask, **What are some of the careers in which people serve full time in our church today?** (Discuss the role of pastor, teacher, DCE, parish worker, District or synodical official, missionary, etc.) Ask if any of the students are considering one of these service-related careers. **Are you encouraged by your family members? by your teachers and pastors?** (Frequently, students receive little positive encouragement to enter a church ministry career. Ask representatives of these areas to visit your class and talk about their work. Ask a guidance counselor to come, too, to discuss the many areas of ministry open to men and women in the church today.)

AM I WILLING TO WORK FOR GOD?
(Objective 4)

Discuss the questions from this section of the Student Book. Ask, **What choices do you have in deciding your future? How do you feel knowing you can depend on God for His help and direction?**

You might end your session by asking the students to pray silently the prayer they have written in this section of their Student Book.

"Oh, that the Lord Would Guide My Ways" (LW 392) reinforces today's theme and helps us state our trust in the Lord. Sing or say the stanzas together aloud or as a silent prayer.

Session 53: Saul: Israel's First King

BIBLE BASIS: 1 Sam. 8--14

CENTRAL TRUTH

Just as God changed Saul's life, He gives us purpose and power for service to Him and to others.

OBJECTIVES

That the students will:

1. Understand that the Holy Spirit of God equipped Saul for service as the king of Israel

2. Realize that God intended Saul to earn the respect of the people before they proclaimed him king in Israel

3. Deduce that God helps us become successful achievers regardless of our status at birth or during life

4. Ask God's direction for their lives

BACKGROUND

God reluctantly planned a time when a king would rule in Israel, for He set down some important guidelines for kings in **Deut. 17:14-20.** Both the people and the kings would have benefited from periodic references to God's Word regarding the role of the king. As you review the period of the monarchy with your students, remind them of the Deuteronomy verses.

The first person chosen by God to be king in Israel **(Deut. 17:15)** was Saul, a Benjamite. Saul was a tall, handsome man whose physical appearance inspired those around him **(1 Sam. 9:2).** Yet he was a very humble person **(9:21).**

Saul's life before he was made king differed noticeably from his life after he was given God's Holy Spirit. The change was predicted by Samuel **(10:6).**

Significant events of this session include:

a. The changing of Saul's heart **(1 Sam. 10:9)**

b. The Holy Spirit coming upon Saul **(10:10)**

c. The designation of Saul as king **(10:20-24).**

In spite of God's designation of Saul as king, not everyone willingly accepted his leadership **(1 Sam. 10:27).** Before long God led Saul in a mighty way against an Ammonite named Nahash who threatened the Israelites in Jabesh Gilead **(1 Sam. 11:6-11).** The event served to solidify Saul's position as king over Israel.

But Saul faced many problems. He had gathered a group of fighting men together at Gilgal to make war on the Philistines. They waited for over a week for Samuel to arrive to offer a sacrifice to the Lord on their behalf. The men grew restless and began to leave. Saul took charge and assumed a privilege that was reserved only for the priests--he offered the sacrifice himself. When Samuel finally arrived, he chastised Saul for his foolish and impulsive behavior and told Saul that his disobedience would cost him the monarchy.

Saul also had to equip his troops with weapons--a formidable task, since the Philistines had denied them access to iron or blacksmiths in an effort to keep them from becoming militarily strong. Saul's early armament was limited to sharpened farm implements **(1 Sam. 13:19-22).**

Nevertheless, God was with Saul and helped him in successful battles against Israel's enemies.

READING THE SCRIPTURES (Objectives 1 and 2)

The activities in this session will help the students see the importance of God's presence and power in their lives for obedience and service to Him.

Before this session the students should have read **1 Sam. 8--14** and completed their Student Book section.

Begin class time with prayer. Thank God for this new day and ask Him to be present and powerful in your lives today. Encourage the students to pray for anyone they might know in need of prayer.

GOD'S INVOLVEMENT IN SAUL'S LIFE (Objectives 1 and 2)

Be prepared to discuss Saul's leadership qualities, the challenges he faced as Israel's first king, and his performance as new king of Israel. Discuss questions 1 and 2 and ask for Scriptural support for their answers. List Saul's strengths and weaknesses on the chalkboard as the students suggest them.

Ask students to share their answers for question 3. **What were Saul's greatest challenges? How did God overcome Saul's weaknesses?** (**1 Sam. 10:6-7** and **chapter 11** give clues.)

Ask, **Does everyone love a winner? What were the reactions of some Israelites to Saul becoming king**

(1 Sam. 10:27 and 11:12)? Were these fickle people? Is it easier to support a winner or a loser? Why do you think some Israelites refused to acknowledge Saul as their king until he was successful in battle? (Their reasons might include lack of faith in God; fear of reprisal from the enemy if they followed Saul and he failed; sheer stupidity; outright disobedience; jealousy; etc.)

GOD'S INVOLVEMENT IN MY LIFE
(Objective 3)

Leading isn't always easy. Can you think of a time when you had to lead others and found that the job included problems that made leading very difficult? (This might be a good time to relate some difficulties to your class that you experienced as a classroom teacher. Help students conclude that lack of cooperation increases a leader's problems.) Discuss question 1 in the Student Book under this section. Share the expectations found in the Bible references.

Explain that God holds us each accountable for our behavior. While some psychologists and humanists excuse people from living up to their potential (for reasons including poverty, broken homes, poor educational experiences, strict parents), God does not accept our disobedience. He is eager to help turn our failures into successes. Discuss questions 2 and 3 and listen to students share answers from their Student Books. Remind the students that God helped Saul, who, as a member of the smallest tribe of Israel chased donkeys and plowed fields for a living, and gave him power to be Israel's king. God is able to do great things for us, too, no matter who we are and where we come from.

I STEP INTO FAITHFUL SERVICE
(Objective 4)

Ask the students to share their answers to the questions from this section. Remind them to take one step at a time in solving their problems, always asking God for help first. Ask the students to report back in a week or two telling how God helped them with these problems they have shared.

You might write the offertory on the chalkboard and sing or say it with your students to close this session: Create in me a clean heart, O God, and renew a right spirit within me. Cast me not away from your presence, and take not your Holy Spirit from me. Restore to me the joy of your salvation, and uphold me with your free Spirit. Amen (*LW*, Divine Service 1, p. 143).

Session 54: Saul: The Failing King

BIBLE BASIS: 1 Sam. 15--31; 1 Chron. 10

CENTRAL TRUTH

God blesses and strengthens those who believe in Him, but He will not tolerate deliberate disobedience. God's grace is never license to sin.

OBJECTIVES

That the students will:

1. Relate God's rejection of King Saul to Saul's deliberate disobedience
2. Understand that God expects His people to be obedient and that His grace enables God's people to lead lives that please Him
3. Confess their sins to God and ask Him to help them lead a Christ-filled life
4. Thank and praise God for His forgiveness and power in their lives

BACKGROUND

This portion of Scripture tells the tragic story of Saul's failure as Israel's king and God's rejection of him. God expects us to obey Him perfectly (**Matt. 5:48**). Saul had to accept the responsibility for his disobedience. God gave him the power of the Holy Spirit to succeed as king, but Saul deliberately sinned against God. The power of the flesh is great (**Rom. 7:18**) and is not to be trusted for it leads us to death (**Rom. 7:24**). But God's grace is always more than adequate for our needs **(Rom. 7:25)**.

Conditions in Israel improved slightly during Saul's early reigning years as king. However, continual disobedience cost Saul the monarchy. In spite of his confession and repentance, he was not allowed to have the monarchy pass on to his heirs **(1 Chron. 10:13-14)**. Instead, God told Samuel to anoint David as the next king of Israel. God took his Holy Spirit from Saul (as he had from Samson) and allowed Saul to experience episodes of depression, fear, and jealousy **(1 Sam. 18:8-16,28-29; 19:9-10; 28:5-6)**. David's successes intensified Saul's anger and jealousy.

Saul tried unsuccessfully to get assurance and direction from the Lord. He even consulted a witch (earlier in his reign Saul had ordered practitioners of the occult removed from Israel in accord with God's command in **Lev. 19:31; 20:6, 27; Deut. 18:10**) and broke the law he had once enforced.

Samuel's message to Saul--probably through an apparition created by Satan **(1 Sam. 28:16-19)**--repeated the message he had delivered previously **(1 Sam. 15:28)** and warned Saul his reign would soon end. Israel lost their king, their trust in God, and their direction for living. Through all this, God still loved them and would provide a great leader for them.

READING THE SCRIPTURES (Objectives 1 and 2)

Assign the reading of **1 Sam. 15:1--13:13** and **1 Chron. 10:1-4** prior to class so that the material can be discussed in class without taking time for an initial reading. Be prepared to point out that the Chronicles account was written for those Jews who returned from the exile to help them understand and have confidence in God's covenant promise to Israel. Before class, also assign Student Book activities for this session.

SAUL--THE DISOBEDIENT KING (Objectives 1 and 2)

The incidents in **1 Sam. 13:3-4** and **15:1-26** tell of deliberate acts of disobedience by Saul that resulted in God rejecting him as king of Israel. Set up a courtroom scenario by assigning students to play the roles of Saul (the accused), Samuel (the prosecutor), God (the judge), a defense attorney, and the jury (the remaining persons in the class). Prior to class have the students who play the parts of Saul, Samuel, the judge, and the defense attorney meet to discuss the incidents and rehearse their roles.

In class the questioning and cross examination should stick to the information given in the texts but may be put into the students' own words. Upon hearing the case, the judge should instruct the jury that they must find the defendant guilty and must order that the defendant forfeit his crown. The jury may argue against or for the judge's decision. However, all who speak must use portions of Scripture to support their opinions.

Be prepared to process this activity with the students in order to help them conclude that God, who is righteous and the absolute authority, has the right to judge a situation and that His creatures should willingly accept His decisions. Ultimately this is the basic issue each of us faces each day: Is God Lord in our lives? It is through Spirit-led obedience that we enjoy God's will for our lives.

I AM DEAD TO SIN AND ALIVE TO GOD THROUGH CHRIST (Objectives 2 and 3)

Discuss Student Book questions 1--3 in this section. Then read **Rom. 5:20--6:14** aloud to the class. Point out that God still expects obedience from His people. The fact that Jesus has died for us and has earned forgiveness for all of our sins does not grant us license to sin **(Rom. 6:1-2)**. On the contrary, through Baptism we have died to the power of sin and have been granted the power of God's Holy Spirit, which enables us to live obedient lives.

(Interesting background reading for the teacher on this topic will be found in The Normal Christian Life by Watchman Nee [Wheaton, IL: Tyndale

House, 1977].)

One way to discover the joy of forgiveness is to confess a sin to God and ask Him to overcome that sin in your life. Ask your students to review **Rom. 6:1-14** again and then go to God in confidence, confessing their sins, accepting His forgiveness, and claiming His power for a new life.

I PRAISE THE LORD! (Objective 4)

Ask the students to share their findings about God's love from this section in their Student Book.

St. Paul concludes **Rom. 7:25** with praise for God in Christ. Remind your students of these important things we can do today and each day:

1. Remember that you have died "in" Christ through Baptism--rejoice!
2. Remember that you are a new person, dead to the power of sin but alive in Christ--thank God!
3. Remember that you do sin because you are still in the flesh. Confess your sin to God and claim His power over sin, each day-- praise God!

Session 55: David: Preparation for Leadership

BIBLE BASIS: 1 Sam. 16--30

CENTRAL TRUTH

God always accomplishes His purposes. Things that we view as obstacles do not stop Him. We can view challenges as opportunities for God to prepare us for greater service to Him and as times when He will demonstrate His love and support for us.

OBJECTIVES

That the students will:

1. Value a person's inner strength and beauty rather than judge outward appearance
2. Identify ways God helped prepare David to lead Israel
3. Identify ways God has already helped them become more mature and faithful to the Lord
4. Recognize David's devotion to the Lord as a strength that contributed to his success
5. Evaluate their own lives and renew their own commitment to God as Lord of their lives

BACKGROUND

It is obvious from **1 Sam. 16:1-2** that Samuel did not enjoy telling Saul that the Lord had rejected him as king over Israel. But God's decision was final, and it was time for Samuel to anoint another in Saul's place. The Lord sent Samuel to Bethlehem under the pretext of offering a sacrifice while He revealed to Him who was to be the next king.

The remaining chapters of **1 Sam. (17--31)** contain a number of vignettes of various experiences that served to prepare David for a leadership role in Israel.

Perhaps the most memorable of these events is the encounter between David and Goliath (**1 Sam. 17:1-58**). The main points of the encounter provide several lessons for the Christian who must stand up to all kinds of evil.

In the first place, David found Goliath's defiance an affront to the Lord God (**1 Sam. 17:45**).

Second, David was prepared to take action against those who would oppose the Lord God (**1 Sam. 17:32**).

Third, David's confidence was completely in God (**1 Sam. 17:47**).

Fourth, David ran into action with boldness and confidence, using those weapons with which he felt comfortable (**1 Sam. 17:48-49**; cf. **Judg. 20:16**).

God looks for no less from His people at any time (**Eph. 6:10-18**). It is our privilege today to face the enemies of God in the power of His might and to battle successfully against spiritual powers.

But we need one more characteristic. We need to know who we are. David's response to Saul's skepticism over his ability to defeat Goliath, and then Saul's provision of unfamiliar weapons and armor were basically the same. "I know who I am and what I can do with what I know" (**1 Sam. 16:32-40**).

Too often we hesitate to put to

use that with which God has blessed us, either to witness for Him, to oppose evil, or even to live our own lives in a way that glorifies God. God has provided each of His people with abilities that will serve Him and the body of Christ. It is our privilege to glorify God with our gifts.

The balance of David's experiences with Saul were marked by Saul's jealous attempts to kill David. Saul's own son, Jonathan, played a significant role in David's rescue on two occasions (**1 Sam. 19:4--7; 20:33-42**). Jonathan was devoted and loyal to David, in spite of the fact that David's success was sure to prevent Jonathan from inheriting the throne. The friendship of Jonathan and David is described in passages such as **1 Sam. 18:1** and **20:42**.

During the time from his victory over Goliath until the death of Saul, David was both a successful warrior and a fugitive. God used all David's experiences to prepare him for his position as king over Israel.

READING THE SCRIPTURES (Objectives 2 and 3)

Assign the Scripture reading and Student Book material for this session well in advance, since there is a good deal of material to cover.

Begin the class with a prayer. Ask for courage to face successfully those things that put our faith in Jesus Christ to the test.

GOD HELPS DAVID LEAD HIS PEOPLE
(Objectives 1, 2, and 4)

Review the main points of this section of Scripture, paying close attention to those points of the story that are listed in the **"Background"** above. Then ask the students to share their answers for questions 1--3 in this section of their Student Books.

On chalkboard or chart, list with the students the qualities they would require in an ideal leader. Reach a consensus on the 10 most important qualities of a good leader. Next have your students listen as you read **1 Sam. 16:7**. Then have them review their lists to determine whether any of their points should be deleted or others added. How do you feel knowing that God looks at your heart?

GOD GIVES CONFIDENCE TO ME
(Objectives 2, 4, and 5)

Discuss Student Book questions 1--3 in this section. Summarize together how God gives us encouragement and confidence in our lives.

Refer to **1 Sam. 16--27**. Give the students about five minutes to list the experiences David had that contributed most in preparing him to be king. **How were these experiences helpful to David? How did God help him?** Then ask your students to share any difficult experiences they may have had in life that have helped to prepare them for adult life. Discuss some of their suggestions with the goal of helping them see God's guidance, protection, and support as He helps them prepare for the future. Two passages for consideration on this topic are **Rom. 8:28** and **2 Cor. 1:1-5**.

One of David's greatest qualities was his respect for and devotion to God. He evaluated most of his experiences from a perspective that acknowledged God as the Lord of his life. His own remarks in **1 Sam. 17:37, 45-46; 24:6; 25:39;** and **26:23-24** are evidence of this. List these verses on the board and ask your students to read them. **What do these verses tell you about David's attitude toward God?** Refer back to Student Book question 3 in this section. **How has God helped you gain confidence and trust in Him?**

O LORD, RENEW MY HEART TO YOU
(Objective 5)

The faith God gave David should be a source of encouragement to you and your students. Ask your students to write a paragraph reflecting on their own lives and their attitudes toward God as compared with David's. **Is there any hope for us? Or is David extraordinary?** The conclusion should be that we are loved by an extraordinary God who blesses ordinary people like David and us. Our greatness comes from God.

Things I Can Do Today

1. Praise God for His love for me.

2. Begin looking at others from God's perspective, focusing on those spiritual qualities of importance in them rather than on their physical appearance.

3. Commit to memory some of the more significant passages from this session.

Things I Can Do Tomorrow

1. Look to God for strength to endure temptation and challenge.

2. Ask God to direct the course of my life to prepare me to be the person he wants me to be.

3. Trust God's promises in difficult times.

4. Make mental notes of the way in which God delivers me from difficulty in order to gain confidence in His presence in the future.

Session 56: David: The Warrior King

BIBLE BASIS: 2 Sam. 2--10; 1 Chron. 11--20

CENTRAL TRUTH

God keeps His promises to His people in a time that accomplishes His own plan and serves to bless His people.

OBJECTIVES

That the students will:

1. Recognize David as a mighty warrior, a capable king, and a sensitive human being

2. Conclude that David's success came from God, whom he trusted and obeyed **(2 Sam. 7:28)**

3. Trace the development of God's plan to provide a country for His people to the military accomplishments of David that secured a place where Israel could grow into a great nation **(2 Sam. 7:10)**

4. Recognize as a Messianic prophecy God's promise to David that a king would come from his seed (**2 Sam. 7:16**; see also **Is. 2:2-4; Micah 4:2; Luke 1:32-33; Ps. 89:35**)

5. Praise and thank God for his blessings and His promises kept to them personally

BACKGROUND

The transition from Saul's leadership of Israel to David's kingship was not accomplished easily. The Lord sent David to Hebron, where he was publicly anointed king. However, Abner, one of Saul's generals, made Saul's son Ish-Bosheth king over Israel. The two factions--the house of Saul and the house of David--were continually at war with each other. David's position grew stronger as time passed, while Ish-Bosheth and Abner's deteriorated **(2 Sam. 3:1)**.

David suffered many disappointments and much treachery at the hands of his own children. But he continued to love them in spite of their deceitful behavior. Though imperfect, his love is a reminder to us of how God continues to love us, His disobedient children.

This period in time was marked with war, murders, and intrigue. David eventually became king over the entire nation of Israel **(2 Sam. 5:3)**. He was 30 years old at the time and ruled 40 years. Though David fought as a warrior throughout his life, he maintained unfailing love for his own family and his subjects. God blessed David's reign with successful ventures **(2 Sam. 5:10, 19)**.

READING THE SCRIPTURES (Objectives 1-4)

The students should have read **2 Sam. 2--10** and completed this section in the Student Book before class.

Be prepared to lead a class discussion on the events leading to David being acclaimed king over Israel. The students are to list events in their Student Books. You might review briefly the history recorded at the beginning of **2 Samuel**. Saul and Jonathan died, David was anointed; the houses of Saul and David were at war constantly;

Abner changed to David's side; Joab murdered Abner; Ish-Bosheth was killed; and all the tribes of Israel came to David.

Pray for God to guide each of you to become more aware of His plan in the Old Testament and His plan for you now. Thank Him for His daily blessings in your lives.

GOD UNFOLDS HIS PLAN FOR ISRAEL
(Objectives 1, 2, and 3)

Direct your students' attention to **2 Sam. 1:1--5:16.** Point out that Israel was divided over the question of who would be king. Judah, comprised of the tribes of Judah and Benjamin, chose to follow David. The northern tribes, known as Israel, followed Abner's lead in making Ish-Bosheth king. After much time and bloodshed, David became king over a united Israel. Suggest that the students might find some parallels in the history of the United States: Civil War, and the recent war in Vietnam, for example. Point out the difference, though: God had selected David as Israel's next king, while His choice of leaders in the United States and Vietnam was not similarly stated. Through this activity, help your students understand the events immediately following Saul's death.

Ask students to share their answers for questions 1 and 2 in this section of their Student Books.

After discussing how God helped David become successful, talk about how God might be involved in the students' lives, too. How is God helping you be a caring, successful, understanding leader? Students' answers should reveal their understanding and conscious awareness of their need to invite God to be <u>in</u> their everyday lives and the importance of depending on Him to provide direction, purpose, and success in their lives. If such understanding is not present, refer to **Eph. 2:8-10; Rom. 6:1-13;** and **Gal. 2:20.**

Share answers to question 4 in this section. You might refer also to **Gen. 15:18** and **2 Sam. 7:10.** (God secured a land for His people.) Then determine whether your students grasp the significance of the fulfillment of God's promise made years earlier to Abraham. Ask them to suggest feelings David may have experienced when he heard God's announcement. Write their comments on the chalkboard. Then compare their responses with **2 Sam. 7:18-29.**

GOD KEPT HIS PROMISE TO DAVID
(Objective 4)

What could be greater than Israel's own land and their king forever? Discuss this section and the students' answers from the Student Books. Jesus Christ, according to His human nature, is called David's son or descendant. Thus God kept His promise to David by establishing Jesus as King of kings and Lord of lords forever.

GOD KEEPS HIS PROMISES TO ME
(Objective 5)

Has it been difficult for the students to find personal importance in the events studied so far? Aside from the good lessons learned, each of us can appreciate God's incredible love for and patience with humankind as He worked to fulfill His plan for salvation. The securing of the Promised Land under David was the culmination of a very important project God began on behalf of us. It set the stage for the coming of the Messiah as it established God's people in the world.

Discuss the students' answers to the questions in this section. Share ways in which God has personally kept His promises to you, too.

I THANK AND PRAISE GOD (Objective 5)

Ask for a volunteer to share a praise-poem he or she has written in this section of the Student Book. Then review David's success formula from **2 Sam. 5:10.**

Close this session with a prayer. Ask God to be a part of all the events in your lives, thank and praise Him for keeping His promises, and ask Him to direct your lives so you may glorify Him and follow the plans He has established for your lives.

Session 57: David: The Man

BIBLE BASIS: 2 Sam. 11--19

CENTRAL TRUTH

Our heavenly Father loves us enough to correct us when we do wrong and rescues us from the slavery of sin.

OBJECTIVES

That the students will:

1. Conclude that David's relationship with Bathsheba was sinful and recognize that many tragic events in David's family life had their origin in David's sin
2. Relate David's fear of discovery to the cover-up he designed resulting in Uriah's murder
3. Acknowledge and accept David's confession and repentance as sincere
4. Understand that sin causes trouble and tragedy in their own lives
5. Confess their own sins to God and accept His forgiveness joyfully

BACKGROUND

From studying David in previous lessons your students should have concluded that David was a just and obedient person who respected God and His laws. This lesson shows that David suffered from the same human weaknesses as we do.

David enjoyed considerable wealth and power as king. On occasion, his idleness allowed opportunity for Satan to tempt him. David committed adultery and murder and suffered miserable consequences of his sins. Through a moving parable, the prophet Nathan brought God's accusation to David. David stood convicted by his own verdict. The agony of his struggle over his sin is recorded in **Ps. 51.** Though David assumes the responsibility for the sin, it should be pointed out that Bathsheba was guilty of immodest behavior.

Paraphrasing Roehrs and Franzmann in the Concordia Self-Study Commentary, this section of Scripture is written to teach and to warn us: **"Let anyone who thinks that he stands take heed lest he fall" (1 Cor. 10:12 RSV)** and for our comfort: there is forgiveness with God for the most despicable sins if we follow David's example of confession and repentance.

The consequences of David's sin should be a lesson to all of us. Others are hurt even when a sinful act appears to be confined to a relationship between two consenting adults. The consequences in this lesson reached David's entire family and resulted in the deaths of several people including Uriah and the first child of David and Bathsheba.

David acknowledged his sin, confessed and accepted his punishment, and acted compassionately toward his children in spite of their rebellious behavior toward him.

READING THE SCRIPTURES (Objectives 1, 2, and 3)

Prepare your students for this session before assigning the Scripture reading and the Student Book section. Tell your students they will find descriptions of behavior here that greatly concern society today: adultery, rape, incest, murder, and rebellion/revolt. The incidents described should be introduced as being very real and should not be compared to fantasies of movies or television. Handle the material delicately. Provide opportunities to discuss attitudes and current information on abortion, incest, rape, murder, etc. Be sure to know what Scripture says about these topics. And evaluate your own personal stand on these themes.

Begin your class session with a short prayer asking God to bless everyone's learning and sharing together today.

Quickly review the main events throughout this section of Scripture. Ask the students to tell what they think of David from **2 Samuel.**

DAVID'S MISERY FROM SIN (Objectives 1 and 2)

Discuss whether the following behaviors of David were against God's law, against human law, or against no law:

a. David's adultery with Bathsheba
b. His attempts at a cover-up
c. David planning Uriah's death
d. The marriage of David and Bathsheba

After the students have classified these events, discuss their answers. Point out that in each case, David's behavior was sinful regardless of which law it violated. God's absolutes convict the disobedient and guide those who are under His grace. God determines what is right and wrong.

Discuss the questions from this section in the Student Book. Although David was not put to death, his sinful behavior did have consequences. Ask the students to find some of those consequences in **2 Sam. 12:15--19:43.** Unlike Cain, David accepted the consequences of his sin and demonstrated understanding toward those who sinned against him **(2 Sam. 16:11; 18:33).**

MY MISERY FROM SIN (Objective 4)

Relating to question 1 in the Student Books, ask your students if they would be willing to volunteer to reveal instances when they attempted to cover up sins. Will they volunteer to tell how they felt in their own experiences? If this is too threatening, ask the students to describe these feelings David might have had as he dealt with his guilt and fear over sin.

Ask, **What is one important thing you have learned from David's experience with sin and its consequences?** Ask someone to volunteer to share what he (she) has learned from his (her) own experience with sin, its consequences in his (her) life, and the mixed emotions accompanying sin.

GOD RESCUES ME WITH HIS LOVE AND FORGIVENESS (Objective 5)

Discuss the questions and answers in this section of the Student Book. Then ask a student to read **Ps. 51** aloud. **How do you feel about David's sincerity in the psalm's words?** Though most will acknowledge and accept David's confession and repentance as sincerely stated, we sinners are never as forgiving as God is. At this time, you might discuss whether we are willing to forgive each other for even less serious offenses.

Point out that although those who have accepted Jesus Christ by faith have had all of their sins forgiven through Christ's death on the cross and His resurrection, our sinful acts still have consequences for us. Assure your students of God's love and forgiveness. At the same time, remind them to think carefully of the misery they may cause themselves and others by behaving thoughtlessly and sinfully. Then <u>reassure</u> them of the good news for us discussed in question 4: through Christ Jesus we are able to be free from eternal death!

Conclude by allowing the students to discuss the joy and happiness they feel when they have confessed and repented of their sins and have the assurance of God's forgiveness and everlasting love. Be prepared to counsel or refer to a counselor a student who may feel the burden of unconfessed sin.

Session 58: Solomon: Judge, Poet, Teacher

BIBLE BASIS: 1 Kings 1:28--4:34

CENTRAL TRUTH

God is "inexorably just, endlessly patient, and inexhaustibly gracious" as He directs the course of history (<u>Concordia Self-Study Commentary</u>, p. 220).

OBJECTIVES

That the students will:

1. List examples of the blessings God gave to Solomon, including wisdom, wealth, honor, and a long life, and be able to give Scriptural references for their manifestations in Solomon's life
2. Ask God for those abilities that will enable them to live prudently and serve God and others
3. Evaluate their own present personal relationships with God

BACKGROUND

As David grew old and it became apparent that he would not live much longer, his son, Adonijah, decided to consolidate the support he needed to become king. When Nathan learned of the subterfuge, he devised a counterstrategy by which he and Bathsheba would alert David to the problem and arrange for Solomon's appointment as king. (Note the absence of God's anointing, a change from the way Saul and David were chosen.)

When he was declared king, Solomon was anointed by the priest, Zadok. David instructed Solomon to keep the covenant God had made with him. Solomon had to secure his position with two enemies of David, Joab and Shimei. The priest Abiather had conspired with Adonijah and also posed a threat. David had shown mercy to Joab and Shimei, but he knew they could pose problems for Solomon. Joab and Shimei were put to death and Abiather was banished. Eventually, Solomon also had Adonijah put to death.

The Lord had always loved Solomon **(2 Sam. 12:25)**. In a dream He offered Solomon anything he desired. In what appeared to be a humble and respectful request, Solomon asked for wisdom to rule God's people and for the ability to judge between right and wrong. He wanted to serve God and the people rather than gain anything personally. God was so pleased with Solomon's request that He also gave him wealth, fame, and promised him a long life if he would remain faithful.

Solomon subsequently demonstrated his ability to govern wisely **(1 Kings 4:29-34)** and the people were happy **(1 Kings 4:20)**.

READING THE SCRIPTURES (Objective 1)

Assign the reading of **1 Kings 1:28--4:34** and the Student Book section before class so that the session material can be thoroughly discussed in class.

Open with prayer. You might thank God for His patience and wisdom in your lives.

To achieve the objectives for this session, summarize briefly the events from this period of Solomon's life:

a. Solomon's request for wisdom **(1 Kings 3:3-15)**

b. An example of Solomon's wisdom **(1 Kings 3:16-28)**

c. Happiness that comes from living wisely **(1 Kings 4:20-34)**

You might relate this story to your students:

A song tells the story of an old man who was laughed at because, when offered a choice between a shiny quarter and a dollar bill, he always took the quarter. A young man befriended this man. When the old man neared death, he gave his young friend two gifts. His first gift was to tell the young man, "Always take the quarter, because as soon as you take the dollar, they will stop playing the game." Before he died, he gave the young man his second gift, four large bags of quarters. The old man had outsmarted his tormentors, though he endured ridicule and shame in the process. He was willing to act wisely rather than reach for what would have been desired by most people. Solomon was initially that kind of a man.

Finally, ask what lessons **1 Kings 3:3-15** and **Matt. 6:33** teach us.

GOD'S BLESSINGS FOR SOLOMON AND HIS PEOPLE (Objective 1)

Ask the students to share answers to questions in this section of the Student Book. Emphasize that through God's love and help, Solomon's activities were blessed and successful.

Of all possible examples, God chose to use the incident where Solomon dramatically decided a case between two prostitutes by threatening to cut their babies in half **(1 Kings 3:16-28)**. When it became clear that Solomon had devised a way to discern the real mother of the living child, he gained the respect of those around him.

Discuss the episode with your students. Since the case made it all the way to the king, it must have baffled the usual judges. But when do you cut the baby in half? Since none of us was there, it is impossible for us to know what Solomon saw in the two women. But God helped him with wisdom and compassion to be a judge of human nature to detect who was lying in this case. Remind the students that God blessed His people through Solomon's kingship.

GOD'S BLESSINGS FOR ME (Objective 2)

Discuss question 1 in this section of the Student Book. **How would you have responded to God's offer and why?**

Ask students to read aloud **Matt. 7:7-8** and **Matt. 18:19-20.** Talk about why the students would ask for those things they wrote in answering this question.

Ask your students what kinds of decisions they make on a day-to-day basis. Why would it be easier to make these decisions by having wisdom from the Lord? What can they do to ask God for His blessing of wisdom in decision-making in their lives?

Talk about questions 3 and 4 in the Student Book. How does **Matt. 6:33**, the Scripture verse highlighted in this session, relate and remind us that God hears us and answers our prayers?

As you talk about questions 5 and 6 together, you might list on the chalkboard those responsibilities the students suggest. Encourage them to think of people and areas other than ourselves for which we have many daily responsibilities. (As Christians we can show joy in our lives from knowing Jesus died for us, and share that through actions and words to our families, friends, neighbors, store clerks, bus drivers, whomever we meet.)

THE LORD IS ACTIVE IN MY LIFE (Objective 3)

Compare **1 Kings 4:20** with **Gen. 22:17.** God's promise to Abraham was fulfilled and, at least initially, Solomon's wise judgment brought prosperity to the nation.

David had emphasized to Solomon that God would keep His promises as long as Solomon remained faithful to God. This was a positive way of emphasizing that Solomon was not to forsake God for the idols of the people around him. It was not a promised reward for self-righteous behavior, for God always provided the resources for success. Everything hinged on a proper relationship with the Lord. In this section, the students will examine their own relationships with the Lord.

Ask a student to read aloud **1 Tim. 4:9-16.** Tell what Scripture says about taking our relationship with the Lord seriously. What will happen if one does not regard it seriously? Read **Gal. 5:19-21** and **2 Tim. 3:2-4** and **8-9.** Lives that resemble the descriptions in these verses are lives of people in trouble.

A benchmark for measuring the Lord's activity in our lives is **Gal. 5:22-23** where Paul lists the fruit of the Spirit. Ask the students for their answers to question 1 in this section of the Student Book. As they volunteer their selected words that describe their lives, write them within a large circle on the chalkboard. Ask the students to then write <u>all</u> the words that describe their lives inside a large circle they draw on a piece of paper. Refer again to **Matt. 6:33.** How does this verse remind us of God's promises to be active in our lives? What things will be given to us?

Question 2 in this section asks the students to write a prayer in which they confess their sins and ask God for the power to overcome the negatives in their lives. Allow a few minutes for students to complete their prayers. They might refer to the circle of words they selected and use those words in their prayer thoughts. Assure your students that God forgives their sins and is eager to have the opportunity to bless their lives with the whole fruit of His Holy Spirit.

Session 59: Solomon: The Builder

BIBLE BASIS: 1 Kings 5--9; 1 Chron. 22; 28:--29

CENTRAL TRUTH

God's gifts to His people include practical and creative abilities and resources that can be employed to glorify Him and move His people to praise Him.

OBJECTIVES

That the students will:

1. Recognize the building of the temple as an important part of God's plan for His people in that the temple and the acts of worship performed there were the focal point of the religious and social life of the people
2. Compute the current value of the materials and labor required to build the temple and thereby recognize its splendor
3. Conclude that God blessed Solomon's ambitious building programs
4. Be aware that Solomon's resources and abilities were related to his relationship with God and that the act of rejecting God for idols would cause the loss of blessings for himself and for all of Israel.
5. Be aware that their resources and abilities are gifts from God to use to His glory
6. Glorify God daily, living as His own temples

BACKGROUND

Solomon enjoyed a privilege David had always desired--that of building a temple for the Lord. David had been denied that privilege because He had shed much blood on the earth (**1 Chron. 22:6-10**). David gathered resources and drew plans for the temple, completing much of the preparatory work for Solomon (**1 Chron. 22:1-4; 14-19** and **1 Chron. 28:11-19**).

The temple required seven years to complete. Solomon's prayer of dedication was a stirring tribute to the Lord, asking His blessing on Israel (**1 Kings 8:22-53**). The service of dedication lasted two weeks and included extensive sacrifices. After the ceremony's pomp and circumstance, the Lord's message came through loudly and clearly. He told Solomon (**1 Kings 9:3-9**) that He accepted the temple as His dwelling place, but only as long as the hearts of the people of Israel were righteous. Should Israel reject the Lord God and follow other gods, the Lord God would reject the temple and make Israel the object of ridicule. Obviously, God was not to be fooled by any outward observance of rituals.

The critical lesson is that God is concerned with our relationship with Him rather than with any earthly splendor offered to Him by those who do not love Him. The temple symbolized the presence of God in Israel, but only so long as the king and his subjects had a proper relationship with the Lord. Idolatry and disobedience were a mockery of God before the other nations.

Today each child of God is also His temple according to **1 Cor. 3:16; 6:19; 2 Cor. 6:16;** and **Eph. 2:21.**

READING THE SCRIPTURES

(Objectives 1 and 4)

Assign the Scripture reading and the Student Book section for this session prior to class. Ask the students to think about what a temple was in this period, what the purpose was for a temple, and what a temple meant to the people.

Begin your class session with prayer. Ask students to pray spontaneously for family members or friends. Thank God for His blessings to you this day.

The temple was the focal point for worship and their integration point with God. But its presence was not as important to God as was His presence in the people's lives. Point out that God wanted a proper relationship with His people. He did not want to be kept in His "proper" place outside of their lives.

THE TEMPLE IN ISRAEL
(Objectives 2 and 3)

Discuss the questions in this section from the Student Book. Ask the students how they would feel had they been one of the temple-builders; one of the worshipers in the temple; someone from a neighboring nation watching the progress of the temple construction.

Ask, **Who really built the temple?** Ask the students to read **1 Chron. 22:1-19** and **1 Kings 6:2-38. Should David or Solomon be considered the real temple builder?** Allow time for discussion. Then, if discussion does not conclude that David's resources came from God as did Solomon's opportunity to actually build the temple, suggest that the real builder was God since it was He who gave David and Solomon all that they had.

Ask, **What is the value of gold today?** As a class, attempt to compute part of the cost of the temple by calculating the current value of the 3,750 tons of gold that David had gathered for the temple (**1 Chron. 22:14**). It might also be interesting to calculate the current value of the silver and the wages paid to the workers over a seven year period.

TEMPLES TODAY
(Objectives 4 and 5)

Briefly, as a class activity, list many different types of "temples" in the world today (grass huts, concrete buildings, tents, outdoor amphitheaters, ornate gold-gilded and stained-glass windowed cathedrals, etc.). Ask the students to share their feelings about the use of extensive funds and high cost materials and labor for building a church as opposed to using the money to serve the needs of the poor, sick, or starving people in the world. Those who carry a burden for the needy will probably consider the use of resources for a worship center to be rather wasteful. To others, though, sacrificial service in the Lord's name is pleasing to God and buildings are never a substitute for service.

God is interested in having us place all that we are and have at His disposal to be used as He wishes. The important point is that we are to present both our resources and our services to the Lord.

Talk about the answers the students have written to the questions in this section of the Student Book. Remind them that no matter where we are, we can worship God in our hearts. Whether we worship in ornate or in simple surroundings, we can be sure that God is with us. And we can be sure that He is pleased when He sees us using what He has given us to glorify and praise Him.

AM I A TEMPLE FOR THE LORD?
(Objectives 5 and 6)

Ask your students to share their answers to these questions in this section of their Student Books. This section of Scripture repeats the emphasis on the relationship that God desired with His people. He wants the same relationship with us--one in which we express our love for, dependence on, and obedience to Him.

Read **Gal. 2:20**, **Rom. 12:1**, and **Col. 1:27** in class. Then ask for volunteers to tell in their own words what it means to be "God's temple." Discuss ways we can respond positively to Paul's exhortation in **Rom. 12:1. How can we offer ourselves as living sacrifices to God?**

You might designate a bulletin board area in your classroom and title it "We Are Temples for the Lord." Tell the students they are to write adjectives that describe themselves as God's temples on the bulletin board or bring in pictures from magazines and newspapers that show how we can be living sacrifices for God. It can become a collage of the students' thoughts and reflections for this session.

Session 60: Solomon: The Fool

BIBLE BASIS: 1 Kings 11

CENTRAL TRUTH

God designed a relationship between Himself and people that brings joy to both. The tragic destruction of that relationship occurs only when we turn away from God.

OBJECTIVES

That the students will:

1. Acknowledge that God was faithful to His promises to Solomon
2. Recognize that Solomon's abuse of the wealth God gave him was a source of his downfall
3. Trace the return of idolatry in Israel to the political marriages of Solomon and his tolerance and approval of his wives' idolatry
4. Conclude that God was justified in taking the kingdom away from Solomon
5. List God's specific blessings to them personally and evaluate their use or misuse of those blessings
6. Remember God's promises to them as they live obediently to God

BACKGROUND

God kept His promise to grant Solomon enormous wealth and fame as well as wisdom **(1 Kings 3:13)**. Unfortunately, Solomon displayed wisdom without character. He critically erred in attempting to solidify his position through political marriages with foreign women. His marriages were forbidden by God's law **(Deut. 17:17; Ex. 34:16; Deut. 7:1-4; Joshua 23:6-13)**, and he tolerated and even provided for his wives' idolatrous worship.

While it is our natural inclination to desire greater and greater wealth and prestige, it is apparent that it can be hard to keep such blessings in a proper perspective. Jesus warned of the difficulties involved in possessing great wealth **(Matt. 19:24; Mark 10:25; Luke 18:25)**.

After reading of the misery caused by the disobedience of Israel during the time of the judges and kings, one longs for a leader who will be faithful in everything. But once again God had to punish for the sake of His people. Solomon's punishment was the loss of his kingdom--none of his sons would rule a united Israel.

READING THE SCRIPTURES
(Objective 1)

Assign the Scripture reading and the Student Book section prior to class.

Pray for God's blessings on your class and your time together to study God's Word. Ask God to strengthen each of your relationships with Him and to send His Spirit to give you power daily to live for Him.

Ask a student to summarize the section of Scripture assigned for today. **How did God keep his promise to Solomon? Because of what one short word was Solomon's punishment given?** (Sin--a small word with gigantic consequences.)

SOLOMON ABUSES GOD'S BLESSINGS
(Objectives 2, 3, and 4)

"Setting the World Right"--A Group Activity

This activity is divided into two subactivities. The first is a group initiative activity in which the students assume the responsibility for managing an enormous sum of money. The second is a discussion of the problems the students experienced during the first subactivity, comparing them to the problems Solomon experienced.

Divide the students into two equal groups. Have the students meet in their groups on opposite sides of the classroom.

Then each group should:

a. Appoint a leader and give their leader a title.

b. Name their group (choose an individual's name, the name of an organization, the name of a country, for example).

c. Decide on their location in the world.

d. Decide how they will use 100 billion dollars which you, the teacher, have deposited for them in a Swiss bank account (there is no guideline as to how the money must be used; however, the groups must account for every penny spent and give a reason for each expenditure).

e. Group resources may be used to purchase food, land, weapons, means of transportation, buildings, electronic equipment, personal conveniences, coal, oil, or gas. Anything may be purchased.

Allow the students to group and go through steps a, b, and c. Then read steps d and e, but add f and g before allowing them to proceed with their spending.

f. All oil and coal is owned by one group in addition to the money in their bank account. All electronic equipment, expertise for building, operating, and repairing it is possessed by the other group. (The teacher decides which group owns which commodity.)

g. No restrictions are placed on trade or bartering between the groups nor does either group have responsibility for the welfare of the other. However, each group must solve one of the problems facing the world today (for example, starvation, energy shortage, arms race, crime).

Allow the groups to interact for about 20 minutes. Then ask each group to report on its transaction, expenditures, and problems solved.

Award a point for each problem for which a reasonable solution was presented; deduct a point for each problem caused. (For example, the group that "solves" the problem of starvation in a country gets a point. The group that goes to war with another country in order to possess something loses a point.) It is the teacher's prerogative to award and deduct points. The group having the most points at the end of the set time limit wins.

Conclude the activity by examining the motive for each action of each group. Did the group sincerely desire to serve others? Did the group actively cause detriment to peace and harmony in the world? Did the group serve its own interest or was it concerned with the welfare of others? Did the group members' behavior build the group or destroy it? Did the leader serve wisely or did he or she represent the group in a way that led to its demise?

Compare the game activity to the actual behavior of Solomon and Israel.

Next, discuss the questions in this section of the Student Book. In spite of his wisdom, Solomon behaved like a very foolish king. Based on his extensive marriages with foreign women and his tolerance of their idolatry, we can conclude that Solomon did not have the commitment to the Lord God that his father David had demonstrated. **1 Kings 11:4** suggests that over a period of time Solomon even became attracted to the false gods of his wives. Constant exposure to something often produces an influence that is at first subtle, soon acceptable, and finally desirable. Brainwashing, as we see it used by cults today, speeds the process of idolatry.

Ask your students to point out where Solomon made his first mistake. (He failed to commit his heart to God as he had asked his people to do in **1 Kings 8:61.** His marriage to foreign wives followed his earlier mistake.)

Eventually Solomon built places for his wives to worship their idols and he joined them. Ask the students to report the information they found on the false gods Chemosh and Molech. Ask a student to read **Lev. 18:21** and **20:1-5.** Ask for comments on the intensity of God's feelings toward the worship of Molech.

Discuss the students' feelings about Solomon's punishment and their reactions had they been Solomon.

AM I USING OR ABUSING GOD'S BLESSINGS TO ME? (Objective 5)

Discuss question 1 from the Student Book in this section. **Do parents sacrifice their children to false gods today?** Read in class **Luke 17:2; Matt. 18:6;** and **Mark 9:42.** What is the significance of these passages for us today?

Ask students to share their

answers for question 2. **Do we place children in the presence of idols by carelessly exposing them to the evil world as shown on TV or in movies?** Conclude that being a Christian parent carries an awesome responsibility for the child's physical, emotional, and spiritual welfare.

Talk about questions 3 and 4 to personally help the students be aware of their blessings and their attitudes toward what God gives them.

GOD'S PROMISES FOR ME TO REMEMBER
(Objective 6)

Ask, **What important promise does God make and keep for each of us?** **John 3:16** reminds us of His promise, too. You might suggest that the students read **John 3:16** (or one of the passages listed in question 1) and personalize it (for example: "God so love me that He gave me His only Son; if I believe in Him, He gives me eternal life.").

Through His Son, Jesus Christ, God offers us all the resources we need to live holy lives **(Gal. 2:20; Col. 1:27; Eph. 1:17-20). What is our response to God?** Praise God that we have a King who is faithful and reliable. Praise and thank God for Jesus Christ--King of kings and Lord of lords!

Session 61: Concluding Activities for Unit 8

USING THIS REVIEW AND EVALUATING SESSION

The following questions may be used to evaluate student knowledge and comprehension of the material in this unit. You may also design questions of your own.

Part I--Short Answer Definitions

Directions: Write a brief sentence to define or explain each word, phrase, or name.

1. monarchy
2. Eli
3. Uriah
4. Jonathan
5. sling
6. Hannah
7. witch of Endor
8. concubine
9. Bathsheba
10. Samuel

Part II--Matching

Directions: Select from the answers in column 2 the name that best matches each phrase in column 1. Write the letter that corresponds to your answer in the blank before the phrase. (There are more names than phrases.)

1

1. shot arrows to warn his friend (G)
2. spared the Lord's anointed (A)
3. an idol whose worship involved child sacrifice (F)
4. asked for wisdom (B)
5. had two injured legs (J)
6. first king of Israel (C)
7. David's general (E)

2

A. David
B. Solomon
C. Saul
D. Uriah
E. Joab
F. Molech
G. Jonathan
H. Ish-Bosheth
I. Mephibosheth

Part III--Short Essays

Directions: Write several short sentences to answer each question.

1. State two reasons why God did not want Israel to have a king.

2. How did God prepare Saul for his position as king in Israel?

3. List several experiences that prepared David to be king and comment on how they were of value to him.

4. State one of the reasons for Saul's downfall and explain how it led to losing the Lord's favor.

5. How did Samuel feel when the Israelites demanded a king? Defend either Israel's or Samuel's position.

6. What were the consequences of David's sin with Bathsheba?

7. Compare and contrast the reigns of David and Solomon.

8. How did God use the monarchy

in Israel to establish a people for Himself?

9. Name two of God's promises to Abraham and tell how they were fulfilled during the period of the monarchy.

Feel free to duplicate the above questions for use in testing. Please add the following credit line: Concordia Publishing House, copyright 1986. Used by permission.

Unit 9: Worship in the Old Testament

Worship is an activity in which human beings ascribe worth to the object of their worship, that which is acknowledged as their God. The act of worship involves the intellect, the emotions, the senses, and the spirit. Worship can be deliberate or spontaneous.

The people of Israel worshiped God in a special manner that God Himself prescribed. God also specified for His people the setting for their worship. Both the setting and the rituals helped Israel remember and understand their relationship with God and His involvement in their lives. The Hebrew worship of God is the subject of this unit. Students will also have the opportunity to evaluate their own worship activities.

The sessions include a look at the worship activities in the tabernacle and Solomon's temple, the subject of giving, and the types of Christ and the prophecies that pointed to Christ.

PLANNING THE UNIT

Session 62: Find some illustrations of the tabernacle and its furnishings to show to the students.

Session 63: Alert students to the request that they identify a song, hymn, reading, or art object that has enhanced their worship.

Session 64: The subject is giving. Bible dictionaries may be helpful. Can you borrow some from the school library?

Session 65: Have a good concordance on hand in the classroom.

Session 66: The suggested culminating experience is to design a worship format for a school chapel service. You may have to get permission for the students to conduct a service.

UNIT ACTIVITIES

If you choose to have the class design a format for chapel worship as the culminating experience, it will be helpful to have them establish groups or pairs that will work together on some of the preliminary planning. This will allow you to use one class period to design the final worship format. The experience of designing and conducting a chapel service should help students appreciate what worship is all about. If you have more than one class, you may have to ask for a series of services or simply select one that will provide a meaningful experience.

Session 62: Worship in the Wilderness

BIBLE BASIS Ex. 25--27; 33:4--40:38

CENTRAL TRUTH

Though God is always with us, He meets us in worship for a special fellowship that glorifies Him and strengthens us.

OBJECTIVES

That the students will:

1. Remember the basic elements of the tabernacle and the ark of the covenant

2. Recognize the significance of the furnishings that God required for the tabernacle and ark of the covenant

3. Recall the significance of what God meant to teach the Israelites as they worshiped Him in the wilderness

BACKGROUND

The people of Israel experienced

many of the same challenges that confront us today. They were influenced by the nations around them, they faced uncertainty as they journeyed to a land promised to them by God, and they had to deal with their own rebellious nature. The Israelites were frightened, rebellious, stubborn, and confused.

The Lord God constantly reassured them by feeding them and by giving them victory in battle. Perhaps the greatest reassurance of His presence was in the place where He dwelt among them, His tabernacle.

The plans for the tabernacle were quite explicit and gave visible expression to the invisible presence of God, foreshadowing the sanctuary where Jesus Christ would serve as our High Priest in heaven **(Heb. 9:24)**.

As a place of worship the tabernacle allowed the Israelites to express their adoration for God and to offer sacrifices to atone for their sins. Until Christ came it was necessary to repeat the sacrifices year after year. The repetition of the sacrifices reminded the people of their sins **(Heb. 10:1-18)**.

The tabernacle consisted of two basic parts, the outer courtyard and the tabernacle proper. In the outer courtyard were the altar for burnt offerings and the bronze laver for ceremonial washings. The tabernacle proper was divided into the Holy Place and the Holy of Holies. Inside the Holy Place was the table of showbread, the lampstand, and the altar of incense. The Holy of Holies contained the ark of the covenant, perhaps the most interesting of all of the furnishings. The ark contained the two stone tablets on which were written the 10 Commandments, a pot of manna, and Aaron's rod. The cover of the ark was a gold-covered board called the mercy seat. The blood of the sacrifice was sprinkled on this cover to atone for the sins of the people. Two cherubim stood over the ark looking down at the mercy seat. It was in the Holy of Holies where God manifested His presence. Access to the Holy of Holies was limited to the High Priest who entered once a year only after being ceremonially purified.

The tabernacle and its furnishings were disassembled and carefully packed each time Israel moved to a new location in their quest for the Promised Land.

READING THE SCRIPTURES

This brief review of the tabernacle and worship practices is designed to give the students an understanding of their own worship and to help them experience greater joy in worship. The activities in this and following sessions will help to achieve that goal.

GOD'S TENT (Objective 1)

God made some very practical arrangements for His dwelling place amid the wandering nation of Israel. The tentlike structure was practical, yet had beauty and dignity. Your students have been asked to do some thinking about the tabernacle's purpose and furnishings. It would be helpful if you would draw on the chalkboard or posterboard an outline of the floor plan of the tabernacle and courtyard in preparation for a discussion of the questions in the Student Book.

Review the questions from the corresponding section in the Student Book with the intent of having the students remember the various furnishings and their purposes.

GOD'S GLORY (Objective 2)

The visible manifestation of God's presence in the temple is stated in **Ex. 40:34-38**. Today God manifests His presence in each believer through His indwelling Holy Spirit **(Col. 1:27)**. He also promises to be with us as we engage in corporate worship in His name **(Matt. 18:20)**.

The purpose of these activities is to help the students recognize the value of the tabernacle and its furnishings in communicating God's purpose and presence to His people as they worshiped Him. Review the questions from the Student Book in class. You will have to do additional research yourself to answer all of the questions that may arise.

Conclude by asking the students to suggest how God would build a temporary place of worship today and whether He could be expected to take up residence in such a place. You may wish to speak with a missionary or military chaplain who has led worship services in a remote place. Another option would be to describe worship experiences in a camp or wilderness setting. What are some of the special feelings that these unusual settings cause?

WHAT DOES IT ALL MEAN? (Objective 3)

Worship in Israel was very different from worship we experience today. The constant repetition of the sacrifices reminded them again and again of ways God had shown His love to them. But it also reminded them of their failure to obey God's laws. Perhaps they lived in fear of God. Yet David's psalms reveal an understanding of God as a loving Father as well as a mighty God **(Psalm 6; 8; 11; 14; 18; 23; and 38)**.

Review the questions for this section from the Student Book. In preparation for this section read **Heb. 10:1-18.** Ask the students to share their answers.

We have been looking at the tabernacle in an attempt to discover ways to bring greater meaning to our worship. Knowledge of God's presence and the assurance of opportunity to communicate with Him can provide meaningful experiences. Conclude by asking the students to describe God. Then have them list some of the things they would like to say to God in worship.

Session 63: Worship in Solomon's Temple

BIBLE BASIS: 1 Kings 5--8; 1 Chron. 22--26; 2 Chron. 3--7; Num. 18:1-32; Heb. 9:1--10:18

CENTRAL TRUTH

God gave Jesus Christ to us as a perfect sacrifice that satisfied Him for eternity **(Heb. 10:10)**.

OBJECTIVES

That the students will:

1. Demonstrate a general understanding of the extensive organizational structure required to staff the temple for all of the rituals required by the Law
2. Distinguish the difference between the single sacrifice of Jesus Christ, which completely satisfied God, and the repeated sacrifices of the Old Covenant performed in the tabernacle and temple
3. Express in writing a recognition of and appreciation for Jesus Christ, their personal Savior

BACKGROUND

This session continues a study that began in the previous session. Under **"WHAT DOES IT ALL MEAN?"** in Session 62 students were asked to give some thought to the repetition of sacrifices in the worship practices of Israel. The present lesson continues that investigation with a focus on the sacrifices and the staff of priests and helpers required to perform the rituals. By comparison the once-for-all sacrifice of Jesus Christ demonstrates the inadequacy of the Old Covenant.

In the wilderness God gave the descendants of Aaron the service of the priesthood **(Num. 18:7)**. The rest of the Levites were to assist the priests. Their reward was the Lord Himself as their inheritance rather than a portion of the land **(Num. 18:20)**.

By the time Israel had a permanent location for conducting their elaborate worship, which was prescribed by God, an elaborate arrangement for the service of the priests and Levites was also necessary. God allowed David to set up the necessary structure as recorded in **1 Chron. 23:13--26:32.** The temple staff was divided into five basic groups.

1. The priests **(1 Chron. 23:13 and 24:1-19)**
2. Assistants **(1 Chron. 23:25-32)**

3. Musicians **(1 Chron. 25:1-8)**

4. Gatekeepers **(1 Chron. 26:1-19)**

5. Treasurers **(1 Chron. 26:20-32)**

The priests were divided into 24 groups and each group would take turns ministering to the people. The assistants were also divided into groups to give each an opportunity for service.

The arrangement was very elaborate as were the priestly garments, the decorations, temple furnishings, and the various sacrifices required throughout the year.

The detail in the Scripture readings for this session can become confusing. The study is important because the students will discover that while the elaborate plans and activities were necessary, they were ultimately inadequate. The very fact that the same sacrifices had to be repeated year after year is evidence of their inadequacy in comparison with the perfect sacrifice of Jesus Christ **(Heb. 10:1-3)**. The sacrifices and observances of the Old Testament were a shadow of the things to come. They should have filled God's people with a longing for the Messiah. In fact, a cloud of witnesses did live by faith in God **(Heb. 11:1--12:3)**.

From our vantage point of knowing Jesus Christ as Savior and Lord, we may find it difficult to appreciate the significance of the worship of Israel. But we can thank God that His Son, Jesus Christ, also died for each of us.

READING THE SCRIPTURES

Prior to class, assign students the Scripture readings and Student Book pages. The students should complete assignments before class to enhance class participation. Arrange to have several Bible dictionaries available in the classroom.

STAFFING A TEMPLE (Objective 1)

Refer to **1 Chron. 23:13--26:32** and ask the students to identify the five basic groups who served in the temple. Then divide the class into five teams and ask each team to study the responsibilities for one of the temple groups and report their findings to the rest of the class. Bible dictionaries may be of help at this point. (The exercise should not take long because the questions were to be answered in the corresponding section of the Student Book. The Levites helped Aaron's descendants in the service of the temple of the Lord [**1 Chron. 23:28-31**]. The Priests were officials of the sanctuary [**1 Chron. 24:5**]. The Singers were responsible for the temple music [**1 Chron. 25:6**]. The Gatekeepers ministered in the temple by guarding the gates [**1 Chron. 26:12-18**]. The Treasurers were in charge of the temple treasuries and treasuries for the dedicated things [**1 Chron. 26:20**].) Ask, **Why was such a large staff necessary?** Answers may suggest that the elaborate system was needed to accommodate the large tribe of Levi. Students should realize that God placed a great deal of importance on the sacrifices and worship because through them the people would grow in their relationship with the Lord.

IMPERFECT SACRIFICES (Objective 2)

As you discuss the first two Student Book questions and elaborate staffing and arrangements, ask the students to read **1 Chron. 23:30-31. Why were there so many sacrifices year after year?** (The worship activities reminded the people of God's involvement in their lives, and the repeated sacrifices reminded them of the need for His continued involvement.) By emphasizing the inadequacy of the Old Testament sacrifices compared with the perfect sacrifice of Christ, the students should begin to understand what Paul meant in **Rom. 3:20** where he stated that **through the law we become conscious of sin.** The need to repeat the sacrifices should have been a clue to the people that they could never become righteous through the Law.

Ask the students to describe the feelings of guilt that may have prevailed among the people of Israel who realized that their sacrifices never satisfied God.

Discuss questions 3 and 4 in the Student Book. Then have someone read **Heb. 10:1-18.** Point out the significance of the once-for-all sacrifice of Jesus Christ.

DRAW NEAR TO GOD (Objective 3)

The splendor of Solomon's temple was only a shadow of the real place where God dwelt. The sacrifices were only a shadow of the perfect sacrifice of Jesus Christ. Today we have access to God through our intermediary, Jesus Christ. The Israelites had no direct access to God. The priest had to speak for them.

Ask the students to identify with the Israelites and imagine themselves as being under the requirements of the Law. Then ask them to imagine that they are hearing the good news about the sacrifice of Jesus Christ for the first time. Have them share some feelings that might result from hearing such news. Point out that they should realize that these feelings are legitimate today as well, because without Jesus Christ we would be lost.

Conclude by asking them to share answers from the question in the Student Book that asked them to identify something that has enhanced their worship experience.

Close the session using one or more of the prayers the students were to write for this session.

Session 64: God Moves His People to Give

BIBLE BASIS: Ex. 25:1-8; 2 Sam. 24:18-25; 1 Chron. 29:1-9

CENTRAL TRUTH

God demonstrated His incredible love for us by giving us Jesus Christ, His own Son. God allows us to experience the joy of giving as we give of our time, talents, and treasures to Him and to others.

OBJECTIVES

That the students will:

1. Recognize the differences between Old Testament tithes, offerings, sacrifices, and gifts
2. Grasp the difference between giving as a duty and giving as a Spirit-motivated response to God's love
3. Examine their own attitudes toward giving and set some personal giving goals
4. Follow the examples of the Macedonians in **2 Cor. 8:5** and, by faith, give themselves to God before offering their financial gifts.

BACKGROUND

Look back to **session 33** as you plan this lesson. Let things that happened then help you plan today's session.

One of the more critical problems in the church today relates to the offering of our time and treasures to the Lord. The problem today is the same as it was in Israel. Though God blesses us with material resources, we lack spiritual understanding. All too often we, in spiritual poverty, fail to enjoy the blessing of giving and do not put to proper use those things with which the Lord has blessed us.

We learn from Scripture that God in His incredible love for us has given us every good thing for our enjoyment. From the giving of Himself in a perfect relationship in a perfect world to the giving of His only Son, Jesus Christ, to redeem us, God has demonstrated His incredible love **(John 3:16).** God also demonstrates His love by giving us all that we need to live each day **(Matt. 6:25-32).**

The normal response from those who belong to God is that they also give, first to God and then also to each other. Giving is the ultimate expression of love **(1 John 3:16-18).**

Occasionally people have the mistaken opinion that the people of Israel gave only because of the requirements of the Law. The Law did require certain gifts and sacrifices, but giving did not end there. True spirituality was expressed by giving in a variety of ways. The converse was also true. Those who were not spiritual denied God that which was due Him and failed to help each other.

The following activities will help your students discover the blessings of giving and the pitfalls of greed.

READING THE SCRIPTURES

Prior to class, assign the Scripture reading and Student Book activities.

The giving of oneself to God is a response of faith, motivated by the Holy Spirit. It is never an act that merits God's grace; it's the result of His grace. Help the students identify (1) what gifts the people gave as recorded in these passages and (2) their reasons for giving them.

GIVE, GIVE, GIVE (Objective 1)

This activity will help the students differentiate between tithes, offerings, sacrifices, and gifts.

Review in class the answers the students have written in the corresponding section of the Student Book. Ask them to explain what is happening.

a. **Gen. 14:20**--Abraham gave a tenth of the spoils of war to Melchizedek, a priest of God. Tithing predates the Law and was a common offering to a deity among the heathen.

b. **Lev. 27:30-34**--God required the Israelites to tithe.

c. **Gen. 4:3-5**--Abel apparently brought a sincere and spontaneous sacrifice to God while Cain did not. There is no evidence that the sacrifices were required.

d. **Gen. 8:20**--Noah spontaneously made an offering in thanks to God.

e. **Ex. 23:15**--Sacrifices were required under the Law (see also **Lev. 4:1 ff.; 16; Num. 28:3-10**).

f. **Ex. 25:2** and **36:5**--Gifts were brought for a specific purpose such as the construction of the tabernacle **(Deut. 15:11)**.

The discussion of the answers to the questions should lead to the conclusion that the Israelites were very much aware of the responsibilities and privileges of giving. Their giving went beyond the sacrifices required for their sins. They had ample opportunity to demonstrate their love for God.

GIVING--MY DUTY OR PRIVILEGE? (Objective 2)

Sometimes we hear people complain, "The pastor is always preaching about money." Perhaps there really is a problem. Does the pastor understand the real motivation for giving? And does the listener understand or experience the joy of giving?

St. Paul quotes Jesus in **Acts 20:35: "It is more blessed to give than to receive."** John tells us that it is no longer necessary to make sacrifices since the blood of Jesus **"purifies us from all sin" (1 John 1:7)**.

We now live under God's grace **(Rom 5:1-2)** and are once again free to express our love for God and each other spontaneously by giving our treasures and talents.

Ask your students to share what they have learned from the Bible study in the corresponding section of the Student Book. The discussion should focus on all of the needs, opportunities, and reason for giving. Conclude by pointing out that people give for various reasons, sometimes for the wrong reasons. For the Christian, giving is a privilege that brings a blessing.

ATTITUDE CHECK (Objective 3)

Ask your students to answer these questions privately but honestly. (Have them write their responses on a sheet of paper only they will see.) Ask if any would be willing to share their answers with the class, but respect their decisions to keep their answers to themselves. Then discuss these questions:

1. **What thoughts come to your mind when you are asked to give a gift from your own baby-sitting or yardwork earnings for the Lord's work?**

2. **What is your personal giving record?**

3. **Does your giving reflect a healthy attitude according to what you have learned in God's Word?**

4. **What would you like to do differently?**

We often give to things to which

we have made a commitment. Teachers and students alike may evaluate their commitment to the ministry of their Lutheran high school on the basis of their gifts of time, talents, and treasures for its support.

I GIVE MYSELF TO GOD AND TO OTHERS (Objective 4)

Read **2 Cor. 8:1-15** to your students. This is a beautiful account of generous giving by the Macedonian Christians to the Christians in Jerusalem, who were in desperate need.

The striking points are in **verses 5, 2, 3, and 4.** The first step is a conscious commitment of oneself to God by faith.

Amazing things happen when we realize, by God's grace, that all we are and have is a gift from God and at His disposal. Then we can give freely to Him and to others in need.

Ask your students to think in their own hearts whether they consider themselves totally available to God.

Each student should have the opportunity to choose a special service project, make some contribution, and experience some of the joy of giving. Such a project will extend over a period of time. The project may involve preparing a food basket, visiting a home for the aging, befriending someone who is alone, or defending someone who is always being ridiculed. The important thing is to start giving to others with the only reward being the joyful experience that comes from giving.

By allowing the students to design individual projects, you will increase the number of joyful experiences that can be shared. This is an important part of the session.

Consider concluding the class by reading and meditating on the words of Luther:

O Lord God, Heavenly Father, I am Thy creature;
do Thou with me whatever Thou dost please;
it is all the same to me, for I know that I am surely Thine.
And if it please Thee that I die this hour or suffer some
great misfortune, I would still be very glad to suffer it.
Never do I want to consider my life, honor, goods, and
whatever I have as higher and greater than Thy will.
Thy will shall please me at all times throughout my life.

From What Luther Says, Vol. III, copyright (c) Concordia Publishing House, 1959.

Used by permission.

Session 65: Types and Prophecies of Christ in the Old Testament

BIBLE BASIS: Gen. 3:15; 22:1-12; Ex. 29:38-42; Lev. 16:6-22; Is. 52:14; 53:7

CENTRAL TRUTH

God reveals Himself to us in ways that help us grow closer to Him and understand His love for us.

OBJECTIVES

That the students will:

1. Identify Jesus Christ in selected sacrifices and prophecies of the Old Testament
2. Recognize the advantage they have in knowing the living Lord Jesus Christ rather than having to anticipate His coming
3. Praise God for His gift of Jesus Christ as the One whose death atoned for their sins, overcame the power of sin, and satisfied God

BACKGROUND

God is determined to enjoy a relationship with the creatures He created. But until Christ came into the world to live a perfect life, suffer and die in our place, and rise again in victory over sin, death, and Satan, there was nothing and no one who could permanently restore man to a relationship with God.

God promised at the fall **(Gen. 3:15)** that He would send One who would redeem humankind. Through the years that preceded the coming of Christ, God gave His people glimpses of what the Messiah would be like.

Those glimpses were found in

sacrifices and prophesies. We call them types of Christ. The types of Christ gave hope to God's people **(Luke 2:25-38)**. We have the privilege of seeing Christ Himself by faith, and have the assurance that the One about whom the Scriptures spoke is here.

This unit on Old Testament worship includes a brief study of some of the types of Christ. In addition, we will look at selected prophecies that complemented the messages of the sacrifices and brought them into sharper focus. Examples of each are listed below.

Types

The burnt offerings (Ex. 29:38-42; Lev. 22:17-20). The sacrificial burnt offering was to be a spotless, young lamb that would be completely consumed by the fire on the altar. The sacrifice represented the complete surrender of Jesus Christ, our spotless Lamb.

The scapegoat (Lev. 16:7-22). The scapegoat symbolically carried away the sins of Israel out of sight of their camp into the wilderness. Jesus carried our sins to the cross and by His death removed them from God's sight.

Isaac (Gen. 22:1-12). Isaac was a type of Christ in that he was the only son of the father of the nation, Abraham. Isaac did not complain when he was about to be sacrificed by his father. Jesus is the only Son of our heavenly Father, who made no complaint when He was sacrificed on our behalf.

Melchizedek (Gen. 14:17-24). Melchizedek was a priest forever **(Heb. 7)** and Jesus is our Priest forever after the order of Melchizedek.

Prophecies

A lamb brought to the slaughter (Is. 53:7). The silent surrender of Jesus Christ, the lamb of God was prophesied by Isaiah (see **Matt. 26:62-63**).

The suffering of the sacrifice (Is. 52:14). Through the prophet Isaiah, God presented some of the most graphic pictures of His suffering Son, including the disfiguring beatings He would suffer. At the hands of the Roman soldiers Jesus was beaten repeatedly **(Matt. 27:30; John 19:1-2)**.

READING THE SCRIPTURES.

Before class assign the Scripture readings and the Student Book exercise to help the students understand that a type is something that foreshadows another yet to come. While the examples are familiar, the ability to understand and appreciate them will vary among the students. Assure the students that God very carefully prepared the way for His Son to be recognized as the Messiah and that Jesus Christ, who fulfills the prophecies and is the perfect sacrifice, is their Savior.

"THE SCRIPTURES TESTIFY ABOUT ME" John 5:39 (Objective 1)

The corresponding section of the Student Book requires the students to read several passages related to Christ and His work. Discuss the readings to determine whether they recognize Jesus in the passages.

Ask the students to identify the thing being sacrificed in **Lev. 22:17-20; Gen. 22:1-12;** and **Lev. 16:6-22.** Then ask how Christ is portrayed in each. They have been asked to find New Testament references that describe Christ in similar terms. You will find a number of those references in the **BACKGROUND** section.

HINDSIGHT, FORESIGHT, AND INSIGHT (Objective 2)

The prophets predicted that Jesus would be rejected by the very ones whom He came to save **(Is. 53:3)**. We who know the whole story have a distinct advantage. We ought to be able to make sense out of the types, prophesies, and events of history and come to the conclusion that Jesus is the Christ. Very logical thinking, is it not? If human reason could be trusted we might reach such a conclusion. But it is the Holy Spirit of God who changes our hearts and gives us the necessary insights to help us recognize Christ in the sacrifices and prophecies.

Ask, **Was it more difficult for the Jews to recognize Jesus than it is for us to know Him?**

Review your class or faculty roster and select the name of a person who is relatively well known. Ask that person for permission to describe him/her to your students in positive terms. Then write a list of descriptive terms (positive ones) about the person. You may include place of birth, family background, attitudes, appearance, mannerisms, and others.

Next divide the class into two teams. Then reveal one characteristic at a time until one of the teams guesses the person. Try to start with the least revealing statements first to make the game last a while. Make your statements interesting such as, "gentle as a lamb," "strong as a bear," "a voice like an angel," and so on.

If you prepare well, your class should guess the person's identity in a reasonable amount of time. If you have more than one class, think of different persons for each and extras as well.

The point of the exercise: God has given us all we need to know about Jesus Christ. As we study Scripture, the Holy Spirit leads us to know God better and better. **Deut. 4:29** and **1 Tim. 2:3-6** show God's love for all people. **Is. 53:3** and **Rom. 1:18-23** describe how some rejected God.

Conclude the activity by reading the beautiful confession of St. Paul in **Rom. 1:16-17.**

WHY DID JESUS HAVE TO DIE?
(Objective 3)

To demonstrate God's free gift of His Son, Jesus Christ, mark the passage **John 3:16** in a Bible and place the Bible in a large box. Wrap the box cover and the box itself with Christmas gift paper so the cover can be easily removed. Place the gift in a prominent place in the room but do not make reference to it.

For the purpose of this activity, focus on two of the things accomplished by the death of Christ:

The blood of Jesus Christ satisfied God. The blood of the sacrificial animal was important, for it was to satisfy God and atone for the sins of Israel **(Lev. 16:1-34).** On the Day of Atonement the high priest would enter the Holy of Holies and sprinkle the blood of the sacrifice on the mercy seat. Our High Priest, Jesus Christ, entered the "greater and more perfect tabernacle," with His own blood **(Heb. 9:11-14)** and satisfied God forever as He atoned for our sins. (Cf. **Ex. 12:13**, the blood of the Passover lamb.)

The death of Christ conquered sin. According to **Rom. 6:4-6** Jesus Christ has also overcome the power of sin, and through our baptism we have been identified with Him and become new creatures. Think of it! Because of Jesus Christ we have a new life before us. By faith we can enjoy God's transforming power in our lives every day.

Jesus Christ is God's gift to us. Present your gift to the class. Have someone open the box and read the marked passage. Follow immediately with the reading of **John 1:12.**

Emphasize that we have not earned this perfect gift from God, but it is ours to receive by faith. Have the class explain this concept to you.

Ask someone to thank God for revealing Christ to us through the sacrifices and prophecies of the Old Testament using the prayer he/she wrote in response to the request in the Student Book.

Session 66: Concluding Activities for Unit 9

BIBLE BASIS: John 4:19-26; Acts 2:42-47

CENTRAL TRUTH

Our gracious God meets us in worship, accepts our praise, and assures us of His love and presence through Word and Sacrament.

OBJECTIVES

That the students will:

1. Design a brief worship format that will enable them to praise God and experience the joys of worship
2. Lead others in worship in a school chapel service

BACKGROUND

Through the death of Jesus Christ our relationship with the Father has been restored. Those who have by faith received Jesus Christ, having been baptized in the name of the Triune God, are once again God's sons and daughters (**John 1:12** and **Matt. 28:19**)

The normal response to God from His children is described in **Acts 2:42-47**. It is normal for us to gather in the name of Jesus Christ to praise God, to teach and learn, to pray, and to enjoy fellowship with each other.

This session is a culminating activity for the worship unit. In it the students will design a brief worship activity that may be used in one of the school's chapel services.

The worship activity should draw on what the students have learned about the Old Testament sacrifices, the perfect sacrifice of Jesus Christ, those who serve us in worship, and the joy of giving.

Depending on the amount of time you wish to spend on preparations for this activity, the format may be simple or complex. The value lies in telling God, Father, Son, and Holy Spirit, what we think of Him. Our worship should tell God what we think He is worth.

The worship format should also provide an opportunity to give something to God. You may have to work with your principal to find a project worthy of your students' gifts and include giving for that project as a part of the worship activity. It would be best if the students could give gifts for something from which they would not derive any benefit other than the joy of giving. Examples include support for a missionary, food parcels for the needy, and services for the elderly.

Unless you prefer to do something else as a culminating activity, base the grade for this unit on the worship format that is developed. (All students will receive the same grade. It will be to their advantage, then, to make the kinds of contributions to the project that will assure a good grade.)

The Student Book asks them to get together in small groups or pairs to plan the worship format. Do this outside of class, and use class time to bring the ideas together. A single worship format should be developed for use in chapel. If you have more than one class, you may wish to select the best format for corporate use or ask for several opportunites to lead chapel.

PLAN A MEANINGFUL WORSHIP SERVICE
(Objectives 1 and 2)

Assign the Student Book activity for this session well in advance.

Ask the students to suggest ways to do the following in worship:

a. Express love for God
b. Express love for each other
c. Show appreciation for what God has done for me
d. Share good news with others
e. Use my talents to praise God
f. Present my gifts to God

Ask the students to nominate worship leaders. Reserve the right to make final choices, but consider the value of the experience for those nominated.

Alert the faculty and student body to the special worship format that will be used and to the project for which support will be invited.

Afterward, involve the students of your class in evaluating the worship experience.

EVALUATE A WORSHIP SERVICE

You may wish to use a different activity to evaluate student progress. The following is suggested for your consideration.

Have your students review a worship service. Use the following outline:

1. Student's name; name of church; location; pastor; date; time

2. Outline the service activities
3. Central theme or focus of the service
4. Opportunities to praise God
5. Opportunities to share faith with others
6. Ways in which God's Word was presented (readings, sermon, etc.)
7. Sacraments, if any, that were celebrated
8. Something that made an impression on you
9. Something that was lacking
10. Your overall impression of the service

The report may also be used to supplement the grade given for the worship format designed by the group.

Unit 10: A People Divided

The focus of this unit is on the kingdom of Israel, also known as the Northern Kingdom. Several kings of Israel represent the condition of the whole monarchy in Israel. It's important that the students realize that God continued to love His people through all the changes they experienced.

Some of the prophets of this period are also introduced, although more prophetic activity will be studied in the next unit, which traces the history of the Southern Kingdom of Judah.

Subjects particularly emphasized during this unit are confession, repentance, forgiveness, prayer, and praise. The accounts of the reigns of the various kings have an underlying theme of rebellion, idolatry, and general wickedness. God's love is always refreshing and reassuring, so look for the things that show His love for His people.

PLANNING THE UNIT

Session 67 lays the groundwork for the rest of the unit with a focus on apostasy. Solomon's multiple marriages, his idolatry, and the civil strife after Solomon's death are studied.

In **Session 68** the New Testament **Book of Jude** is studied to help the students understand apostasy in relation to their own lives.

Session 69 is a study of the first king of the 10 tribes, Jeroboam.

Session 70 focuses on Ahab and Elisha, the king who thought Jeroboam's sins were trivial and the prophet whom God sent to keep the king in line.

In **Session** 71 your students will discover how God serves His servants as they see Him minister to a depressed Elijah.

Session 72 concludes the study of the Northern Kingdom. It looks at the events immediately preceding the captivity of Israel.

Session 73 provides an opportunity for review and evaluation before beginning your study of Judah.

Session 67: The Kingdom Torn Away

BIBLE BASIS: 1 Kings 11:9--12:33

CENTRAL TRUTH

God, our loving Father, protects His children from those who would destroy them.

OBJECTIVES

That the students will:

1. Recognize Solomon's idolatry as the primary reason for the division of Israel
2. Trace the origins of the division of the kingdom to Rehoboam's unreasonable attitude and Jeroboam's lust for power
3. Conclude that God designed the division of the kingdom to protect those who believed in Him

BACKGROUND

In Session 60 you read that Solomon was guilty of serious disobedience by marrying foreign wives **(1 Kings 11:4-6)**. Later Solomon gave in to horrible idolatrous practices, changing from a tolerant king to a worshiper of false gods **(v. 5)**. Solomon brought the Lord's punishment upon himself, and as He did with Saul, God took the kingdom away from him.

The study of the division of the kingdom covers two sessions and focuses on apostasy with references to Israel, other Old Testament events, and our own times.

God did wait until Solomon's death to take the kingdom from him, but as Solomon's integrity crumbled, so did the security of the nation. When the split occurred, the northern tribes (10 in all) were called Israel. The Southern Kingdom was called Judah after the single tribe of which it was comprised. (Judah had assimilated the small tribe of Benjamin.) Eventually Samaria became the capital of Israel while the capital of Judah remained at Jerusalem.

Israel's history was brief (lasting some 200 years) and marked by bloodshed and idolatry. Judah survived for about 325 years and experienced some brief revivals before being taken into captivity.

READING THE SCRIPTURES

Assign the Scripture readings and the related Student Book activities prior to class time.

In this session you'll lay the groundwork for a general discussion of apostasy as it is covered in **session 68**. **Sessions 67** and **68** cover both the historical and the comtemporary perspectives.

Sometimes we're tempted to help students understand the seriousness of apostasy by condemning those things in their world that are, from an adult perspective, capable of leading them into sin. **Sessions 67** and **68** will lead the students from the specific problems in Judah to a generalization about apostasy, then back to the specific by asking the students to make applications to their own lives.

AN OLD PROBLEM (Objective 1)

Review the list of Solomon's weaknesses **(1 Kings 11:1-10)** with your students to see if they understood what they read. Solomon's weaknesses were lust, disobedience, disregard for God's warning, bad companions, and apostasy.

Ask the students to share their definitions of apostasy--the sin of knowingly and deliberately rejecting God and His truth for idols and lies. It's the abandonment of the true faith for that which is false while pretending to be true to God.

A DRAMATIC SOLUTION (Objectives 2 and 3)

One might think that Solomon would have a stronger commitment to God since the Lord had spoken directly to him on two occasions **(1 Kings 3:5** and **9:2)**. It's frustrating to see disobedience continue when God so clearly shows His love and states His expectations of His people.

God continued in His resolve to accomplish His plan for salvation through His people. In order to do so, He had to deal with Israel's disobedience once again. His immediate response to Solomon was to raise up several enemies to spoil the peace won by David. God's next response was to take the kingdom from Solomon. Point out to the students that God would not tolerate anything that would destroy His people.

THE DIVISION BEGINS (Objectives 2 and 3)

The students have been asked to identify Rehoboam and Jeroboam, the two principle characters in the events that led to the actual division of the kingdom. Rehoboam's serious error in judgment coincided with God's plan to take the kingdom from him **(1 Kings 12:13-15)**.

Ask, **How do you feel about asking advice from your parents, your teachers, and other adults when you're faced with important decisions?** Discuss how Rehoboam's decision fit into God's plan for His people. **How do you think Rehoboam felt about such a decision after he had asked advice from the elders? Have you ever asked someone for advice, rejected that advice, and then later wished you had heeded it?**

The northern tribes were prepared

to rebel against Rehoboam. In response to his decision they shouted, "To your tents, O Israel!" The slogan was that of David's enemies too (**1 Kings 12:16; 2 Sam. 20:1**). It was a cry of rebellion and preparation for civil war. (What are some slogans you may have heard on the news used by rebels and revolutionaries in our country? in other countries? What do these slogans mean?)

Rehoboam's mistake led to the division of the kingdom, but Jeroboam made two mistakes that led to the loss of a dynasty as well as an inheritance with the Lord. Ask your students to describe Jeroboam's two rebellious acts. (He fortified cities against Judah and he tried to keep the two nations separate by introducing two golden calves, instituting worship away from the temple and from God (see **EX. 32:1-4**).

Since God had already promised the 10 tribes to Jeroboam, it was unnecessary for him to force the issue. His actions caused him a great loss.

Ask, **Why did Jeroboam rebel?** Jeroboam's behavior demonstrated self-interest and self-reliance and none of the understanding of God's will that had been evidenced by David.

The division of the kingdom was complete and the nation was on a course that would lead to its destruction.

Session 68: Blatant Apostasy

BIBLE BASIS: Jude 1-25

CENTRAL TRUTH

God, our loving Father, protects His children, especially from those who would harm them spiritually.

OBJECTIVES

That the students will:

1. Develop a working definition of the term apostasy as a result of studying Israel's history and the letter of **Jude**.
2. Select examples from their own world that could lead to apostasy
3. Praise God for His protection from those things that would destroy their faith in and their relationship with Him

BACKGROUND

A brief look at the New Testament **Book of Jude** will provide a study of apostasy in terms that the students will both understand and be able to apply to their lives.

Jude is believed to have been a brother of Jesus. His important message to the church pointed to false teachers who could destroy the faith. Jude refers to several Old Testament events to help his readers understand the problem. Jude's letter can help us as we face a host of temptations and misleading teachings, especially from the cults that are becoming popular today.

In the last session you described apostasy as the deliberate rejection of God (rebellion against Him) and of truth in preference for idols and lies. Idol worship in the Old Testament also included sexual immorality and other excesses. The examples from the Old Testament and the problems identified by Jude tell us that things just don't change.

Godless men eased their way into the early church. They misled people into sins of immorality, taught that Christ was not God, and generally disrupted the Christian church and its practices (**Jude 4, 12, and 16**).

While Jude had wanted to write a more positive letter, he felt compelled to address the problems that threatened to destroy the faith. His letter built on past experiences, things with which his readers were familiar. Because of their familiarity, Jude omits comment on them and assumes they are enough of a warning.

Jude's examples included references to rebellion, immorality, and criticism of the things of God, all of which were ploys of Satan.

Jude concludes by listing those things that help us and those things we can do to help each other. His conclusion is a source of encouragement.

The questions in the Student Book provide a means of analyzing the problems faced by Jude's readers and a basis for relating them to our own times.

READING THE SCRIPTURES

Assign the reading of **Jude** early enough to enable the students to do the research that is necessary to answer related questions in the Student Book. Be alert to a defensive attitude on the students' part when they are asked to evaluate their own life-styles in terms of things that can lead to apostasy. Do not create conflict. Rather, lead them to discover things that threaten their faith and then to their best source of help, their Friend Jesus.

You may be able to set your students at ease by referring to things in your own life that you have recognized as potentially dangerous to your faith. Help your students talk about their faith in Jesus Christ in terms of real life experiences.

I WANT TO REMIND YOU (Objective 1)

Reminders are good for us. We're forgetful, and repetition of important information helps us assimilate and remember. Jude's reminder comes when there is a threat to the Christian church.

Ask, **What threat is identified in Jude 4?** (Certain men had slipped into the fellowship who were godless, immoral, and denied the deity of Christ.)

To reinforce his evaluation, Jude refers to three situations from Israel's history. Ask, **How do these three references relate to your definition of apostasy?** (They are examples of rebellion, immorality, and idolatry: rebellion in the wilderness, immorality in Sodom and Gomorrah, and the idolatry of the angels who followed Satan. **Jude 5-7.**) Ask, **How did God deal with each of these sinful situations?**

The men Jude saw as infiltrators into the church had also earned God's wrath. Jude reinforced his remarks with three more examples in **verse 11.** Ask your students to state the examples and explain the significance of each.

a. The way of Cain **(Gen. 4:3-14)**--no respect for God as shown by his sacrifice, the murder of Abel, and his reaction to his punishment.

b. Balaam **(Num. 22--24** and **31:16)**--tried to make a profit by cursing God and leading Israel into idolatry.

c. Korah's rebellion **(Num. 16:1-35)**--against the authority of God vested in Moses and Aaron.

Again, God punished each for his wickedness.

Conclusion: God's attitude toward apostasy has never changed and His resolve to protect His people has never weakened.

Jude also points out that there are other behaviors that are marks of the apostate **(v. 16)** including grumbling, finding fault, having evil desires, and flattering others in the hope of gaining an advantage. Point out that these examples describe a life-style. The fact that a person may complain or have an occasional bad thought doesn't mean he or she is guilty of apostasy.

DID YOU KNOW THIS? (Objective 2)

Jude's reminder humbly implies that he is only reinforcing something his readers already know. Could he say the same to us? Sometimes students complain that they are forced to learn things they will never use. Introduce this part of the lesson by pointing out that Jude expected his readers to have a knowledge of the history of God's activities that would enable them to make application to their own lives.

Select from the things adults face today some things that could lead to apostasy. It might be the temptation to compromise a Christian principle for the sake of financial gain (e.g., accepting or selling stolen goods). Ask students to share examples they wrote in their books. Prepare a list of your own just in case they are reluctant to suggest some. One example might be the life-styles of some of the rock music stars to whom many young people devote themselves.

To learn more about rock music and cults, write to Commission on Organizations, The Lutheran Church--Missouri Synod, 1333 S. Kirkwood Rd., St. Louis, MO 63122-7295. You might also purchase books in the "How to Respond to . . ." series from Concordia Publishing House.

Ask the students to identify potential dangers in some of the things facing them.

ABOUT THE SALVATION WE SHARE
(Objective 3)

Apostasy leads to misery and emptiness. If that's true, why was it so popular in Israel **(Jude 12-13)?** The apostate usually deliberately rejects truth and, therefore, cannot make sound judgments **(Jude 10)**. But God does not leave us defenseless in the face of trouble. The salvation we share is sure. God is powerful.

Ask a student to read **Jude 24.** Then have a student list on the chalkboard all those things that Christ does for us (keeps us from falling, presents us before God without fault and with great joy).

Have another student read **Eph. 6:10-18.** Ask, **What is the armor that God gives us?**

Ask whether any of your students ever think of putting God's armor to use. His spiritual support is very powerful, but often we neglect to use it. **What are some practical ways we can use God's armor?** (Prayer, worship, fellowship, the Lord's Supper, and the study of His Word.)

Close with a prayer asking God to protect the faith of your students.

Session 69: Jeroboam--Setting a Course for Israel

BIBLE BASIS: 1 Kings 12:20--14:20

CENTRAL TRUTH

God is always faithful to His Word and His judgments are righteous.

OBJECTIVES

That the students will:

1. Select from the record of Jeroboam's rule those acts that caused him to lose his position as king
2. Recognize that Jeroboam brought God's judgment upon himself
3. Discover that even among the northern tribes God had His remnant of faithful people.

BACKGROUND

Jeroboam was an impatient man who apparently didn't trust God to do as He promised. His behavior was a sign of things to come in Israel. (The term Israel from now on refers to the nation comprised of the 10 northern tribes.) Frequently a new king took the throne in Israel after murdering the king before him. Apostasy continued to be characteristic of the northern kings.

The division of the kingdom took place in 931 B.C. and Jeroboam, a talented leader **(1 Kings 11:28)**, became king of Israel. To prevent the people of the northern tribes from going to Jerusalem to worship, Jeroboam made two golden calves and had them set up in Bethel and Dan. He also established a festival and appointed his own priests.

God wouldn't tolerate such rebellion and sent an unnamed prophet to warn Jeroboam that He would bring judgment against Jeroboam's idolatry. Jeroboam's attempted retaliation toward the prophet was thwarted by God. The prophet declined Jeroboam's offer of hospitality and headed back toward Judah. Unfortunately, the courageous prophet was tricked by a false prophet from Israel and died because of his disobedience.

The experience meant nothing to Jeroboam, who continued rebelling against God. Jeroboam seemed to be determined to do evil. The false prophet's deception is a clue that false prophets were accepted in Israel.

Jeroboam's rebellious behavior set the course for the future kings of Israel.

READING THE SCRIPTURES

Assign the Scripture readings and the Student Book activities for

session 69 in advance of this class session.

The next several sessions provide a look at those things that characterized Israel. The questions in the Student Book help the students review the Scripture account and serve as topics for class discussion.

REBELLION (Objective 1)

The brief account of Jeroboam's reign highlights the acts of rebellion of which he was guilty and God's reaction to them.

1. **What were Jeroboam's rebellious acts?** Ask the students to share those they found and discuss each one.

a. **1 Kings 12:25**--he fortified Shechem against Judah encouraging civil war

b. **12:28**--he established idolatry

c. **12:31**--he appointed non-Levite priests

d. **12:32-33**--he instituted a new religious festival

e. **13:4**--he tried to harm a prophet of God

f. **v. 33**--he ignored God's warning

2. God gave Jeroboam at least two warnings through His prophets. (The history of Israel contained more warnings which Jeroboam also ignored.) Discuss the following with your students:

a. **1 Kings 13:1-10**--A prophet predicted that Josiah, king of Judah, would destroy altars to Jeroboam's idols and burn the bones of the priests who sacrificed on the altars. **2 Kings 23:15-20** records the fulfillment of the prophecy nearly 300 years later.

b. **1 Kings 14:1-16**--Jeroboam's son became ill and died. The prophet Ahijah warned Jeroboam (Jeroboam had sent his wife to see the prophet) that this was the only son who would receive a decent burial because God would take the kingdom from Jeroboam and lead the nation into captivity.

Conclusion: God gives ample warning even to those who are very rebellious. Such patience is another example of God's incredible love for His people.

RETRIBUTION (Objective 2)

God is consistent. He didn't punish idolatry on one occasion only to overlook it on another. He always dealt with it like the cancer it was to His people. Eventually Jeroboam had to pay for his rebellion and idolatry. God's warning remains clear today **(Heb. 10:26-31)**.

1. Have the students describe Jeroboam's attitude based on **1 Kings 13:33**. (He was determined to do as he pleased, and he was pleased to rebel against God.)

2. The price for Jeroboam's rebellion (and Israel's) was steep. **What were the costs of Jeroboam's sin (1 Kings 14:12-16)?**

a. **14:12**--Jeroboam's son would die, he would have no heir to the throne (fulfilled in **1 Kings 15:28-30**)

b. **14:15**--the Lord would strike Israel; they would lose their land and be scattered in captivity (In fact, they never returned from captivity to be a nation.)

3. Do your students know and understand the cause of God's anger? God made it plain in **1 Kings 14:15b**. (He hated their idolatry.)

4. Discuss the students' answers to how they would have reacted to God's warnings had they been Jeroboam.

5. Ask the students to share the prayers they wrote. Look for an emphasis on confessing the sin of rejecting God, repenting, and asking God for forgiveness.

REMNANT (Objective 3)

The picture is bleak! In fact, the repetition of the foolish behavior of God's people can make study of this Old Testament period discouraging! It appears that no one in Israel cared about God anymore.

But all is not lost. Remember that God loves His people. A faithful few know that, and they haven't given up.

1. Read **2 Chron. 11:13-17** to your students. (Remember that there are some of the same accounts and sometimes additional information in

Chronicles.) Ask, **What do these verses tell you about the people?** (A remnant of priests and Levites **set their hearts on seeking the Lord** and came to Judah to worship the true God; they were faithful, persistent, sincere.)

2. Ask the students to describe the remnant and tell why it was important. (Without a remnant, God would have no people through whom He could accomplish His plan.)

3. Finally ask, **After all your studies on rebellion among the descendants of Abraham, has it occured to you that we may have rebelled against God in some ways?** Be prepared to share experiences and discoveries from your own life.

Close by reassuring your students that because of Jesus Christ, God forgives them and accepts and keeps them as His own dear children.

Session 70: Ahab and Elijah

BIBLE BASIS: 1 Kings 16:29--22:40

CENTRAL TRUTH

God restrains evil and provides spiritual leaders for His people.

OBJECTIVES

That the students will:

1. Recognize that the morality of Israel reached a new low under the rule of Ahab
2. Identify the prophet Elijah as a person God used to restrain evil forces in Israel
3. Praise God for those who courageously preach and teach His Word

BACKGROUND

Time doesn't permit studying each king of Israel and Judah. Ahab has been selected because of the evil he perpetrated in Israel and also because of the remarkable man God introduced to confront Ahab--the prophet Elijah.

1 Kings 16:30 describes Ahab as one who did more evil than any king before him. The same was said of Ahab's father, Omri (**1 Kings 16:25**). The other kings of Israel had **[walked] in the ways of Jeroboam** (**v. 19**), but Ahab was so evil that he made Jeroboam's sins look trivial (**v. 31**).

Ahab selected Jezebel, daughter of the Sidonian king Ethbaal, to be his wife. Ahab openly defied God by building a temple to Baal in Samaria, Israel's capital. God was angered by his behavior (**v. 33**).

The Lord God still had faithful people in key places. One was Obadiah, a devout leader who was in charge of Ahab's palace. Obadiah had rescued 100 of the Lord's prophets when Jezebel was on a prophet-killing rampage (**1 Kings 18:4**). God used both Obadiah and Elijah for important purposes. Obadiah worked quietly for the Lord. Elijah was a public figure and became a thorn in Ahab's flesh.

This session intentionally overlooks Elijah's activity in Israel recorded in **1 Kings 18--19** because that section of Scripture is covered in **session 71**.

Three incidents from Ahab's life have been selected for study at this time.

1. Ahab's battle against Ben-Hadad (**1 Kings 20**)
2. Ahab's acquisition of Naboth's vineyard (**chapter 21**)
3. Ahab's last battle and death (**chapter 22**)

In spite of his wickedness, Ahab received some favors from God. One occurred when God assured him of a victory over Ben-Hadad, King of Syria. Apparently God wanted Ahab to kill Ben-Hadad. When Ahab made a treaty with Ben-Hadad instead of killing him, God sent a prophet to tell Ahab that he would die for his disobedience (**1 Kings 20:42**). Ahab became sullen and angry.

Sometime later Ahab became obsessed with the desire to have a vineyard that belonged to a man named Naboth. When Naboth declined Ahab's offer to buy, Ahab began to pout. The evil Jezebel conspired to have Naboth killed in a way that resembled the circumstances around the death of Christ (false witnesses). The irony of the situation is that Naboth was accused of blaspheming God and the king while the king and much of the nation were engaged in open idolatry. Obviously the elders and nobles were as wicked as Jezebel or were too frightened of her to refuse to commit murder. The incident was typical of the cruel and ruthless behavior of which Jezebel was capable. She also urged her husband into evil **(1 Kings 21:25)**.

Elijah brought God's message of judgment against Ahab and Jezebel. Ahab would share the fate of Jeroboam **(v. 22)**, and Jezebel would be eaten by dogs **(v. 23)**, a prophecy which was fulfilled in **2 Kings 9:30-37**.

Ahab did a surprising about-face and humbled himself before the Lord. His punishment was delayed (an example of God's amazing mercy and incredible love).

Ahab's last battle is described in **1 Kings 22:29-38**. After disregarding the word of the Lord brought by the prophet Micaiah, Ahab entered the battle dressed like a common soldier. A random shot from an enemy archer struck Ahab, causing a fatal wound **(1 Kings 22:34-38)**.

READING THE SCRIPTURES

Assign the Bible reading and Student Book questions in advance. Use information from the **"BACKGROUND"** to help you lead a discussion of the material.

FROM BAD TO WORSE (Objective 1)

1. The Scripture verses in the guide show aspects of Ahab's behavior and attitudes.

a. **1 Kings 16:31**--Ahab considered Jeroboam's sin trivial, married Jezebel, and began to serve and worship Baal.

b. **v. 32**--He built an altar and a temple to Baal.

c. **v. 33**--He erected a monument to Ashera.

d. **v. 34**--He rebuilt Jericho which Joshua had cursed--**Joshua 6:26**.

2. Ask the students to share the evils described in:

a. **1 Kings 20:42-43**--Ahab failed to kill Ben-Hadad.

b. **21:4** and **16**--He coveted Naboth's vineyard and approved his murder.

3. Ask volunteers to read their character descriptions of Ahab.

GOD'S ENVOYS FOR ISRAEL (Objective 2)

God always has His remnant of believers and gives them various assignments. Both Elijah and Obadiah were prominent during Ahab's reign but served God in different ways.

1. **Who were the two men of God mentioned in 1 Kings 18:1-5?** (Obadiah and Elijah)

2. a. Elijah appears to be the more prominent of the two servants of God. He risked his life when he confronted Ahab on Mt. Carmel.

b. Obadiah, the other servant, rescued and cared for 100 prophets. According to **1 Kings 18:9-14**, Obadiah served God with some fear of discovery. You might point out to the students that heroes have fears just like everyone else.

3. Discuss this question and ask your students where Elijah got his courage. They should realize that it came from the Lord, a fact that will be even more apparent in the next session.

GOD'S ENVOYS FOR US

Those who serve as God's representatives are God's gifts to us **(Eph. 4:11-13.)**

1. Ask, **Have you ever thought of your parents, teachers, pastors, or Christian friends as gifts from God?** Remind them that God's envoys often challenge us and say things we don't want to hear. When people speak God's truth to us they are a blessing from God. **Who has been a blessing to you from God?**

2. Ask, **Why is it important for us to have Christian friends, caring parents, pastors, and teachers?** Sometimes when we're trying to become independent, we overlook the wise counsel of God's envoys. Fortunately most of us mature in time to benefit from much of what God has to say. In the meantime, though, we can miss a lot of what God has to offer through people He uses as His envoys. Close this session by having numerous students pray the prayers they wrote about God's

envoys in their lives. Give as many students as possible the opportunity to share their prayers. Sometimes having a time for spontaneous prayers gives an extra opportunity for those who want to pray extemporaneously. You might suggest that the students form a circle and hold hands while they pray. (If your students aren't accustomed to this way of praying, it might take some encouragement and preparation.) An experience like this might be very meaningful but shouldn't be forced on them. You may wish to suggest to the students that they encourage a close feeling with God and with their family members by using the circle prayer idea at home.

Session 71: Elijah--God's Servant

BIBLE BASIS: 1 Kings 18:16--19:21

CENTRAL TRUTH

God ministers to those who serve Him to refresh, assure, and empower them.

OBJECTIVES

That the students will:

1. Recognize that God used Elijah, an ordinary person, in an extraordinary way
2. List the ways in which God ministered to Elijah
3. Conclude that God will also care for them in all their needs

BACKGROUND

God enabled Elijah to do extraordinary things even though he was subject to some of the same weaknesses each of us experiences. By reading Elijah's encounter with the prophets of Baal and the subsequent events, we discover what Elijah was like and what God did for and through him.

God sent Elijah to confront Ahab about his worship of Baal. Elijah proposed and won a dramatic contest with the prophets of Baal (**1 Kings 18:16-42**).

After the contest, the priests of Baal were slaughtered and Elijah told Ahab that the drought which had plagued Israel was over.

Rather than fearing the Lord at the news of the defeat of the prophets of Baal, Jezebel vowed to kill Elijah. The man who had just witnessed a dramatic display of the Lord's power now fell apart at the threat of the wicked Jezebel and ran away into the wilderness (**1 Kings 19:1-4**).

The man of God now suffered from fatigue, hunger, loneliness, and perhaps arrogance. Elijah wanted to die.

But God met each of his needs. First Elijah slept and then God gave him water and food (**1 Kings 19:5-9**). After Elijah had regained his strength, God discussed his problems with him.

Elijah believed he was the only faithful person in Israel (perhaps he meant the only faithful person with the courage to act). God gently showed Elijah that He was present in a whisper (**1 Kings 19:12**) and then assured him that he was not alone. God had a remnant of 7,000 people in Israel who had the courage to refuse to worship Baal. Finally God gave Elisha to be a friend to Elijah (**1 Kings 19:21**).

God always sees to our needs. We despair when we are hungry, tired, frightened, and alone. (The late Vince Lombardi is credited with the statement, Fatigue makes cowards of us all. If that is true, we can understand why Elijah behaved the way he did.) But God is always there to minister to our needs. God invites us to look to Him for refreshment (**Is. 40:31**).

READING THE SCRIPTURES

This session can be very meaningful for your students. It addresses some very common problems. Many teenagers experience loneliness and depression. They have practical problems--poor eating habits, busy schedules, and lack of sleep. The lack of spiritual food and failure to rest in the Lord are even more serious problems.

Assign the Scripture reading and the correlating Student Book activities prior to class.

Lead your students through the story of the contest between Elijah and the prophets of Baal. Point out the tension in the situation, the long hours Elijah spent, the emotional and physical drain resulting from the contest and the slaughter of the 450 prophets of Baal, and finally the grueling run in front of Ahab's chariot. Throughout this session, help the students apply to their own lives the meanings of the ministrations and assurances God gave to Elijah.

ORDINARY MAN--EXTRAORDINARY GOD (Objective 1)

As we learn in our study of the judges, God sends some very ordinary people to do some tough jobs, but He always endows them with His extraordinary power.

God sent Elijah to Ahab to arrange a contest with the prophets of Baal. The purpose was to show a wavering people that the Lord God was the One they should follow **(1 Kings 18:21)**.

Discuss the students' answers in their Student Books.

Ask your students to outline the general rules of the contest: The 450 prophets of Baal would prepare a sacrifice for their god. Elijah would prepare a sacrifice for the Lord. The one who consumed the sacrifice with fire would be acknowledged as the true God.

Point out that Elijah gave the prophets of Baal plenty of advantages: They could go first, they took all day, he gave them helpful suggestions (actually he taunted them), and he soaked the Lord's sacrifice with copious amounts of water.

The Lord God burned Elijah's sacrifice while Baal remained silent.

Ask your students if they are convinced by God's demonstration. (Be prepared to respond to those who think the account is only a story without historic accuracy.)

After the contest, the prophets of Baal were killed. **Deut. 13:1-11** gives the reason for the harsh penalty--the souls of the people were at stake. Have the students share the comments they wrote in their Student Books about the danger of the idolatrous priests. As the rains came, God filled Elijah with the strength and endurance to run before Ahab's chariot as Ahab returned to Jezreel. (Elijah assumed the humble role of a servant who ran before his master's chariot.)

GOD SERVES HIS SERVANT (Objective 2)

After the contest, Elijah became frightened by Jezebel's threat **(1 Kings 19:2)** and fled to the wilderness only to become so depressed that he wanted to die. It is no wonder! He was frightened, fatigued, hungry, and lonely. He may have even felt like a martyr.

Ask your students to identify the needs that Elijah had.

God responded in very practical ways by allowing him to rest, by giving him food, by reassuring Elijah of His presence, and by providing him with a friend.

Point out that these are basic needs each of us has. Hunger and fatigue can cause us to be discouraged. Loneliness is a problem from which many of us suffer even when we are surrounded by friends. Have the students read **Eccl. 4:9-12** and list the values of companionship. God provided a companion for Elijah so he could share his experiences with another.

Draw your students' attention to the fact that God met each of Elijah's needs. God also knows the needs that each of us has and is capable of satisfying them.

HOPE IN THE LORD (Objective 3)

The Scriptures contain some beautiful promises for those who believe in the Lord.

Review each of the following passages, assuring your students that the promises are for each of them.

Matt. 20:25-28--Jesus came to serve us.

2 Cor. 1:3-5--God comforts us in every need and makes us a comfort to others.

1 Peter 5:7--Jesus cares for us and wants to carry our anxieties (burdens).

Is. 40:27-31--God knows our needs and strengthens us.

Discuss questions 1--3 and the students' answers from the Student Book.

Be alert to anyone who hints at having significant anxieties and unresolved problems. Further counseling may be necessary.

Close your session with one of the prayers written by the students.

Session 72: Israel Taken Captive

BIBLE BASIS: 2 Kings 17

CENTRAL TRUTH

God is very patient with His people, communicates very clearly what He expects of them, allows them ample opportunity to repent, remains patient with those who do not repent, but finally brings judgment on those who insist on continuing in sin.

OBJECTIVES

That the students will:

1. Make the transition from the time of Ahab to the time of Hoshea and the fall of Samaria, recognizing what precipitated the fall
2. Recognize the totality of the destruction of the nation resulting from the captivity and resettlement
3. Show appreciation for God's patient love and respect for His righteousness through a personal confession and prayer

BACKGROUND

2 Kings 17 provides a good summary of the history of the Northern kings and the reasons for the fall of the nation. Hoshea was not any more evil than his predecessors, but he made some mistakes that led to the invasion of Samaria by the Assyrian king Shalmaneser.

Hoshea became king in 731 B.C. and inherited an obligation to pay tribute to the Assyrian king. Counting on what proved to be an empty promise of help from Egypt, Hoshea refused to pay the tribute. Shalmaneser threw Hoshea in prison and attacked Samaria (not just the city, but also the surrounding region).

Shalmaneser took Israelites captive and relocated them outside of Israel. Foreigners were brought in to resettle Samaria. Israel ceased to exist as a nation.

The new inhabitants were heathen and God would not tolerate their worship of idols **(2 Kings 17:25)**. In response to a request for the people for help, the king of Assyria sent a priest from captivity to teach the new inhabitants of Samaria how to worship the Lord.

Their worship was not limited to the Lord God, since they also persisted in their worship of idols. But at least those Israelites who remained had an opportunity to worship their God.

Viewed only from the perspective of the captivity, this is a depressing account. But God's plan was not thwarted, for when His time was right, He did bring deliverance for <u>all</u> of his people in Jesus Christ **(John 4:1-42)**.

We are privileged to have the whole history of God's plan in view. Pray to God that we may, by His grace, remain faithful to Him and live with Him for eternity.

READING THE SCRIPTURES

Assign the readings and corresponding pages from the Student Book well in advance, for the students' work outside of class is essential to the discussions that are part of the following activities.

Explain to the students that they will deliberately ignore accounts of the kings of Israel because of similarity. Since this is not a strict study of the history of Israel, you will sample those events that demonstrate God's love and purpose for His people throughout Old Testament history.

THE END OF THE LINE (Objective 1)

Ask someone to describe the sinking feeling that comes when a person makes a mistake that causes a team to lose a game. Then ask, **Do you think Hoshea experienced such feelings when he realized that Shalmaneser called his bluff (2 Kings 17:4)?**

Now go back and find out how Hoshea became king **(2 Kings 15:30)**. (He revolted against Pekah and assassinated him, proving that he was accustomed to taking a chance.)

Point out that parts of Israel were already in captivity **(2 Kings 15:29)** when Hoshea became king. Therefore Hoshea, counting on a promise of help from Egypt, may have felt that he was not risking much.

Hoshea's gamble was costly from both a personal and a national standpoint. Determine whether your students understand this by asking

a. what it cost Hoshea personally **(2 Kings 17:4b)**

b. what it cost Israel **(17:5-6)**

NO WAY BACK (Objective 2)

It wasn't unusual for a conquering nation to select the best and brightest from a defeated nation and move them to another location (see the **Book of Daniel**). Relocating the people of a conquered nation served the interests of the conquerers in several ways:

a. They acquired slaves.

b. They used the special skills of their captives.

c. They deprived the conquered nation of leadership.

During the war in Vietnam, whole villages were relocated to get the people out of war zones and win their cooperation. Thus an old idea continues to have value.

1. Ask your students to describe what the Assyrians did to the people of Samaria **(2 Kings 17:5-6)** and what advantages they gained. (Point out that in this case the name <u>Samaria</u> refers to more than just the city. It refers to the nation.)

2. The vacuum created by deporting people of Samaria was filled by importing people from other areas. Ask the students to describe the problems that resulted from bringing in foreigners **(17:25-26)**. (God sent lions to kill some of the idolatrous people.)

The report given to the king of Assyria is rather interesting. Those who did not know God often believed that gods had jurisdiction over a particular area.

Explain to your students that the people who were resettled in the area were willing to include the God of Israel in their worship if it would bring them peace.

3. Ask the students to share their speculations on why God sent lions to bother the idolaters.

4. Reinforce the previously formed definition of apostasy by referring to **2 Kings 17:41.** Apostasy was still a problem at this time.

5--6. **2 Kings 17:23** concludes a summary of the whole problem in Israel and tells the tragedy of the situation in a short statement. Those who were carried off did not return. Those who remained intermarried with the heathen imports. The result was a mixed breed of Samaritans. No wonder conflicts arose between the Jews and Samaritans at the time of Christ! Review the passage with the students.

7. Ask the students to share some of the examples of God's love they found in this session.

CONSISTENCY (Objective 3)

The apostle Paul assures us that God is consistent **(2 Cor. 1:18-21)**. He never wavers from His promises but fulfills them in Jesus Christ, God's greatest <u>YES</u> to the world.

When God promised to punish idolatry, He was faithful and kept that promise. Human beings cannot be counted on to be that consistent.

Read Paul's statement **(2 Cor. 1:18-21)** to your students and ask them to tell you what they think it means.

What happened in Israel was tragic. It did not have to be that way. God longed to love His people, but He could not tolerate their idolatry because of its eternally destructive consequences.

It would be even more tragic if we did not learn from Israel's mistakes. Your students should have looked at a number of God's promises. Review the following passages with them. Emphasize that the Lord is faithful and can be trusted.

1. Jesus Christ, the visible expression of the invisible God **(Col. 1:15)** is consistent **(Heb. 13:8)**.

2. God is always with us **(Heb. 13:5b)**.

3. God always loves us **(Ps.**

118:1).

4. God always helps us (**Ps. 118:6-7**).

In many of the sessions the students have been asked to write prayers. **Heb. 13:15** tells us why. Prayer is an essential part of our relationship with God.

Through Jesus, therefore, let us continually offer to God a sacrifice of praise--the fruit of lips that confess His name. Heb. 13:15

Close this session by praising God.

Session 73: Concluding Activities for Unit 10

The following test is a suggested instrument for evaluating student progress in this unit.

Part 1. Multiple Choice

Directions: Read each question carefully. Select from the possible answers following a question the one answer that is most correct. Write the letter that corresponds to your answer in the blank before the statement or question.

(d) 1. This man once served Solomon. a. Rehoboam b. Ahab c. Shalmaneser d. Jeroboam
(c) 2. The statement "To your tents, O Israel!" was a cry of: a. poverty b. unity c. rebellion d. despair
(a) 3. Jezebel came from: a. Sidon b. Moab c. Egypt d. Ethbaal
(c) 4. The real cause for the division of the kingdom was: a. Solomon's marriages b. golden calves c. apostasy d. heavy taxes
(b) 5. The place Jeroboam went to escape death: a. Sidon b. Egypt c. Assyria d. Bethel
(a) 6. The larger kingdom after the division was: a. Israel b. Judah
(d) 7. Elijah engaged in a contest with the prophets who served this god: a. Molech b. Anammelech c. Nibhaz d. Baal
(c) 8. This was the capital city of Israel: a. Bethel b. Jerusalem c. Samaria d. Dan
(b) 9. This was the capital city of Judah: a. Bethel b. Jerusalem c. Samaria d. Dan
(c) 10. This man built two golden calves: a. Aaron b. Rehoboam c. Jeroboam d. Ahab
(b) 11. God promised to make this man a great king if only he would obey God as did David: a. Rehoboam b. Jeroboam c. Ahab d. Hoshea
(d) 12. Samaria was attacked by: a. Ahab b. Ethbaal c. Hoshea d. Shalmaneser
(a) 13. Which king humbled himself before the Lord? a. Ahab b. Jeroboam c. Rehoboam d. Shalmaneser
(b) 14. Why did Naboth refuse to sell his vineyard? a. it was not his b. God's law forbade the sale of family property c. Naboth did not like Jezebel d. Naboth had promised the land to his sons
(c) 15. Rehoboam followed the counsel of: a. the elders b. God c. his friends d. Elijah
(a) 16. The man who rescued and fed 100 prophets of God was: a. Obadiah b. Elijah c. Elisha d. Ahijah
(a) 17. What did the 450 prophets do to try to convince their god to burn his sacrifice? a. cut themselves b. threatened to kill Elijah c. offered a child sacrifice d. prayed silently
(b) 18. Why did Elijah kill the 450 prophets? a. he was jealous of them b. God's law required it c. Ahab ordered him to do so d. the people demanded their death
(b) 19. Which was not a reason for Elijah's depression? a. he feared Jezebel b. he was the only faithful person in Israel c. he was fatigued d. he had been through some demanding circumstances
(d) 20. Who was the last king of Israel? a. Ahab b. Jeroboam c. Shalmaneser d. Hoshea

Part 2. Short Essay

Directions: Write brief answers for any six of the following questions. Identify which questions you are answering.

1. **What were the main causes for the division of the kingdom?** (Solomon's apostasy, Rehoboam's unreasonable attitude, Israel's rebellion.)

2. **Jeroboam apparently did not believe God would give him the kingdom of Israel. What did Jeroboam do to secure his position?** (Fortified towns, established worship away from Jerusalem, appointed his own priests, built golden calves.)

3. **What evidence is there that there was a remnant of believers in Israel?** (Priests went to Jerusalem to worship, God told Elijah that there were 7,000 faithful, some believers remained in Samaria after the captivity.)

4. **Describe how God ministered to Elijah after the contest with the 450 prophets.** (Allowed him to rest, fed him, revealed Himself in a whisper, gave him a companion.)

5. **How did Hoshea gain the throne in Israel?** (Conspired against and murdered his predecessor.)

6. **Why did the Assyrian king think Hoshea was a traitor?** (Hoshea stopped paying tribute and attempted to make an alliance with Egypt.)

7. **What warning did Elijah deliver to Jezebel after she had Naboth murdered?** (Dogs would devour her by the wall of Jezreel.)

8. **How did God prevent Israel from ever becoming a significant nation again?** (The Assyrians carried off a number of the people and repopulated Samaria with heathen people with whom the remaining Israelites intermarried.)

9. **The names Israel and Samaria can have more than one meaning and are sometimes used interchangeably. Explain their meanings and uses.** (Israel was a name for Jacob and his descendants. It was also the name of the United Kingdom. When the kingdoms split, the 10 northern tribes were called Israel. Samaria was the capital of the Northern Kingdom and the name eventually referred to the whole area of the Northern Kingdom.)

10. **Describe religious life in Samaria after the fall of the Northern Kingdom.** (Heathen people repopulated the area and brought their idols with them. Those Israelites who remained may have included some faithful to God. God caused the king of Assyria to send a priest back from captivity to assist with worship of God. Idolatry was rampant.)

Unit 11: The Kings and Prophets of Judah

This unit focuses on the kingdom of Judah, also known as the Southern Kingdom. Several kings of Judah have been selected for study. Their lives and experiences should provide a suitable review of the conditions in Judah from the time of Rehoboam until the Captivity.

This unit is a continuation of the previous one. The two units provide a cohesive view of the divided kingdom without frequent switches between the two.

Session 74: The Southern Kingdom--Asa

BIBLE BASIS: 1 Kings 15:9-24; 2 Chron. 14--16

CENTRAL TRUTH

"The Lord Almighty is with us; the God of Jacob is our fortress." Ps. 46:11

OBJECTIVES

That the students will:

1. Become familiar with the main characteristics of the reign of Asa.
2. Identify the blessings of the Lord as the reasons for Asa's success.
3. Compare the intensity of their own commitment to Jesus Christ with the commitment to God confessed by the people of Judah in **2 Chron. 15:12.**

BACKGROUND

After our brief look at several of the kings who led Israel to ruin, we now focus our attention on Judah. Although the history of Judah also ends with captivity, there are some bright moments along the way.

Asa, a descendant of David, was the third king of Judah. Under his leadership, some decisive action was taken to return Judah to the worship and obedience of the Lord God. The account of his reign in **1 Kings 15:9-24** is very brief, but **2 Chron. 14--16** provides essential supplemental information.

Initially Asa's behavior was pleasing to God. Besides making efforts to remove the altars of the false gods physically, he also gained the cooperation of the people. Asa's reforms appealed to large numbers of people from Isráel who relocated in Judah. The people were so enthusiastic about the covenant they made to seek the Lord that they threatened to kill those who dared to do otherwise **(2 Chron. 15:3)**.

The people of Judah enjoyed a period of peace. Then, for some reason, Asa made a treaty with Ben-Hadad of Aram. In so doing, Asa demonstrated an independence from God that led to the loss of the Lord's support. When the seer Hanani announced God's judgment, Asa lost his temper and threw Hanani in prison.

Asa's stubborn streak was further evidenced when he refused to ask the Lord for help when he suffered from a severe disease that affected his feet. Asa died without a change in attitude.

Our perspective of Asa's entire life leaves us with some perplexing questions. Why was Asa so stubborn? Why did he persist in his miserable rebellion? The Lord cannot be a part-time participant in our lives. When He is in control, His blessings overflow.

READING THE SCRIPTURES

The successes and failures of the people of Judah and Israel sometimes appear to be rewards for good behavior and sanctions for disobedience. Take time to point out that God did not behave capriciously, loving His people one moment and hating them the next. His love was constant. The breakdown in the relationship between God and His people was always the result of their rebellion and rejection of Him. When they separated themselves from Him, they suffered. Asa is yet another example of this.

In this session you will help your students recognize how important it is to acknowledge their dependence upon Jesus Christ and seek to involve Him in all that they do.

ENTHUSIASTIC BEGINNINGS (Objective 1)

1. Point out that unlike Rehoboam, Jeroboam, Ahab, and Hoshea, the description of Asa is rather positive. Discuss these positive things.

2. Under Asa's leadership the people made a covenant with the Lord. Ask your students to describe the covenant **(2 Chron. 15:12)**. The intensity with which they lived up to the covenant is striking **(v. 13)**. Judah's behavior sounds a little like the Spanish Inquisition. However, differences exist. God had commanded His people to rid the land of idolaters and idols. Furthermore, Judah's authentic dedication to the Lord attracted others who loved the Lord **(v. 9)**. Discuss the passages with your students, focusing only on the attitudes of Asa and the people. (Students will be asked to make personal applications later.)

WITH THE LORD (Objective 2)

Judah was at peace with surrounding nations. This peace was a blessing from God **(Ps. 29:11)**. Help your students understand that peace was not a reward for good behavior but a characteristic of a relationship with the almighty God. Peace is something we, too, can enjoy. Ask students to read the following passages and tell what they mean:

Rom. 5:1 (We have peace <u>with</u> God.)

Eph. 2:14-18 (Jesus Himself <u>is</u> our peace and is the one who brought us peace with God.)

Gal. 5:22 (We also enjoy the peace of God, no matter what the circumstances.)

Point out that because of Jesus Christ we are no longer God's enemies (which once was the case because of sin) and that we can enjoy the peace of knowing we are in God's grace.

Conversely, the misery God's people suffered was the result of rebellion and independent action (which included idolatry and alliances with heathen people). If time permits, discuss parts of **Deut. 28.** Sometimes God intervenes to protect His people from themselves and the evil of this world. Sometimes His intervention is traumatic, but for the good of His people.

EAGER FOR THE LORD (Objective 3)

The enthusiasm of the people for the Lord was beautiful. **2 Chron. 15:15** describes how eagerly they sought the Lord.

1. Point out to your students that their eagerness was not shallow emotion but serious and profound. Ask your students how **2 Chron. 15:16** demonstrates the depth of commitment expressed by the people of Judah. (They were prepared to put to death those who would cling to idols.)

2. People from Israel came to Judah because of what God was doing for Asa.

Ask your students if they know of anyone today who attracts others because of the evidence of God's presence in his or her life.

(They may identify one of the popular evangelists on television, but steer them to think of someone among their own acquaintances. If they are unable to identify someone, ask, **Is it because the Lord is not working in people today?** The answer should be obvious. Perhaps we should be looking around more carefully for godly people.)

3. Paul describes the attractiveness of the Christian in **2 Cor. 2:14-16.**

4. Ask volunteers to share their answers. Throughout history, people have courageously demonstrated their faith in Christ. Sometimes teenagers fear criticism for expressing their faith. Others may have an immature concept of their relationship with Jesus Christ. Either way, they may be missing some of the joy that comes from knowing Jesus Christ as Savior and Lord.

5. Conclude by discussing Peter's encouraging words from **2 Peter 1:3-11** where we learn that God has given us everything we need for life and godliness. For this we praise and thank Him!

Session 75: Jehoshaphat--a Step Forward

BIBLE BASIS: 1 Kings 22:41-50; 2 Chron. 17:1--21:3

CENTRAL TRUTH

"Give thanks to the Lord, for His love endures forever" (2 Chron. 20:21b).

OBJECTIVES

That the students will:

1. Select from the accounts of Jehoshaphat's reign the events that help them form an impression of his character
2. Identify ways in which God showed His love and support as well as occasions when He had to discipline His people
3. Conclude that God is <u>THE</u> source of power and joy for their own lives

BACKGROUND

Once again the account in **2 Chronicles** provides more detail about the life of the king of Judah. Jehoshaphat was another king who was, at least initially, faithful to God.

Jehoshaphat, son of Asa, succeeded his father as king. Some disagreement appears between **1 Kings 22:43** and **2 Chron. 17:6** about the removal of the high places and Asherah. The difference may be the degree to which Jehoshaphat accomplished his goal **(2 Chron. 20:33).**

Jehoshaphat provided a team of priests and Levites who traveled throughout Judah instructing people in the Law. Knowledge of God's Word was and is an essential ingredient in knowing God Himself (**Rom. 10:14-17** and **2 Tim. 3:14-17**).

Jehoshaphat strengthened Judah by building fortifications, an effective supply system, and a large army. The Lord God Almighty was his most important asset (**2 Chron. 17:10-19**).

Considerable attention is given to the alliance between Jehoshaphat and Ahab and their disastrous venture against Syria (**2 Chron. 18:1-19:3**). The battle was mentioned in **session 70** without reference to Jehoshaphat. Attention is given now because it is an example of a mistake Jehoshaphat made that caused God to be angry with him. It is appropriate for each of us to carefully evaluate the significance of our associations with others.

We learn an important lesson from **2 Chron. 20:21**, the central truth for this session. A large army comprised of Moabites, Ammonites, and Meunites decided to wage war against Judah. Perhaps they were encouraged by Syria's victory over Judah and Israel when Ahab was killed (**2 Chron. 18:28-34**). Jehoshaphat had learned his lesson and once again turned to the Lord for help. Having placed their trust in the Lord God, the people of Judah faced their enemies with the words, "Give thanks to the Lord, for His love endures forever." Their words acknowledged God's activity in their lives and identified His enduring love for them. They were in a beautiful position. Though facing a formidable enemy, they rested in the Lord and relied on His love and power.

READING THE SCRIPTURES

Prior to class, assign the Scripture readings and the Student Book activities for this session.

Pray that you and your students may become more aware of God's love, support, and discipline in your lives. Ask God to bless your learning and sharing during this session so that His power, peace, and happiness may be in your daily living.

WALKING IN DAVID'S WAY (Objective 1)

The Student Book asks for a description of all the things Jehoshaphat did that showed he walked in the ways of David.

1. Review the following passages with your students:

a. **2 Chron. 17:3-6** (He did not worship Baal, he did worship and obey God; he tried to rid the land of idolatry.)

b. **Verses 7-9** (He sent priests and Levites out to teach God's law to the people.)

c. **2 Chron. 19:4-11** (He set up God-fearing judges in the land.)

2. Jehoshaphat was a good leader in other ways and, because of God's favor, he was able to fortify cities and build a strong army. Point out to your students that when we are in a right relationship with God, even the routine and practical parts of life go better.

3. If time allows, ask the students to share their descriptions of Jehoshaphat.

ACHIEVING SUCCESS IN THE LORD (Objective 2)

Based on their study of the history of Israel, some of your students may have the impression that "God loves me when I'm good and hates me when I'm bad, and since I'm bad a lot, God always hates me!" This idea may come from the reward/punishment experience of the Israelites. This activity reinforces the concept that was developed in **session 74**, pointing out that God is loving and generous to His people and delights in helping them with the difficulties they face in life.

Review the questions in the Student Book to help the students realize that:

1. Jehoshaphat

a. Made an improper alliance with Ahab.

b. Ignored God's warning.

c. Participated in a war that ended Ahab's life.

2. God chastised Jehoshaphat (**2 Chron. 19:1-3**).

3. In the war with the Moabites, Ammonites, and Meunites, Jehoshaphat:

a. Placed himself in God's hands.

b. Followed the Lord's commands.

c. Enjoyed the Lord's victory.

4. On the one hand, Jehoshaphat operated independently and made mistakes. On the other, he depended on the Lord and had the privilege of enjoying what God did for him. His dependence on God did not merit God's blessings. God's grace provided the blessings.

GOD IS MY STRENGTH (Objective 3)

The Student Book contains a simple fable about an imaginary king and his son to help the students understand that God has chosen them in Christ to be His children and that all of His blessings are theirs because God has chosen to share them. They need not live in fear that God will zap them if they make a mistake. They must realize what they will lose if they choose to live apart from God.

Review the fable and questions. Summarize, assuring the students that Jesus Christ, in God's greatest demonstration of love for them, bore the punishment for their sins and is also, by His Holy Spirit, prepared to live His life in them. It is in Christ that they have all of what God has to offer.

Conclude this session by saying together the words of **2 Chron. 20:21b: "Give thanks to the Lord, for His love endures forever."**

Session 76: Ahaz--a Step Back

BIBLE BASIS: 2 Kings 16; 2 Chron. 28

CENTRAL TRUTH

God chooses to love us in spite of our natural inclination to live apart from Him.

OBJECTIVES

That the students will:

1. Recognize the devastating effect on Judah caused by the disobedience of Ahaz

2. Identify God's rescue of the captives from Israel as a demonstration of His love for and intent to preserve His people

3. Apply what they have learned about God's mercy to their own lives, remembering God's unfailing love for them

BACKGROUND

Our study of the kings of Judah skips over the reign of Jotham primarily because of the brief record of his reign in both **2 Kings** and **2 Chronicles**. Jotham's son, Ahaz, was as distinguished for his unfaithful behavior as Asa was for his good deeds and accomplishments.

For reasons not mentioned in either account, Ahaz became heavily involved in idolatry, going so far as to sacrifice his own son to an idol **(2 Kings 16:3)**. Furthermore, he was responsible for the spread of idolatry throughout Judah.

God responded by bringing Aram (Syria) against Judah. Israel also attacked Judah and took a large number of women and children captive after inflicting heavy losses on Judah's soldiers.

God intervened and through a prophet convinced the army of Israel to return their captives to Judah.

Ahaz persisted in his rebellion against God by attempting to form an alliance with Assyria. In so doing he closed the Lord's temple and instituted the worship of Assyrian gods in Judah.

The reign of Ahaz lasted 16 years. In that time he caused considerable damage. Though Ahaz was buried in Jerusalem, his body was not placed with the other kings.

READING THE SCRIPTURES

Assign the Scripture readings and corresponding Student Book activities prior to class.

Thank and praise God for His constant love for and preservation of us.

In this session you will have the opportunity to discuss the responsibilities of leadership and the effect a leader has on his people. In a Student Book activity, the students are asked to trace the spiritual development of members of their own families. If they understand more fully what happened in a few generations in their families, they may better understand the reasons behind changes among the kings of Israel and Judah. The remaining activities will help them understand the reign of Ahaz.

HEAVY CASUALTIES (Objective 1)

Normally we hear casualty reports only in connection with a combat operation, where the success of a battle is measured by the cost of human lives. To some extent the reign of Ahaz can be evaluated on the basis of his casualty reports.

1. The Student Book asks the students to evaluate how Ahaz's sins cost the nation of Judah. **What did Ahaz do wrong?**

a. **2 Chron. 28:2** (He was like a king of Israel, made idols,and worshiped Baal.)

b. **2 Chron. 28:3** (He offered his own sons as sacrifices.)

c. **2 Chron. 28:4** (He instituted idolatry all over the nation.)

d. **2 Chron. 28:5-8** (He got Judah into a costly war.)

Point out that the heavy casualties included human lives and souls. Battle casualties were one thing, but Ahaz's leading many people into spiritual death through idolatry was another.

2. Students should list details of Judah's heavy casualties--many people taken captive, 120,000 soldiers killed in one day, etc.

3. Your students might be interested in tracing several generations of their own families to develop a "religious family history." Since we look at the kings quite critically, we might look at our own families to see how spirituality fluctuates from generation to generation. You might use this as an optional activity. Consider those students in your class who may be adopted or have few or no living family members. Adapt activities to fit the needs and considerations of your students.

GOD'S MERCY FOR JUDAH (Objective 2)

At this point, you might review with your students the meaning of mercy.

Unger's Concise Bible Dictionary describes mercy as a "form of love determined by the state or condition of its objects. Their state is one of suffering and need, while they may be unworthy or ill-deserving."

God cares about us. Even when we sin He loves us, though He hates the sin **(Rom. 5:8)**. God's mercy also relates to our physical needs as evidenced by His concern for the women and children who were taken captive. Discuss the following with your students:

a. **How did God show mercy to Judah (2 Chron. 28:9-15)?**

b. **Why did God criticize Israel (same passage)?**

c. **How does this event in Scripture show God's love for His people and His authority over the nations?**

Ask your students how they can apply to their own lives the lessons God tried to teach Judah.

a. about the assurances of God's love

b. about the assurance of God's hatred for sin

c. about God's authority in the world

GOD'S MERCY FOR ME (Objective 3)

1. Ask the students to share how they feel knowing about God's mercy to His people in Judah. **What does this mean for us?**

2. Talk about the different synonyms used in the **Psalms** for the word mercy.

a. **Ps. 52:8**--unfailing love

b. **Ps. 57:3**--love and faithfulness

c. **Ps. 106:1**--love

3. The students were to write something they have learned during this session. If time permits, ask them to share their discoveries. Be encouraging and at the same time make sure their findings are doctrinally sound.

Session 77: Hezekiah

BIBLE BASIS: 2 Kings 18-20; 2 Chron. 29:-31; Is. 36--39

CENTRAL TRUTH

God's love keeps us from destruction. God has put our sins out of His sight (**Is. 38:17**).

OBJECTIVES

That the students will:

1. Become familiar with Hezekiah's style of leadership and his courageous dedication to the Lord
2. Rejoice over the Lord's love for His people and their love for Him
3. Begin to form a concept of leadership for their own lives as members in God's church

BACKGROUND

The faith of the people of Judah resembled a roller coaster. The king's leadership was a key factor in determining the spiritual characteristics of the nation.

Session 77 focuses on some characteristics of leadership essential for the church. Students should begin evaluating their own experiences and performances and ask, "How can I serve God in my congregation?" "How can I serve God wherever I am?"

We learn important things about Hezekiah from the Scripture accounts:

1. He knew himself. Hezekiah knew he was God's child, and he was responsible to God. When he became king at 25, he immediately and decisively reopened the temple in Jerusalem (**2 Chron. 29:3**).
2. Hezekiah chose quality assistants and told them what he expected of them (**2 Chron. 29:4-19**).
3. He credited God for the good things that happened (**2 Chron. 29:36** and **31:21**) and humbled himself before God when he did evil (**Is. 38:15-17** and **2 Chron. 32:24-26**).
4. He did not allow anyone or anything to intimidate him or cause him to deviate from what he knew was right (**2 Chron. 31:21** and **32:7-8**).
5. Although Hezekiah committed himself to obey God's law, he also knew the spirit of the Law (**2 Chron. 30:1-4**), and when unable to fulfill it to the letter, he prayed for everyone's pardon (**2 Chron. 30:18-20**).

Though God blessed Hezekiah (**2 Chron. 31:21**), He did not overlook his sins. God showed mercy to Hezekiah when he repented. And by placing Hezekiah in a position of leadership, God preserved His remnant in Judah (**2 Kings 19:30-31**).

READING THE SCRIPTURES

Before this session, assign the Scripture readings and the related Student Book activities.

Parents and church congregations invest in young people when they provide training in God's Word. One of the goals of Christian education programs is to provide future leaders for the church.

Pray that God will bless your efforts as you help prepare your students to assume responsible leadership roles in His kingdom.

A LEADER FOR GOD'S PEOPLE (Objective 1)

Some characteristics of a good leader are listed in the **"BACKGROUND"** and will help answer questions from the Student Book's corresponding section. Review the questions and share answers together. Help the students develop an impression of the eager, aggressive, positive leadership Hezekiah demonstrated.

No attempt has been made to relate any of Hezekiah's leadership characteristics to any of the excellent materials available for leadership training. For your own resource, you might want to consult a manual that looks at civilian and military leadership styles: To Get the Job Done: Reading in Leadership and Management (second edition), edited by John B. Washbusk and Barbara J. Sherlock (Annapolis: Naval Institute Press, Annapolis, MD 21402, second edition, 1981).

GOD LOVES HIS PEOPLE (Objective 2)

The account of Hezekiah's reign is refreshing.

1. Ask the students to read their comments on **2 Chron. 29:36.** Have they grasped the spirit of love conveyed in this verse?

2. Another evidence of the love relationship is found in the giving attitude that God worked in His people. Reinforce the earlier session on "giving" by discussing **2 Chron. 31:2-14.** Point out that a healthy relationship with the Lord is demonstrated by the very generous sharing of God's blessings with others. Remind them that a generous giving attitude flows from a right relationship with God; it does not earn a relationship with God.

3. God is never fooled by outward behavior. God knows our hearts. When Hezekiah sinned, God dealt with his sin, and Hezekiah knew thatit was for his own good. Discuss the students' comments on **Is. 38,** which describes how God dealt with Hezekiah's sin. Then ask them to read **Matt. 5:48.** Being right with God "most of the time" is not enough in God's sight. God commands us to be perfect, and our perfection is found only in Christ **(Col. 1:28; Eph. 4:13).**

4. The reign of Hezekiah provides examples of God's power and love--such as the destruction of Sennacherib's army and the extension of Hezekiah's life.

YOU--A LEADER (Objective 3)

Point out to your students that God saved Judah from certain defeat at the hand of Sennacherib of Assyria **(Is. 37:21-28).** Similarly God has saved us through Jesus Christ **(Col. 2:13-15)** from all the powers and authorities that threaten us. He makes us Alive in Christ.

Remind your students that they have been saved by God's grace so they could be new people--people who could do things that glorify Him.

Discuss questions 1 and 2 from the Student Book. Focus on **2 Tim. 3:17** and **Eph. 2:10.** How can you convince your students that God has great leadership expectations for them? At this point the emphasis is that we are expected to be active. Both passages imply that, while God has things for us to do, our activities do not merit His love--they grow out of His love!

Leadership is one of God's gifts to the church **(Rom. 12:4-8).** Ask questions such as, **What kind of leading do you think God has in mind for you? What new insight have you gained from 2 Tim. 3:14-17?** How will we be better able to understand God's will for our lives and be prepared for **His service?** (Through careful and continuous study of His Word.)

Remind the students that each person is special because of what God has done!

Finally, remind your students that God never promised that life would be easy. Jesus warned His disciples that they would be persecuted because they belonged to Him **(John 15:20).** The Apostle Paul wrote of his eagerness to share in the sufferings of Christ **(Phil. 3:10).** God promises to be with us.

Remind your students also that God stands ready to help in time of need (example: **2 Cor. 1:3-5**). Hezekiah, living right with the Lord from his youth, called upon Him for help. Our confidence in God grows and our relationship with Him strengthens with time. It is important to take this relationship seriously and rejoice in it!

Close your class session with a prayer of praise to God for His love and power.

Session 78: Manasseh--a Reversal

BIBLE BASIS: 2 Kings 21:1-18; 2 Chron. 33:1-20

CENTRAL TRUTH

The Lord is moved by the prayers of His repentant people and graciously forgives them **(2 Chron. 33:13).**

OBJECTIVES

That the students will:

1. Recognize the depth of God's love for His people in the way He forgave the sincerely repentant Manasseh.

2. Be assured of God's love for them in spite of anything they have done.

3. Realize God's desire for them to repent and return to Him.

BACKGROUND

Initially Manasseh appears to be on a collision course with destruction. The **2 Kings 21:1-18** account does not mention that he repented of his sins **(2 Chron. 33:10-13)**. Once again **2 Chronicles** provides important information.

Occasionally people (often teens) presume that their sins are greater than God's capacity to forgive. The Biblical account of Manasseh's life assures us that God's capacity to love and forgive is greater than any sins we could ever commit. We also learn from **2 Chron. 33:17-25** that our sins can cause problems that are not easily corrected.

Some of the things Manasseh did are prevalent in our own society-murder of children, sorcery, witchcraft, astrology and other occult activities. Little in our time is a new invention when it comes to doing evil! We need to be aware of the horrible implications of abortion, astrology, drug abuse, and the various occult practices that are prevalent today, even among some who confess to be Christians.

God subjected Manasseh to a humiliating, though temporary, captivity during which Manasseh repented and humbled himself before the Lord.

READING THE SCRIPTURES

This session's Scripture account seems far removed from us, especially when we read verses such as **2 Kings 21:16 ("Manasseh . . . shed so much innocent blood that he filled Jerusalem from end to end")**. You will lead the students through the account of Manasseh's reign primarily from the perspective of **2 Chronicles 33**. Focus on how God brought Manasseh to repentance and how He loves each of us in spite of our sins.

THE DEPTH OF GOD'S LOVE (Objective 1)

As you discuss **Luke 7:36-50,** point out that Jesus forgave the woman's sins just as God forgave Manasseh's sins. Some of your students probably carry burdensome guilt feelings and need to be assured and reminded of God's love and forgiveness. This session provides such opportunity.

1. Enumerate Manasseh's sins.

a. He did evil, like the nations expelled from Canaan.

b. He rebuilt the altars and symbols of the idols and worshiped them.

c. He even built altars to idols in the temple.

d. He sacrificed infants to idols, practiced sorcery, witchcraft, and divination and consulted mediums and spiritualists.

e. He set up carved images in God's temple.

Remind the students that they studied God's Word concerning mediums and witchcraft in **session 54.** Sometimes TV programs such as <u>Bewitched</u> try to make witches look cute, but there seems to be a serious movement promoting witchcraft and mediums in today's society.

2. Ask for students' impression of Manasseh, but don't spend too much time concluding the obvious.

3. You might have to do extra research to prepare for discussions on some of the sins the students might have listed for this question. If you feel the time is appropriate, talk briefly about abortion, drug abuse, astrology, etc. and what God's Word says about these subjects. Avoid discussions for the sake of entertainment. Be prepared to help students find counseling if they face serious problems.

4. God tolerates gross sin for only a limited period of time. **2 Chron. 33:10-11** tells how God stopped Manasseh from further sin. The account is brief. **Why do you**

think Manasseh was led away in shackles with a hook through his nose? (Apparently he was either very violent or was being humiliated.)

5. Ask, **How did Manasseh's response to God differ from some of his predecessors' responses?** (He did repent according to **2 Chron. 33:12-13** and, according to the reforms he tried to accomplish, he was sincere.)

6. The fact that Manasseh wasn't able to effect the reforms he initiated shows how far things had degenerated in Judah. He wasn't able to change his son Amon, who was the next king in Judah. The record of his reign also ends with a sense of failure.

You might ask, **How do you feel about punishing people who are sorry for committing crimes? Do you think someone should be punished for breaking a school rule after he or she apologizes?** (Students might feel there is a difference between breaking a school rule and committing a "bad crime." They often can't understand why they are punished for breaking a school rule.) Remind your students that God certainly forgives all our sins because Christ died for those sins. But we must experience the consequences of our sins and expect to bear the cross caused by those consequences.

Ultimately, each of us must realize we are responsible for our own actions and the events caused by them. Point out that very seldom do we do things that do not affect at least one other person.

7. God loved Manasseh in spite of his sins. The Lord spoke to Manasseh, He listened to Manasseh, and He brought him back to Jerusalem.

GOD'S LOVE FOR YOU REQUIRES NO WAITING! (Objectives 2 and 3)

We live in a hurry-up society. We often demand instant gratification; yet ironically we don't care to be hurried by others and often procrastinate. Help students understand that God wants to have a proper relationship with us right now.

1. **2 Chron. 33:10** tells about God's special love effort to Manasseh. God spoke to Manasseh, either directly or through a prophet, to tell him to stop his wicked ways.

2. This section provides personal time for the student to acknowledge his or her sin, repent, and claim God's forgiveness. Ask, **What kinds of feelings do you have after you've confessed, told God you're sorry, and then believe that through Jesus He forgives all your sin?**

3. Ask a student to read **Eph. 2:4-5** with feeling. Then ask a volunteer to restate the passage as he or she might use it to meaningfully witness to someone. Are your students relating to this message personally?

Ask for volunteers to describe Paul's prayer from **Eph. 3:14-19.** God's love is profound--so deep that our minds can't imagine it, and God wants to fill us with His loving presence in Christ.

Encourage students to think of creative descriptions of God's love by asking them to complete a sentence such as, "God's love for me is like . . ." Emphasize human needs, getting past completions such as "God's love is like a warm puppy."

You might close this session with a personal prayer. Or read the words of the hymn, "Chief of Sinners Though I Be" (LW 285) to summarize this session.

Session 79: Josiah

BIBLE BASIS: 2 Kings 22:1--23:30; 2 Chron. 34--35; Jer. 3:6-13

CENTRAL TRUTH

"The anger of the Lord will not turn back until He fully accomplishes the purposes of His heart" (Jer. 23:20). The purpose of God's heart was to lead Judah to repentance--and that happened later through the Babylonian Captivity. God **"will not always accuse, nor will He harbor His anger forever" (Ps. 103:9).**

OBJECTIVES

That the students will:

1. Become familiar with the reign of Josiah and see in it the fulfillment of God's prophecy and the hopelessness of Judah's future

2. Realize that God's patience with sin and rebellion is limited

3. Rejoice in Christ through whom they have peace with God and hope for the future

BACKGROUND

To review, Manasseh never effectively carried out his reforms, possibly because idolatry was so firmly established with the people and he didn't have enough time to accomplish his goals. Manasseh's son, Amon, reigned only two years, perpetuating the evil of his father. Amon was assassinated and his eight-year-old son Josiah became king of Judah.

Josiah proved to be a king who **"walked in all the ways of his father David" (2 Kings 22:2)**. Josiah possibly was influenced by good men like the high priest Hilkiah **(2 Kings 22:4)**.

Josiah began to rid the land of idols, altars, and people who served the idols. He repaired the temple and reinstituted worship of God with a ceremony to celebrate the Passover.

While the temple was being repaired, the high priest recognized a discovered book to be "the Book of the Law." After Josiah heard the contents of the Book of the Law, he knew the nation was in trouble because the people had **"not kept the Word of the Lord" (2 Chron. 34:21)**. The prophetess Huldah confirmed Josiah's fears predicting Judah would be destroyed. God told Josiah the destruction of Judah would take place after his death.

Knowing all this, Josiah renewed the covenant with the Lord and had the people do the same. He aggressively campaigned to rid the land of every form of idolatry. In the process, Josiah fulfilled God's prophecy to Jeroboam (compare **1 Kings 13:1-5** with **2 Kings 23:15-18**).

Obviously God couldn't tolerate any more idolatry even though He had responded to Manasseh's sincere repentance. The **Book of Jeremiah** gives evidence that the people had only feigned repentance, perhaps out of fear of what Josiah would do. The **Book of Jeremiah** describes best what the people of Judah were like. **2 Kings** and **2 Chronicles** give good descriptions of Josiah's character.

READING THE SCRIPTURES

Because of God's announcement of judgment on Judah the approach to this session is quite Law-oriented. It is tempered by the reference to **1 Peter 1:3-5** and the assurance of hope we have in Jesus Christ.

The activities are designed to help the students understand the difference between the attitude of Josiah and that of most of the people of Judah, and the need for God to put an end to the devastating idolatry in Judah. (God accomplished this later. After the Babylonian Captivity, we find no evidence that the nation returned to the idols of the precaptivity days.)

A PROPHECY IS FULFILLED (Objective 1)

1. Ask the students to compare the prophecy of God given to Jeroboam in **1 Kings 13:1-5** with its fulfillment some 300 years later in **2 Kings 23:15-16**. (They should discover that the prophecy was completely accurate, as were the prophecies about the Messiah.)

2. Ask the students to share their summaries telling what Josiah did well.

3. **Jeremiah** provides necessary information about the people of Judah. Prior to this, we have seen God as a forgiving Father to His children. Now He has reached His limit and will tolerate no more sin. According to **Jeremiah 3:6-10** the people of Judah only pretended to abandon their idols. Jeremiah's prophecy compares idolatry with adultery. Point out that God compares His relationship with a believer to the intimate relationship that should exist between husband and wife--a relationship that should not be violated. God also compares the captivity of Israel with divorce.

Divorce was to occur only when there was infidelity. Israel and Judah were both unfaithful partners with God and it was necessary for Him to break His relationship with them. Discuss the analogy; make sure the students understand the sanctity of marriage and the importance of a pure relationship with the Lord. Ask the students to describe Judah's attitude.

4. Point out that to have a proper relationship with God it was essential that the people return to true worship. The returned exiles needed such encouragement and Josiah provided that with the celebration of the Passover.

AN APPROACHING DISASTER (Objective 2)

1. God's intent was clear according to **2 Chron. 34:23-28.** Ask, **Would you believe a prophet who predicted the destruction of your country because of the sins of the people?**

Then ask, **What would you do if God warned that He would destroy this country in the next generation?**

2. Ask your students how they might react when threatened by an approaching disaster (fire, flood, terminal illness, loss of parents, nuclear war, and others you might add). Then have the students describe how Judah reacted (compare **2 Chron. 34:29-33** with **Jer. 3:6-10**) to find the real reaction of the people).

3. Finally, ask the students to describe Josiah's reaction and share their comments on it. **Whose reaction was more sincere, Josiah's or the people's?** (Based on **2 Chron. 34:27-28** Josiah's was more sincere.) Point out that many people would have said, "If God intends to destroy us anyway, why not enjoy life before we go?" Josiah did not react that way, but worked hard to restore true worship of God, perhaps even hoping that God would change His mind.

GOD GIVES US HOPE FOR THE FUTURE (Objective 3)

For the insincere believer, this session should be a "shake him and wake him!" time. For all of us, this session serves as a warning and as an assurance. There is hope in Christ for those who believe. God did spare Josiah from the misery of the destruction of Jerusalem.

1. **1 Peter 1:3-5** also holds a word of hope for the Christian who faces the sin and rebellion of the world. Ask, **Where is your hope found?** It is, of course, in Jesus Christ, in whom we have a sure hope for an inheritance that will never be spoiled or taken away. Point out that according to **verse 5** we are shielded by the power of God until the time comes for us to join Him forever.

2. **How are you like the kings or the people of Judah?** This is a personal question and perhaps not easily discussed. A student may want to talk privately with you about a sin he or she feels separates him or her from God. By all means be a compassionate Christian listener and refer the student to a counselor if you feel the need. Otherwise you might focus your discussion of the question on how we are all spiritually phony from time to time. Don't allow the conversation to remain shallow, but emphasize the need for authenticity of faith in Christ.

Close with a prayer of thanks for our sure hope in Jesus Christ and a request for God's protection for each person in your class.

Hymns 368 ("My Hope Is Built on Nothing Less") and 442 ("In You Is Gladness") from Lutheran Worship reinforce the Gospel message in this session. You might sing or say some of the stanzas together.

Session 80: The Fall of Judah

BIBLE BASIS: 2 Kings 23:31--25:30; 2 Chron. 36; Jer. 2--39

CENTRAL TRUTH

The Lord lovingly corrects His people with justice **(Jer. 10:24).**

OBJECTIVES

That the students will:

1. Review the final years of Judah to identify the events that led to the Babylonian Captivity

2. Conclude that God was just in punishing His people through the destruction of Jerusalem and the Babylonian Captivity

3. Remember that because He loves them so, God lovingly corrects them too, and forgives their sins for Jesus' sake

BACKGROUND

After Josiah's death, Jehoahaz reigned as king only three months before he was deposed by the king of Egypt. The next king, Eliakim (renamed Jehoiakim by the Egyptian king), did evil in the Lord's sight. In the 11th year of Jehoiakim's reign the Babylonians attacked Judah and took Jehoiakim away. This began the Babylonian Captivity.

The Babylonian king, Nebuchadnezzar, placed Jehoiachin on the throne and, in his three month reign, he also did evil. Nebuchadnezzar took Jehoiachin captive and replaced him with his uncle Zedekiah.

Zedekiah reigned wickedly for 11 years. He rebelled against God and Nebuchadnezzar until finally God's and Nebuchadnezzar's patience ran out. Jerusalem was attacked and Judah's end had come.

The **Book of Jeremiah** contains repeated warnings and prophecies from the Lord as well as additional detail about the responses of the people of Judah. The people were thoroughly wicked and stubborn, refused to listen to the prophets of the Lord, and chose instead to continue to sin.

Jeremiah knew both the beauty and the horror of the Lord's power. Knowing that God's judgment was unavoidable, he prayed that the Lord would correct with justice and not with anger **(Jer. 10:24)**. Though God would have been justified in totally destroying Judah, He was merciful. Judah remained in captivity for about 70 years before God brought the people back to His land.

READING THE SCRIPTURES

In this session you will acquaint the students with the kings and the events that immediately preceded the Babylonian Captivity and help the students understand that God was justified in dealing with His people in such a harsh manner.

Ask, **What punishment do you think Judah deserved?** You may discover that the students agree with God that Judah should have been punished, but they may <u>not</u> agree with the <u>severity</u> of the punishment. **How do you think God would be just in dealing with our country?**

THE END (Objective 1)

1. The following four kings ruled after Josiah:

a. Jehoahaz reigned three months and was an evil king.

b. Jehoiakim reigned 11 years and was an evil king.

c. Jehoiachin reigned three months and was an evil king.

d. Zedekiah reigned 11 years and was an evil king who rebelled against Nebuchadnezzar.

This rather mechanical exercise provides a perspective of Judah's end times. It builds the case for God's decision to punish Judah.

2. The events that led to Judah's captivity consisted largely of Nebuchadnezzar's attacks on Judah and the rebellion of Zedekiah (which served to convince Nebuchadnezzar that he should take the whole nation into captivity).

a. **2 Chron. 36:5-7** and **2 Kings 24:1-2** (Nebuchadnezzar invaded Judah and made the nation a vassal state. However, Jehoiakim rebelled after a few years.)

b. **2 Chron. 36:9-10** (Nebuchadnezzar took Jehoiachin captive along with articles from the temple.)

c. **2 Chron. 36:11-14** (Zedekiah rebelled against Nebuchadnezzar. As a result, the Babylonian army laid siege against Jerusalem and defeated the army of Judah.)

3. The accounts of the last days do not describe how much the people suffered because of their sin. Ask a

student to read **2 Kings 25:1-21** aloud. Then ask the students to enumerate the ways the people suffered. They might include war, starvation, death, desertion by the king and his army, fire, destruction of the temple, loss of their possessions, and captivity.

Emphasize that the situation was very grave and that the people were severely punished for their gross sins. The most severe punishment was the loss of fellowship with the Lord God.

As a transition to the next activity, ask if anyone is familiar with any of Germany's actions during World War II, specifically the usage of concentration camps in which six million Jews died. Periodic news releases still recall the horrible treatment of Jews and others during World War II. Remind your students that Germany suffered during the war and remains a divided country today. Ask, **Do you feel that the ways the Germans have suffered are just in relation to the crimes that they committed?** The purpose of this question is to determine whether the students identify with a somewhat more contemporary event than those accounted in **Kings** and **Chronicles**. If you notice little reaction, you may use the event as a parallel to the quickly forgotten Law of God in Israel and Judah. Are your students willing to allow that God was justified in his dealings with Israel?

GOD IS JUST (Objective 2)

1. The **Book of Jeremiah** contains excellent descriptions of God's view of what had gone wrong in Judah.

a. **Jer. 5:1-6** and **11-13**. (God describes the people of Judah as dishonest, disinterested in the truth, incorrigible, stubborn, and rebellious. Review the exact words used by comparing several translations.)

b. **Jer. 7:1-15** and **30-31**. (The people look on the Lord's house as a magic charm that keeps them safe from punishment while they take advantage of the helpless, steal, murder, commit adultery, perjure themselves, and worship idols. They simply refuse to be accountable for their sins.)

2. Divide the class into two groups.

Group 1: Enumerate the sins of Israel for which God's punishment is deserved.

Group 2: Suggest excuses for the people and provide reasons why God should not punish them.

One requirement: Each group must use Scripture as the source for their statements.

Allow each group about 10 minutes to research and complete their activity. Then have the groups read their accusations and defenses. (This may seem impossible for the defense group--you may have to help them think of some excuses. The prophets often list excuses of the people, so direct them to research the prophetic books.)

Use another 10 minutes for the groups to present their materials. Then point out what **Jeremiah** says in **10:23--a man's life is not his own to direct his steps.** We are responsible to God for what we do and He may judge us as He sees fit.

3. Jeremiah pleaded for mercy, asking that God punish justly and not out of the emotion of His anger. Sometimes we fear a person's anger more than the punishment we get for doing wrong! Uncontrolled anger has been the reason behind a variety of crimes (e.g. child molesting, rape, murder, assault). Point out how Jeremiah pleaded for mercy and that God is always just in His dealings.

GOD IS LOVE (Objective 3)

Summarize the fact that just as God loved His people in Judah and took care of them, He loves and cares for us today.

HOW? Ask students to share responses they have written in their Student Books.

Conclude with a prayer, asking for God's mercy and thanking Him for His loving justice in your lives.

Session 81: Concluding Activities for Unit 11

The following test is a suggested instrument to evaluate student progress for Unit 11--The Kings of Judah.

Part 1: Matching

Directions: In the blank before the phrase in column 1 write the letter of the name from column 2 that matches most correctly.

Column 1

1. Allied with Ahab (B)
2. Last king of Judah (F)
3. Discovered the lost Book of the Law (C)
4. Brought about reforms in Judah (A)
5. Practiced sorcery (D)
6. God delivered him from Sennacherib (G)

Column 2

A. Asa
B. Jehoshaphat
C. Josiah
D. Manasseh
E. Ahaz
F. Zedekiah
G. Hezekiah

Part 2: Short Answer

Directions: Write in the missing name to correctly complete the sentence.

1. The king who destroyed the altar at Bethel and burned the bones of the false priests was (Josiah).

2. The Major Prophet who spoke to Josiah was (Jeremiah).

3. The chief male idol in Judah was (Baal).

4. The prophetess consulted by Josiah was (Huldah).

5. The idol to whom children were sacrificed was (Molech).

6. The country where Jehoahaz was taken captive was (Egypt).

7. The country where Judah was taken captive was (Babylon).

8. Sennacherib was king of (Assyria).

9. The king whose feet became diseased was (Asa).

Part 3: Short Essay

Directions: Write several short sentences to answer each question.

1. Why did the reforms brought about by several of the kings of Judah not last very long? (Idolatry was widespread and the reforms were usually reversed by a succeeding king. The people apparently didn't truly repent, but pretended to obey the king to avoid punishment.)

2. Defend or criticize God's decision to punish Judah by placing the people in captivity. (Look for an answer that suggests that God's decision was just. Some students may also know that after the Captivity, the people did not return to the idols of the precaptivity days.)

3. How does the account of Manasseh's reign in **2 Kings** differ significantly from the account in **2 Chronicles**? (The account in **2 Kings** doesn't mention the fact that Manasseh humbled himself before the Lord near the end of his reign. Unfortunately, Manasseh's sins had already caused some horrible problems in Judah.)

4. During the reign of Asa the people made a covenant. What were the terms of the covenant and how was it enforced? (The covenant required that the people seek the Lord with all their heart and soul. Failure to do so was punished by death.)

5. Why did God abandon Judah and allow the people to be taken captive? (The people committed idolatry and would not return to God. The further they strayed from God, the more they violated His Law and mistreated each other. Finally there was no hope for them.)

Unit 12: Overview of the Prophets

PLANNING THE UNIT

Special Preparations

For **session 87** the students are required to do independent study on one of the Minor Prophets and prepare a report that will be turned in on the scheduled session day. The report may serve as a basis for a grade for this unit. If additional evaluation is desired, you may administer a quiz on the Major Prophets.

The outline for the independent study report is contained in the material for **session 87.**

Take time to identify some resource materials for your students. Speak with the school librarian to have some books placed on temporary reserve so that they are available to all students. Suggest to the students that they also check their church libraries or talk to their pastors about research materials.

Bibliography

Laetsch, Theo. Bible Commentary: The Minor Prophets St. Louis: Concordia Publishing House, 1956.

(This excellent book is now out of print and may be difficult to locate. You may wish to check with local pastors to determine whether you can borrow a copy if one is not available in the school library.)

Session 82: Isaiah

BIBLE BASIS: Is. 1--12; 49--57

CENTRAL TRUTH

"Come now, let us reason together," says the Lord. "Though your sins are like scarlet, they shall be as white as snow; though they are red as crimson, they shall be like wool" (Is. 1:18).

OBJECTIVES

That the students will:

1. Recognize that Isaiah was called and inspired by God to speak to God's people
2. Relate God's declaration of judgment in **Is. 1--5** to their knowledge of the history of Judah
3. Praise God for the assurance of His presence, mercy and deliverance through Immanuel

BACKGROUND

The central truth for this session repeats Isaiah's message. The prophet announced God's judgment and His assurance of God's love, mercy, and deliverance.

Isaiah tells us that he lived during the reigns of Uzziah, Jotham, Ahaz, and Hezekiah **(Is. 1:1).** In chapter 6 he describes his call by God and says it occurred in the year that Uzziah died, which was about 740 B.C. If tradition is correct, Isaiah died as a martyr during the reign of Manasseh who came to power after the death of Hezekiah (687 B.C.).

God's presence and power in His temple are majestically described in **Is. 6:1-4.** The text inspired Martin Luther to write the beautiful hymn "Isaiah, Mighty Seer, in Spirit Soared" (LW 214). Isaiah is revealed as a sinful man cleansed by God and equipped for service **(Is. 6:5-9).**

The first five chapters of Isaiah give an overview of his message of judgment and hope. **Is. 1:4-6** describes how thoroughly sin had infested the people of Judah--they were totally immersed in it from head to foot. Their sacrifices had become meaningless attempts to fool God, who knew their real condition.

God promised to judge His people, but He also promised deliverance. God's hatred for sin and His determination to obliterate it are obvious, as is His incredible love for His people.

READING THE SCRIPTURES

Because it's impossible to cover

the **Book of Isaiah** in one session, study will be limited to an overview of the book's major messages. Since the students are by now familiar with the history of God's people, it should be relatively simple to relate the messages of Isaiah to the experiences and the behavior of the people of Judah.

GOD'S CALL (Objective 1)

1. Ask your students to describe what Isaiah saw according to **Is. 6:1-4.** They should realize that God revealed Himself as a magnificent king and in a way that Isaiah could relate Him to being greater than the kings on earth. God also revealed His power through the singing of the seraphim.

2. People often act as if they will never have to be accountable to God for what they do. Isaiah had a different experience. In the Lord's presence, he knew he was doomed because of sin. Those who are clothed with the righteousness of Jesus Christ will not have to fear **(Eph. 3:12).** Those who don't have a relationship with God through faith in Christ are doomed.

3. Isaiah was sinful. It is also possible that Isaiah identified with those who lied to God about their devotion to Him while they worshiped idols.

4. Ask your students whether they think God calls His servants in dramatic ways today. Some people have made decisions to serve the Lord in the midst of a dramatic circumstance (e.g., Luther), but those experiences are not universal. <u>Every</u> believer in Christ has been gifted by God to serve the body of Christ. In addition, some are called for special service.

5. Ask your students whether they see themselves as available to God as Isaiah was. People have made commitments to service in emotional circumstances. According to tradition, Isaiah was sawed in half. Perhaps he would have been less enthusiastic about serving the Lord had he known that martyrdom awaited him. Yet many people have eagerly served the Lord even in the face of certain death **(Eph. 3:13).**

GOD'S JUDGMENT (Objective 2)

1. Review the problems of the sins of Judah as listed in:

a. **Is. 1:4-7** (Their sin has totally corrupted them.)

b. **2:6-8** (They are into idolatry and the occult.)

c. **1:10-15** and **21-23** (They are not sincere in their worship and are dishonest in their dealings.)

Is it possible that Isaiah is also describing us? Ask your students whether they are like the people of Judah in terms of the sincerity of their worship and behavior.

2. Ask the students whether they understand God's response as described in:

a. **Is. 1:24-25** (God would treat them as enemies and purge them of their wickedness.)

b. **Is. 2:12--4:1** (This lengthier section describes the Day of the Lord in terms that predict the reversal of all of the things on which they now depend including leaders, commerce, wealth, and reputation.)

GOD'S PROMISE (Objective 3)

God's tender attitude toward His people is seen in His offer to reason with His people **(Is. 1:18).** There's no way any of us could ever argue about our condition with sins as red as scarlet and crimson. But it's God's plan that we be made pure through the death of His Son so that we can be white as snow or pure wool.

1. Ask your students to relate God's promise **(Is. 7:14)** to its New Testament fulfillment **(Luke 1:26-38).**

2. <u>Immanuel</u> means "God with us." Ask your students the significance of the name and then direct them to **Col. 1:15-23** and **Heb. 1:1-4.** Jesus Christ is God! And He is with us! No idol is capable of that or any other act.

Review with your students what God was like and what He did in

3. **Is. 53:2-3** (He was a plain man who came to serve--not to be served--without splendor.)

4. **Verses 4-9** (He served us by carrying our diseases, sorrows, and sins, and He did it without complaint,

though it was the loneliest and most painful experience imaginable.)

5. **Verse 9b** (Christ was different from us because He had never done anything wrong; the sinless Lamb of God carried our sins.)

God's love is incredible. God's love surpasses our ability to understand it **(Eph. 3:19)**. How can we ever thank Him for what we cannot begin to understand? Ask your students to consider living their lives as a constant thank-You to God. Invite a student to share his or her prayer of praise.

Session 83: Jeremiah

BIBLE BASIS: Jer. 1; 13:1-11; 16:2-9; 20:7-18; 23:5-8; 25:1-14; 26; 29:10-14

CENTRAL TRUTH

From eternity the Lord has known those who belong to Him; He formed them in the womb and set them apart for Himself **(Jer. 1:5)**.

OBJECTIVES

That the students will:

1. Become acquainted with Jeremiah as a person and identify with some of the challenges he faced as he served the Lord
2. Analyze several of the messages that God delivered through Jeremiah
3. Conclude that God creates life and already knows us in our mother's womb
4. Commit themselves to telling one person this week of God's love, forgiveness, and salvation through Christ

BACKGROUND

Jeremiah was a unique person. God chose him to perform a task for which he was not especially suited. Yet he obeyed the Lord, who supported him throughout his life. Jeremiah was timid, sensitive, and lonely, but he spoke God's Word with authority.

God called Jeremiah when he was a young man (perhaps about 20 years old) probably in 627 B.C. Josiah was king of Judah at the time. Though Jeremiah was reluctant to take on the Lord's assignment, he found he could not do otherwise **(Jer. 20:9)**. With the Lord's assurance and power, Jeremiah began a long career as God's prophet **(Jer. 1:18)**.

The Lord gave Jeremiah a variety of messages that exposed the sins of the people, warned them of God's impending judgment, and assured them of God's deliverance. Unfortunately, Jeremiah's words fell on deaf ears and rather than repent, the people tried to get rid of Jeremiah **(Jer. 26:7-9)**.

For this session the focus is on representative prophecies and the man who delivered them. Attention is purposely given to the difficulties Jeremiah experienced. He seemed more fragile than St. Paul, who also suffered as a result of his service to the Lord **(Phil. 2:14-18** and **2 Cor. 11:23-32)**.

The study of **Jeremiah** should reinforce the students' understanding of the previous sessions on the kings of Judah, but should also provide the opportunity for you to help your students deal with the pressures they experience when they try to live according to their convictions and faith in this hostile world.

READING THE SCRIPTURES

Through this session the students will become better acquainted with Jeremiah. He was much like they are in that he possessed the usual human weaknesses. After helping your students understand what Jeremiah was like and the things God had to say through him, you will have the opportunity to help them understand just how intimately God knows each of them. God also has special plans for each of His children today!

A FIRED-UP PROPHET (Objective 1)

The following activities will review student answers and put everything into a proper perspective.

1. Ask your students why Jeremiah was so reluctant to serve God **(Jer. 1:6)**. Notice that he claims to be

too young rather than admit to sin as did Isaiah. Perhaps Jeremiah was intimidated by those to whom he would speak.

2. God reassured Jeremiah by the promise of His presence, rescue, and message **(Jer. 1:8-9)**. Ask your students whether such a promise was just for Jeremiah and whether they can count on the same support. Have them read **John 14:26-27** after they give their answers. Then ask if they have a different opinion about God's presence and power for their lives.

3. Ask your students whether they could live with the restrictions God placed on Jeremiah: he could not marry and have children **(16:2-4)**; he could not attend funerals, mourn, or show sympathy **(16:5-7)**; he could not go to parties **(16:8-9)**.

4. There were reasons for these special restrictions. Sometimes God taught His people a lesson through the lifestyle of a prophet in addition to his words (see **Hosea**).

5. The next two questions in the Student Book are designed to help them understand how difficult it was for Jeremiah to speak God's message. Ask the students to describe the responses Jeremiah received from the people (**Jer. 20:8**--insults; **26:8-9**--threats of death).

6. Jeremiah was hurt and frustrated by the reception he received to the point that he cursed the day he was born and those who allowed him to be born **(Jer. 20:14-18)**.

7. Nevertheless, Jeremiah persisted in his service to the Lord. **Jer. 20:9-13** tells us that the prophet could not help but speak the inspired message that God had placed in him. Ask someone to read **Luke 19:28-40**. Point out that when Jesus made his triumphal entry into Jerusalem His followers shouted praises for what they had seen Him do. Jesus' remark to his critics shows us that God's Word and His praises cannot be stifled, for even the stones He created could cry out at His direction. Yet teenagers (and adults) find it difficult to sing out God's praises. Have the students comment on why we are afraid to praise God in public. **Why are we embarrassed? ashamed? How do you feel when your family prays before eating in a public restaurant? or when you see someone else praying before or after eating in a restaurant? or when we hear someone joyfully say, "Praise the Lord!"? Should we feel "funny" about thanking and praising God?** (Perhaps we do not know Him well enough to describe Him or thank Him.)

THE LORD SAYS . . . (Objective 2)

We are more effective witnesses when we quote the Lord than when we try to convince people by our own reason **(1 Cor. 2:13)**. Jeremiah also spoke the message of a greater authority, God Himself. God gave Jeremiah a variety of messages in a variety of styles.

1. One example of style is found in **Jer. 13:1-11**. This is an object lesson God used to show how his people had been ruined by sin and lost their close relationship with the Lord. Ask for a volunteer to explain the meaning of the lesson of the linen belt.

2. Jeremiah predicted a 70-year captivity by the Babylonians. The first captives were taken during the reign of Jehoiakim. Point out that Jeremiah was even given details about the length of the captivity. There could be no mistaking the seriousness of God's warning. Yet Jehoiakim refused to believe Jeremiah and burned the scroll that contained his message from God **(Jer. 36:20-26)**.

3. God's message even extended to the period after the captivity. Have someone read aloud **Jer. 29:10-14** and then **Deut. 4:25-31**. They should note that God did not change the terms of His relationship with them. He always wanted their complete devotion. He wants no less from us.

4. The students have been asked to speculate as to why God always added reassurances to His warnings. God has always held out hope to His people and has hoped that they will return to Him.

I KNEW YOU (Objective 3)

1. **Jer. 1:5** reveals that God knew Jeremiah even before He formed Jeremiah in his mother's womb. God, the Creator of life, knows all of those whom He creates. It is reassuring to know that He has known us from eternity. This passage could lead to a discussion of the doctrine of foreknowledge and election. Review the doctrine in the Formula of Concord.

2. Ask someone to read aloud **Rom. 8:28-39**. This passage is further assurance for us that nothing can take us away from our Lord, not even the worst threats or persecutions of mankind. This promise presumes that we cling to the Lord and desire to be kept close to Him. Perhaps it would be of value to ask the students how important their relationship with God is to them.

3. Jeremiah cried out to the Lord over the threats and mistreatment he experienced. It isn't easy to live the Christian life; Christians are frequently subjected to ridicule and even persecution. The apostle Peter advises us to anticipate trouble **(1 Peter 4:12-19)**. Ask your students whether they have ever made a conscious effort to prepare themselves for the ridicule they may experience for wanting to live a Christian life. Suggest to them that they should prepare for and anticipate ridicule and identify in advance resources for help and encouragement for such times. Resources include God's Word, worship, Holy Communion, prayer, and fellowship with other believers. Have the students suggest others.

I'M ON FIRE FOR THE LORD (Objective 4)

1. Everyone has misgivings about serving the Lord and perhaps about being a Christian. If time permits, have the class divide into two groups (with chairs in a circle) to discuss some of the misgivings they have had and how the Lord and others have helped them through such times. Have someone report from each group to share comments. What encouragement can students share with each other?

2. Expect the Holy Spirit to work through you and through your students as you pray for Him to help you focus on Christ at the right time and in the right place.

Session 84: Ezekiel

BIBLE BASIS: Ezek. 1--3

CENTRAL TRUTH

God reveals Himself to us as the King of kings and Lord of lords in all that He does.

OBJECTIVES

That the students will:

1. Place Ezekiel's ministry in its proper historical context

2. Become familiar with the unique and varied ways in which God revealed Himself to Ezekiel and through him to the exiles

3. Conclude that the conditions of Ezekiel's call still apply to God's people today

BACKGROUND

Ezekiel became the prophet of the Exile, the period when Judah was in captivity. God gave him the task of delivering His message to those Jews in captivity through words and symbolic actions. He was responsible for those people who had been taken captive during the time of Jehoiachin. During the fifth year of captivity God came to Ezekiel by the River Chebar in Babylon. God called Ezekiel in about 593 B.C., when he was about 30.

Since a single class period doesn't allow for an in-depth study of **Ezekiel**, the greatest part of the book has been deliberately ignored. Instead you'll focus on Ezekiel in his proper historical context, examine the nature of his first vision, and study the conditions of his call.

Ezekiel's first vision is a mystery. Even he had difficulty describing it and didn't comment on its significance. He used the phrase "what looked like" as he reported what he saw, revealing the difficulty he had with accurate descriptions. The creatures he saw appeared to be serving the almighty God. In the presence of the Lord's glory, Ezekiel fell on his face. By His Holy Spirit, God raised Ezekiel to his feet, put His Word in him, and sent him on his way.

Ezekiel's job was to deliver God's message. If the message was ignored by the people, Ezekiel wasn't held accountable. But if Ezekiel failed to deliver God's message, he would be held accountable for the blood of those who died. We, too, are charged with bringing the Gospel message to the people of the world in which we live **(Matt. 28:19-20)**, and it is God who causes our labors to bear fruit **(Rom. 7:4)**.

Ezekiel was like a watchman in a tower. And God asks us to be like Ezekiel today, using that same privilege of warning people of the dangers of sin and alerting them to the coming of their Savior, Jesus Christ.

READING THE SCRIPTURES

After your opening prayer, ask your students, **If you were God, what would you do with the people in captivity?**

Remind the students of the idolatry and disobedience that caused their captivity. You can expect answers to vary. Some students will want to impose severe punishments while others will want to show kindness to the exiles. Make your transition to the study of **Ezekiel** by pointing out that God appointed a prophet to speak to those people who were cut off in a foreign land. God's appointment of Ezekiel is another demonstration of His incredible love for His people.

GOD IS WITH EXILED EZEKIEL
(Objective 1)

The first two verses of **Ezekiel** help pinpoint exactly who and where Ezekiel was and when he was there.

1. Ezekiel was 30 years old, living by the River Chebar in Babylon, when he saw visions of God.

2. King Jehoiachin had been in exile five years already when Ezekiel had his vision. This information helps us identify the year as 593 B.C. Ezekiel was a priest whose father's name was Buzi. He experienced the Lord's presence and described it as the Lord's hand upon him in **1:3**.

3. Ask, **What kind of impression do you have of Ezekiel now? What do you think he was like?** (Ezekiel was relatively young and educated since he was a priest. Assuming he had been taught the truth about God, he should have possessed reasonable knowledge of God and His relationship to the Israelites. If Ezekiel was one of the faithful, it's apparent that the good and the bad suffered the same misfortune. This will also be apparent in the next session on Daniel.)

GOD SHOWS HIS PRESENCE TO EZEKIEL
(Objective 2)

Ps. 137 expresses how lonely the people of Judah were, longing for God's holy city, Jerusalem. We get lonely and depressed at times, too, and need reassurance and direction for our lives. You might briefly discuss how each of you sometimes feels, relating to the feelings of the people of Judah. What causes our feelings of loneliness?

It was important that the people realize that the God they had rejected was in reality the King of kings and Lord of lords. Ezekiel's encounter with God in his vision overwhelmed him and he even had trouble interpreting what he saw. But God's revelations to Ezekiel left no doubt that He was the Sovereign Lord.

1. Point out that what Ezekiel initially saw was a mystery. The students may not understand what Ezekiel saw, but they should have been able to list the parts of the vision. (He saw a windstorm, an immense cloud, flashing lightning, and a fire that gave off brilliant light like molten metal.)

2. Next he saw some unusual messengers. They were creatures with the form of a man with four faces and four wings. They had straight legs

with feet like those of a calf but made of burnished bronze. On their sides, beneath their wings, they had human hands. They moved in a straight line. Ask the students to supplement this information with what they find in **1:10-14.** You might want to read the interpretations of this vision from several good commentaries.

3. Next Ezekiel saw the wheels within wheels which, like the creatures, were moved by the Spirit of God.

4. The wings of the creatures sounded to Ezekiel like rushing waters, the tumult of an army, and the voice of God.

5. Finally Ezekiel saw the majesty of God, who revealed Himself in something resembling a human form **(1:26)**. Added to the fire and brilliance of the first vision was a rainbow symbolizing God's mercy. This vision resembles God's righteous and awesome judgment along with His continuing love and mercy. Your students may have missed some of this interpretation. Ask them to tell what Ezekiel saw and suggest they focus on the significance of the figure and the rainbow.

Ask volunteers to show and tell about their pictures. Was this an easy task? Probably not! Point out that the difficulty they had illustrating the vision was probably similar to Ezekiel's difficulty describing his vision verbally.

GOD CALLS EZEKIEL TO SERVE HIM
(Objective 3)

1. God did three things with Ezekiel.

a. He stood Ezekiel on his feet **(2:2)**.

b. He told Ezekiel He was sending him out to the exiles **(2:3)**.

c. He established him as a watchman for the exiles **(3:17)**.

2. God gave Ezekiel an enormous responsibility, a heavy burden of sharing God's Word. Furthermore, the manner in which he was to share God's messages was varied and unusual. Ask your students to comment on the fact that if Ezekiel failed to share God's message, the blood of those who died without that message would be charged against him. Ask, **Have you ever thought witnessing for Jesus Christ was <u>this important</u>?** Read **James 5:20** aloud in class. Ask, **How does this Scripture passage emphasize the job God asks us to do when He commands us to "go and tell all nations" about the Savior? How do you feel when you read and hear the Scripture messages for us that direct us to be God's messengers?**

3. Ezekiel was to portray the siege and the fate of Jerusalem symbolically by lying on each side a specific number of days, by eating and drinking in rationed portions, etc.

Ask, **What do you think God expects of each of us today (Matt. 28:19-20; John 6:44-45; Gal. 6:6)?**

What specific messages does God give us to tell others? (A few of the many in Scripture might include **1 John 5:1-12; 3:23; Mark 16:16; John 3:15-16; 16:31;** and **17:20**).

4. Your students should see that Ezekiel's ministry was dramatic and unusual. God gave him overwhelming responsibility as the watchman for God's people. Since God planned to take Judah back to His land, it was important that someone speak to them of God's plan and why He was doing what He was. Previously they hadn't understood the plain words of the prophets; perhaps now they would learn something from Ezekiel's symbolic behavior. Encourage your students to read the remaining chapters of Ezekiel in their own time.

Close this session with a prayer asking God to reveal His will to each person.

Session 85: Daniel

BIBLE BASIS: Dan. 1--6

CENTRAL TRUTH

God will keep in perfect peace those who trust in Him **(Is. 26:3)**.

OBJECTIVES

That the students will:

1. Recognize Daniel as a man of God who was faithful to the Law of God, faithful in worship of God, and a faithful manager of the gifts from God

2. Be aware that they, too, have God's power to live as His men and women

BACKGROUND

Each of God's prophets played a significant role in the plan God had for His people. Daniel was living proof of the truth of Isaiah's words, **"You will keep in perfect peace him whose mind is steadfast, because he trusts in You" (Is. 26:3).** Though Daniel faced some severe trials, he always seemed to remain confident in the Lord. He was quite different in temperament from Jeremiah.

Daniel was one of the princes of Judah who had been taken captive by Nebuchadnezzar in about 605 B.C. He was picked for special training because he possessed the capacity and appearance for leadership in the king's service.

From the beginning of Daniel's account, it is obvious that he had a proper relationship with the Lord, for he was convinced of the need for and blessings of obedience and trust in the Lord. He trusted God for his health, security, and everything else that he needed for life.

Dan. 6:22 is an indicator of the nature of Daniel's relationship with God for he says, **"My God sent His angel, and he shut the mouths of the lions. They have not hurt me, because I was found innocent in His sight. Nor have I ever done any wrong before you, O king."** Daniel is not describing self-righteousness, but righteousness of faith, which resulted in his living faithfully before God and man. The first six chapters of the book contain several interesting accounts of incidents in the lives of Daniel and his friends Hananiah, Mishael, and Azariah. The accounts are refreshing, interesting, and inspiring. The last six chapters, which are deliberately ignored in the present study, contain apocalyptic messages that are interesting and may be a topic for another occasion.

READING THE SCRIPTURES

Help the students realize that being a child of God is not only interesting and exciting, but also the way to great joy and blessing. Daniel is an example of one of God's men. Jesus Christ is the only one who ever lived completely as God intended for human beings to live. The exciting thing is that God is willing and eager to produce real life in us so we can be His men and women too! Assign the Scripture readings and the related Student Book activities before this session. Be ready to share your own excitement about what God has done for you in your own life!

FAITHFUL TO GOD, BLESSED BY GOD
(Objective 1)

1. If time permits, ask a student to read aloud **Dan. 1.** Ask, **How would you describe Daniel and his friends?** (They were princes of Judah who had been taken to Babylon as captives; they were handsome, healthy, and talented.)

2. Daniel could have been tempted by the special privileges he was offered when he was selected for special training. Nebuchadnezzar was determined to take advantage of the "brain drain" he had caused in Judah and designated the most promising for further training.

Ask, **What did Daniel refuse?** (He refused the rich food and wine of the Babylonians, preferring to be a vegetarian.) **Why do you think Daniel would refuse such good food?** (The type of food and the way it was prepared probably violated God's law.) Read together and discuss further insights from these passages: **Gen. 9:4; Lev. 7:22-27; 17:10-16; Deut. 14:3-21.**

3. God blessed Daniel and his friends with success. They had not merited God's blessings, which flowed from their relationship with God. Do your students understand the relationship between obedience and success?

4. According to **chapter 6,** Daniel was faithful also in worshiping God. Point out that Daniel's friends also went through a severe test of

their faith related to worship. Then ask, **What do you think these young men saw in God that made them so adamant in their worship?** Have the students describe the plot of the jealous satraps (minor administrators) and tell what they might do in this situation.

How do Daniel's worship habits --praying three times a day in this case--compare with your own personal worship habits? Remind your students that Daniel didn't have complete worship opportunities because he was away from God's temple. Daniel continued to worship the true God even when he faced death.

5. Daniel was also faithful with the gifts God gave him. Students may not realize they have a responsibility to be faithful stewards of their own spiritual, intellectual, and physical gifts. It may appear that Daniel really did not do anything special, but it should be pointed out that he worked hard, using the gifts God gave him. In this way he won the respect of others.

Dan. 1:17-20 indicates that God blessed Daniel with knowledge and understanding in many areas, including the interpretation of dreams.

Ask a student to read **2:17-28. To whom did Daniel give credit for his special abilities? Why is it important that we give God credit for the abilities we have?** (It is a form of praising God, testifying to His love for us, and it prevents us from becoming arrogant.

If the students still need help seeing how Daniel was faithful with his gifts, have them read **6:3**, which describes how Daniel distinguished himself.

OUR STRENGTH COMES FROM GOD

1. To reinforce this fact, mention once again that God was the source of Daniel's special abilities and talents.

2. Divide the students into small groups (five or six people in each group). Ask them to take turns saying at least one positive thing about each person in their group. This might be difficult at first, but will accomplish the purpose of making each student feel good about himself or herself. When finished, ask, **How did you feel about what your classmates said about you? How did you feel saying complimentary things about your classmates?**

Then ask the students to share how they feel about all the good things God has done for them from the Scripture references they were to look up.

2 Cor. 13:4-5 (Jesus Christ is in us with His power.)

Eph. 1:13 (We are marked with the seal of God's Spirit.)

1 Cor. 2:12, 14-15 (Through God's Spirit we can make spiritual judgments and know God's truth.)

Matt. 18:19-20 (When we pray together in Christ's name, God grants our requests.)

1 Cor. 12:1-11 (A list of the spiritual gifts.)

2 Cor. 12:9 (Our weakness is God's opportunity to demonstrate His power.)

3. Ask, **Have you discovered anything about your relationship with God that you didn't know before? Are you excited about the possibilities for living that God offers to those who belong to Him?**

At this time you might talk about some of the temptations the students face today that could compromise their relationship with God. Ask, **What are some things that tempt you?** For some it might be food, clothes, makeup, rock music, popularity, sports, or money. Remind them how Daniel wanted God to be first in his life and as a result he prospered.

If the students don't understand what God offers them, suggest they begin to use some of the gifts God has promised. One way to use God's gifts is by praying together.

Close with a prayer. Ask God to help each of you better understand how to be his men and women, and for the grace to live lives that glorify Him through the use of the gifts He has given you.

Session 86: Jonah--A Minor Prophet

BIBLE BASIS: Jonah 1--4

CENTRAL TRUTH

God is willing to warn the wicked because He wants all people to be saved and come to the knowledge of truth **(1 Tim. 2:4)**.

OBJECTIVES

That the students will:

1. Become familiar with the main points and lessons of the **Book of Jonah**.

2. Recognize Jonah's reluctance to share God's Word and recognize similar problems in their own lives.

3. Praise God that Jesus died for them **(Rom. 3:29-30)**.

BACKGROUND

The Minor Prophets include twelve men, one of whom is Jonah. The name Minor Prophets doesn't describe their importance, but relates to the length of their writing. It has been appropriately pointed out that the Wise Men **(Matt. 2:5-8)** were led to the Christ Child in Bethlehem on the basis of **Micah 5:2**.

The **Book of Jonah** has been selected for study in this session because of the lesson it teaches. The students might already be familiar with Jonah from hearing about his three-day and -night stay in the belly of a great fish. The lesson of the book, however, is that God's love for humanity extended beyond the Jews to include all people.

Jonah was a bigot--or at least a religious snob. He ran from God because he didn't want God to forgive the people of Nineveh. (Nineveh was the capital of Assyria and that nation was an enemy of Israel and Judah.) It's interesting that Jonah acknowledged God as Lord and then refused to accept God's will. It's inconsistent to confess God (Jesus) as Lord and then refuse to obey Him.

God was determined to have Jonah preach to the people of Nineveh, so He brought Jonah back to face his responsibilities. Jonah cried out for help from the belly of the fish **(Jonah 2)**. He should have recognized that his situation was as bad as that of the people of Nineveh.

Jonah grudgingly carried out God's command and then sat down to sulk while God showed mercy to Nineveh. God taught Jonah a lesson, pointing out that he was more concerned with his own physical comfort than he was over the 120,000 children in Nineveh whose lives were at stake. Those children were too young to even be responsible for their actions, but Jonah had no feeling of mercy for them. God even cared for the animals **(4:11)**.

The book ends without telling us whether Jonah learned his lesson. It's important for us to be willing to share God's Good News about Jesus Christ with others. It becomes even more important for God to love others through us when we have an inclination to be religious snobs.

READING THE SCRIPTURES

Assign the Scripture readings and the Student Book activities before class time. Mention that the students especially read and carry through paragraph 1 under **"Saying No to God."** Expect the students to do this--don't give the impression that it's an option!

It's usually easier for us to find weaknesses in others than in ourselves. The activities in the Student Book for this session are designed to do two things.

First, the students are required to tell the story of Jonah to a friend who isn't in this class. Will they actually do this? It's not an optional activity, though some may think it's silly or feel too embarrassed to do it. The experience should make them come to grips with a reluctance to witness. Second, they should recognize that the result of witnessing is not always the success story that we find in the account of Jonah. It's God who brings results. We may never see any results. It's our responsibility to share Jesus Christ--to plant the seed of God's

Word--with other people.

SAYING NO TO GOD (Objective 1)

1. Ask for volunteers to share the account of Jonah's experiences as they told it to their friends.

2. Ask volunteers to relate the reactions of their friends to the account. The focus of this activity should be on the experiences of sharing God's Word and the responses to that Word. The students may not have many reactions to share because there may not have been many spontaneous reactions. Point out that the lack of reaction is exactly what Philip experienced when he approached the Ethiopian **(Acts 8:26-40)**. That's why it's so important for believers to spend time explaining what they know to others. Assure your students that they have something important to share with others as a result of their study of God's Word. Ask, **If your friend were starving, would you give him or her a part of your own food? If your friend's clothing all burned in a fire, would you give him or her clothes from your own closet? Isn't it even more important to share the Word of God especially when you consider that your friend might be dying eternally?**

God's responsibility is in making the seed grow, nurturing the already-planted Word in a person.

3. Jonah's sincere message from God to Nineveh convinced the people to believe.

GIVING IN TO GOD (Objective 2)

God chooses to work through us. He chose Jonah for a special purpose and wasn't about to accept Jonah's refusal to cooperate.

1. **Jonah 4:1-3** reveals that. Jonah couldn't tolerate Nineveh. He was a bigot. There may be some disagreement about this description, but Jonah was angry enough about the situation to express on two occasions the wish to die (**4:3** and **4:8**). Ask your students if they've ever experienced such deep feelings against anyone. Have someone read **Rom. 12:9-21** and ask whether they think God really means what He says.

2. Ask your students to describe their feelings as they shared the story. The feelings often include fear, embarrassment, or inadequacy. Hopefully none had an attitude of disinterest. Point out that their reasons are as valid as Jonah's. But we really have no excuse for failing to share God's Word with others. We never know when in our daily lives something we say or do will eventually affect someone. We sometimes never know the results of our "seed planting" and the Holy Spirit's nurturing. Any time we see someone who needs to know about Christ, we should consider the possibility that God has placed us in his or her presence for a very important reason--to let that person know of both sin and God's love.

3. Jonah was extraordinarily concerned about himself. Teens sometimes tend to be introverted and self-centered, preoccupied with their own growing up and all their life hassles. Ask whether they've noticed anything they're overly concerned about. Talk about some of the things that get in the way of sharing Christ with others. Can you remember some things from your own experiences through your teen years to add to the discussion?

4. Encourage the students to redirect their energies toward helping others and at the same time share God's Word. Relate the idea of being good stewards (managers) of time and abilities. Are any students involved in their church's youth group, service-related projects, hospital candy-striping programs, VBS programs, neighborhood help-groups, or their Sunday school department?

BELONGING TO GOD (Objective 3)

1. Point out to your students that as far as the Jews were concerned, they were the only ones who enjoyed God's favor. The term gentile referred to a heathen, someone who didn't know God. Most of us who are Christians are in that category. Ask your students to imagine what it would be like if they had no hope for eternal life simply because they

weren't of a particular race. Those who are members of a minority group may be able to share what it's like to experience discrimination. Ask for comments only if you feel they will contribute to the understanding of God's great love for us.

2. Review **Rom. 2:17-24.** The Jews misinterpreted the value of circumcision, the seal of the covenant God established with them. A spiritual circumcision was more important to God than the physical act. Faith in God was more important than an empty performance of a ritual. The Gospel is for the Jew and the Gentile **(Rom. 1:16).**

3. God commands and expects us to go and make disciples of all nations, to baptize and teach them of the Triune God, and to remind each other to remain faithful to God.

If time permits, have someone read **Acts 10:1--11:18.** This is the account of the way God taught the Apostle Peter that Jesus Christ came also for the Gentiles.

Close this session by praising God. Sing or say the words of the common doxology together (LW 461).

Session 87: Concluding Activities for Unit 12

Several possibilities exist for culminating activities for the unit **"Overview of the Prophets."** Here are some suggestions.

1. Have the students give brief oral summaries of the independent study reports they did on the Minor Prophets. (The report guidelines are outlined below.)
2. Administer the suggested test.
3. Use a combination of 1 and 2 above.
4. Use the session to catch up on work not completed in prior sessions.

INDEPENDENT STUDY REPORT GUIDELINES

The purpose of the independent study report is to help the students learn to do Bible study on their own. If they also give an oral report, they will discover that it is possible to share God's Word successfully with others and begin to feel more at ease doing so.

The report should have been assigned when the present unit was introduced. The Student Book contains instructions for the preparation of the written report on one of the Minor Prophets. Since **Jonah** was covered in the preceding session, his book was not among those from which the students could choose.

1. Review the instructions in the Student Book with the students.
2. Prepare a list of reference books available in the classroom or on reserve in the library. Suggest that students also ask for assistance from their church library if one is available. Remind them to check with their pastor, church secretary, or church librarian about books that may help them with this project.
3. Set a due date for the report, explain how the report will be graded, and explain how the report grade will relate to tests as a means of determining their final grade for the course.
4. Let the students know whether they will be expected to make an oral presentation on their reports and whether they will have a unit test in addition to the report.
5. When grading the reports you may wish to evaluate the following:
   a. Is the report complete (were all directions followed)?
   b. Does the student have a grasp of the theme and purpose of the book?
   c. Did the student write in his/her own words?
   d. Has the student made an appropriate personal application?

SUGGESTED UNIT TEST ON THE PROPHETS

Part 1. Multiple Choice

Directions: Read each question carefully. Select from the possible answers following the question the one that is most correct. Write the letter that corresponds to your answer in the blank before the question.

1. Major prophets were generally:
   a. military men
   b. more important

c. authors of longer writings
d. authors of more than one book

2. The prophet who complained about the way his audience treated him was:
a. Isaiah
b. Jeremiah
c. Daniel
d. Ezekiel

3. The prophet whose lips were touched by a hot coal was:
a. Isaiah
b. Daniel
c. Ezekiel
d. Jeremiah

4. Which prophet was also a priest?
a. Daniel
b. Ezekiel
c. Jeremiah
d. Jonah

5. Which prophet wrote the beautiful prophecies about the Messiah?
a. Jonah
b. Daniel
c. Jeremiah
d. Isaiah

6. Which prophet confessed his sin at the time of his call?
a. Daniel
b. Jeremiah
c. Isaiah
d. Jonah

7. Which prophet was told that God knew him even before he was formed in his mother's womb?
a. Daniel
b. Jeremiah
c. Ezekiel
d. Jonah

8. Which prophet was a prince of Judah?
a. Isaiah
b. Daniel
c. Ezekiel
d. Jeremiah

9. Which prophet used object lessons to convey God's messages?
a. Isaiah
b. Daniel
c. Ezekiel
d. Jeremiah

10. Who were the two prophets who were called to serve God while in captivity?
a. Isaiah and Jeremiah
b. Jeremiah and Ezekiel
c. Daniel and Isaiah
d. Ezekiel and Daniel

Part 2. Matching

Directions: Column 1 contains a list of statements from or about the books of the prophets. Column 2 contains a list of prophets (and the abbreviations for their names). Read each statement and identify the prophet to whom the statement belongs by writing the appropriate abbreviation for his name in the blank before the statement.

Column 1: Statements

1. I have made you a watchman. (Ez)
2. You must not marry and have sons or daughters. (Je)
3. My God sent His angel, and He shut the mouths of the lions. (Da)
4. Surely He took our infirmities and carried our sorrows. (Is)
5. Forty more days and Nineveh will be destroyed. (Jn)
6. Son of man, stand up on your feet. (Ez)
7. His Word is in my heart like a burning fire. (Je)
8. Three times a day he got down on his knees and prayed, giving thanks to his God. (Da)
9. I am angry enough to die. (Jn)
10. There is a God in heaven who reveals mysteries. (Da)

Column 2: Prophets

Is. = Isaiah
Je. = Jeremiah
Ez. = Ezekiel
Da. = Daniel
Jn. = Jonah

Part 3. Short Essay

Directions: Write brief answers for five of the following questions. Identify the questions you are answering.

1. How did Daniel demonstrate that he was God's man?

(He was faithful in obeying the Law, in worshiping God, and in using the gifts God gave him.)

2. What similarities were there in the ways God summoned Isaiah and Ezekiel to be His prophets?

(Both saw visions that conveyed some of the majesty and power of God.)

3. Describe the character of Jeremiah and compare it with Daniel's.

(Jeremiah complained about his suffering and rejection. Daniel appeared to be calm and confident in God.)

4. Explain some possible reasons why Daniel refused to eat the Babylonian food.

(It may have been butchered in a way that violated God's Law or may have been meat that was forbidden according to the Law.)

5. What was the reassuring part of Isaiah's message?

(Messianic prophecies.)

6. Why did Jonah run from God?

(He did not want to preach to the people of Nineveh because he knew they would repent. Jonah did not want God to show them any mercy.)

7. Why did God wish to save the city of Nineveh?

(God loves all people. There were over 120,000 children in the city as well as animals, and God had compassion on them.)

8. Why was Isaiah frightened when he saw a vision of God?

(He knew that he was a sinful man in the presence of the righteous and almighty God.)

Unit 13: The Exile and Return

Sessions on **Esther, Ezra,** and **Nehemiah** will provide a glimpse of what life was like for the exiles and how difficult it was to re-establish God's people in the Promised Land.

Session 88: Esther

BIBLE BASIS: Esther 1--10

CENTRAL TRUTH

God has called each of us to be His royal priest to serve Him and the body of Christ at the right time in His perfect plan. **(Esther 4:14b)**

OBJECTIVES

That the students will:

1. Become familiar with the main points of the **Book of Esther,** especially as they relate to a history of God's people in exile
2. Recognize Esther as God's woman, a person who was obedient to her guardian and to the Lord
3. View themselves as persons who have a unique purpose in God's kingdom here on earth

BACKGROUND

The book of **Esther** provides supplementary information on the history of God's people in exile. Previous information has come mainly from studies of the prophets.

The events in **Esther** probably took place shortly after the rebuilding of the temple. Thus some of the Jews had already returned to their homeland. But it is apparent that a number of them had chosen to remain in captivity.

This story shows the great courage of God's people and His continuing love for them. The Jewish feast of Purim commemorates God's deliverance of His people from the wicked Haman.

The principal characters are: Xerxes, king of Persia who ruled 486-464 B.C. over what was previously Babylonia; Mordecai, a Jew who was Esther's cousin and guardian; Esther, a beautiful Jewish girl who won a beauty contest to become queen; and Haman, one of Xerxes' administrators whose pride resulted in his death after his plan to kill all the Jews was foiled by Esther and Mordecai.

Near the end of a long and ostentatious party, Xerxes wanted to show off his queen, Vashti. When she refused to appear, the king's advisors suggested that she be severely punished lest the other women of the land begin to disobey their husbands **(Esther 1:1-18)**. In a search for a replacement, Esther became a favorite of the king. Following the advice of her guardian, Mordecai, she did not reveal that she was Jewish and related to Mordecai.

When Haman was promoted to a significant post in the government, Mordecai refused to bow to him. Haman's anger over the matter was so fierce that he plotted to kill all of the Jews in the Persian empire.

Mordecai urged Esther to intervene, suggesting that God had placed her in her royal position for just this reason **(Esther 4:14b)**. Aware that she was risking death, Esther devised a counter plot to foil Haman.

Esther's courage and devotion to her cousin are admirable. Though the name of God is never mentioned in the book, we can see how God acted on behalf of His people.

READING THE SCRIPTURES

The Student Book contains questions that will lead the students through the events in the **Book of Esther.** You may have to help them understand the story line. You will also have to help them apply the lessons to their own lives.

A THREAT TO GOD'S PEOPLE
(Objective 1)

1. It might be said that Esther won a beauty contest **(Esther 2:1-9 and 18)**. Have the students describe Esther.

2. Mordecai was an alert man who seemed to step in when there was trouble **(Esther 2:8, 21-23; 4:1-17)**. Review each of the references with the students.

3. Haman was ambitious and vain. His pride went out of control and turned against him. Ask students to think of times they have lost their tempers and then regretted what they did.

4. The flavor of the Persian court is seen in the celebrations that Xerxes sponsored **(Esther 1:2-11; 2:17-18)** and in the fact that anyone who entered the king's presence uninvited would be put to death unless the king extended his golden scepter. Point out that the security around the President of the United States is also very strict today in order to protect the President, just as it is tight around each country's head of government. Xerxes also had to be protected from terrorists **(Esther 2:21-23)**.

5. Ask the students to explain how Esther used her position to her advantage **(Esther 5:1-7; 7:1-10)**. She maneuvered things so that Xerxes offered to grant her request before she presented it.

6. Mordecai worked behind the scenes most of the time but eventually God rewarded him **(Esther 6 and 10)**. Ask, **Is such patience typical today?** It sometimes seems that in our society instant gratification or reward is expected, and we resent having to wait for anything.

GOD'S WOMAN (Objective 2)

1. Ask the students what they think of Esther's initial reluctance to enter the king's presence. Ask, **How did Mordecai convince her that she had no choice (Esther 4:12-13)? Did Mordecai leave her a way out?** Yes, he did, for he was convinced that rescue would come from elsewhere if necessary.

2. Mordecai must have seen a relationship between the death of Esther's parents, her exceptional beauty, and Vashti's refusal to obey the king. It placed one of God's people in a position to influence Xerxes to spare the Jews. Ask your students to think about situations that seemed to have coincidentally worked out to their advantage when something bad was bound to happen. Recall a couple of your own in case they are unable to recognize God's working on their behalf.

3. Earl Nightingale, a motivational speaker, suggests that the higher you look in a good organization the more dedicated the people are. Esther was prepared to give her life for her people. Help the students understand that Jesus did the same **(Phil. 2:6-11)**. Can God expect anything less from us?

4. Are there any "risky" things

that need doing around school? Describe the West Point Military Academy Honor Code. (It basically says that there will be no cheating and no lying of any kinds. Cadets who know of violations of the Honor Code are expected to report them.) Mordecai lived by his own honor code (**Esther 2:21-23**). He sought no rewards.

Discuss with the students the reverse honor code that protects those who do wrong (there is considerable peer pressure to conceal violations of school rules). Assure them that you are not trying to get people to tattle (or squeal, rat, or whatever they call it), but that it is appropriate to defend the truth and live honorably.

A ROYAL POSITION (Objective 3)

This is an opportunity to reinforce a concept discussed previously. In **1 Peter 2:9** we are described as a royal priesthood. Some of the responsibilities of God's royal priests are listed below. Ask for comments on them and suggestions how each can be carried out in real life. Be careful to place them in a Gospel context, but also point out what happens when we abandon our royal privileges.

1. The royal privilege to praise God (**1 Peter 2:9b**)
2. The royal privilege to love others (**John 15:9-17**)
3. The royal privilege to follow Christ (**John 8:31-32**)
4. The royal privilege to obey those in authority (**1 Peter 2:13**)
5. The royal privilege to know and obey God (**Acts 5:29**)
6. It is easier to want to live a royal life when one has the support of others who are living similar lives. Can the class become a support group to each of its members? Can friendships be established to offer support for living the royal life? Pose the question to the class, pointing out that Esther and Mordecai provided support for each other.

Challenge your students to accept and use their royal privileges by joining in the project for people belonging to God as described in the Student Book. What results can you expect if just your class members join in this demonstration for Christ? if the whole school would join?

Close with a prayer requesting God's continuing presence and reminders of our royal privileges.

Session 89: The Homecoming of God's People

BIBLE BASIS: Ezra 1--10

CENTRAL TRUTH

God assures His people that His promises are true by reminding them of His faithfulness in the past.

OBJECTIVES

That the students will:

1. Recognize that the return of the Jews to Judah was the fulfillment of God's promise to His people
2. Identify the people and events that impeded progress on the rebuilding of the temple
3. Explain the contribution that Ezra made in stabilizing the resettlement of Judah
4. Be reminded of the peace, joy, and happiness we'll experience when God takes us to live with Him in heaven--our eternal home

BACKGROUND

The prophets had foretold God's intent to bring His people back to the land He had given them (**Is. 44:24--45:13; Jer. 50:18-20; Ezek. 37**). During the reign of Cyrus, the Persian king who had conquered Babylon, the exiled Jews were allowed to return to Judah.

Ezra 1:1 credits God with Cyrus' decision to allow the Jews to return and to supply them with all that they needed to resettle the land. Zerubbabel and Jeshua led the first group to return.

In spite of the decree of Cyrus, some people in the land tried to thwart the effort to rebuild the temple (**Ezra 4:1-4**).

Building of the temple was held up until the new king, Darius, found the original memorandum by Cyrus authorizing the project. Darius put an end to the bureaucratic interference and issued a decree to allow the Jews to rebuild God's temple **(Ezra 5:1-6:12).**

Ezra arrived on the scene after the temple had been rebuilt and the Passover had been celebrated. Ezra was a priest and a highly qualified teacher of the Law **(Ezra 7:6).** When he came to Jerusalem, Ezra also brought another group of Jews with him.

Ezra was immediately confronted with a problem. With their leaders setting the example, the people intermarried with the heathen around them, a practice that God had forbidden centuries before **(Ezra 9:1-4).** Ezra confessed the sin of the people to God and the confession of the people followed--in a downpour **(10:9).**

READING THE SCRIPTURES

The accounts of the exile, return, and reconstruction are a similar but scaled down version of the original formation of the nation of God's people. The nation that God brought out of the Egyptian captivity to conquer a land and build His temple was now brought out of the Babylonian captivity to face new enemies in the land where they would rebuild His temple.

Help your students identify God's faithfulness to His promises and His continuing incredible love for His people.

A PROMISE KEPT (Objective 1)

1. Ask for volunteers to read the following prophecies related to the return of the exiles from captivity: **Is. 44:24--45:13; Jer. 50:18-20;** and **Ezek. 37.** As each prophecy is read, ask someone else to explain its meaning.

2. The Isaiah prophecy also includes the name of the king who will release God's people. Ask students to comment on the importance of such minute detail in God's prophecies.

3. Tell the students that during World War II, Hitler believed that the Third Reich would last a thousand years. He was even convinced that his destiny was in the stars (he consulted a number of people involved in occult practices.) The name given to Japanese suicide planes during the same war was Kamikaze (meaning "divine wind"). The Japanese also believed that the gods were with them.

Almighty God made promises to His people that true. Ask your students to rate God's credibility in comparison with some of the political leaders of the past or even the present.

4. Not all of the Jews returned from the exile. Aside from those who died in captivity there were those who started to enjoy the life they were living. The study of **Esther** revealed that things were actually going well for the Jews. Ask the students to suggest what kinds of things might convince the Jews to remain in Babylon.

THE TEMPLE REBUILT (Objective 2)

1. Some of your students may be living in homes different from those they lived in earlier in their lives. Ask several to describe from memory the house or neighborhood they lived in previously. Point out that memories of times and places are never completely accurate. The Jews probably remembered the splendor of Jerusalem and the temple and some may have had only their parents' memories to go by. Have someone describe the destruction of Jerusalem as it was recorded in **2 Kings 25:13-21** and **2 Chronicles 36:18-21.**

2. The people first resettled their homes and towns **(Ezra 2:70).** Ask the students whether they think the temple should have come first. (Legitimate needs had to be taken care of first.)

3. Ask, **Why do you think the altar was the first thing to be rebuilt in the temple area?** (God did not need a temple, but He did require sacrifices and worship.)

4. God's two leaders at this time were Zerubbabel and Jeshua.

5. The students need to be reminded that they are not living in a neutral world. The world is actually hostile toward God and His people.

Ask the students to identify the hostility in **Ezra 4:1-5**.

(**Ezra 4:6-24** does not fit chronologically into the account since it names two kings who came after Darius.)

6. God helped His people through Darius by enabling him to find and support the original memorandum of Cyrus.

A NATION RESTORED (Objective 3)

Have the students tell you what Ezra's qualifications were. God anticipated His people's needs and had a skilled teacher waiting to move into position to accomplish His plan. He also caused Cyrus and then Artaxerxes to be very generous to the Jews.

When Ezra arrived in Jerusalem, he faced the problem of intermarriage that had been taking place between the Jews and the heathen of the land. In order to illustrate this, ask the students to imagine that they have been given a new home that has been completely furnished. They can move in immediately, but they must decide what furniture they wish to take with them from their present homes. (Hopefully there are some who are not willing to give up some of their current furniture or other possessions.) Explain that when people of differing faiths marry, there is a similar chance that each will insist on holding on to all or part of their previous beliefs. If that results in a mixture that makes either faith difficult to distinguish, neither is viable any longer. For the Jews it was potentially disastrous as Ezra pointed out. Do the students feel that the dissolution of the mixed marriages was unfair? Recall the consequences that Solomon faced.

Where is God's incredible love in all this? Ask for opinions and look for answers similar to the following: God kept His promise; God brought the people safely home; God protected them from their enemies; God gave them wise and courageous leaders; God accepted their sacrifices; God governed their sacrifices; God governed them through people who were committed to His law.

A PERFECT HOMECOMING (Objective 4)

Have you talked about death and dying with your students? It helps to know that we're not the only ones who are afraid of death. We can support each other and strengthen each other's hope and trust of someday living eternally with God. Remind your students to ask questions and to depend on their pastors, teachers, and family and friends for Christian support and care, especially when they have fears and doubts. Direct their attention to the key Scripture passages for this session (**John 17:17b** and **Deut. 7:9**).

For an optional discussion starter, you might refer to three hymns that describe our heavenly home: "Jerusalem the Golden" (LW 309), "Jerusalem, O City Fair and High" (LW 306), and "Jerusalem, My Happy Home" (LW 307).

Close your session with a prayer or a simply stated benediction such as **The Lord bless and protect each of us while we go about our daily work. The Lord give us each peace and love and joy in knowing His words are true and His promises are forever. Amen.**

Session 90: Secure in the Lord

BIBLE BASIS: Neh. 1--13

CENTRAL TRUTH

The joy of the Lord is the strength of His people (**Neh. 8:10b**).

OBJECTIVES

That the students will:

1. Desire the qualities of faith and leadership with which God blessed Nehemiah

2. Follow the history of the reconstruction of Jerusalem

3. Praise God for His incredible love for His people

BACKGROUND

Nehemiah was a contemporary of Ezra. Unlike Ezra, who was a priest, Nehemiah was a layperson. Nehemiah made his first trip to Jerusalem in 445 B.C. and remained there for twelve years. During that time he supervised the rebuilding of the wall around Jerusalem. Nehemiah left Jerusalem at the close of the first century after Cyrus released the Jews from captivity. Fortunately Nehemiah returned because he found it necessary to correct a number of errors that had crept in during his absence.

Nehemiah had a unique leadership style. It was his style to begin his activities with prayer **(Neh. 1:4; 2:4, 12; 4:4-5, 9; 6:9)**. It was his style to plan carefully and creatively **(Neh. 1:11; 2:4-9, 13-16; 4:7-23)**. It was his style to work hard **(Neh. 4:6, 23)**. It was his style to obey Lord **(Neh. 5:6-13; 13)**. It was his style to give credit to the Lord **(Neh. 6:16)**.

The account of Nehemiah's work shows how he led and motivated a weary people, all the time refusing to be intimidated by his enemies.

It is appropriate that we conclude a study of the Old Testament history of God's people with Nehemiah because he is a positive example of how God's people can deal with the challenges of everyday life. Nehemiah enjoyed a right relationship with the Lord, in whom he rejoiced and from whom he gained strength.

READING THE SCRIPTURES

It is possible to summarize all that God expected of His people in the example of Nehemiah. Nehemiah loved the Lord, depended on Him, and obeyed Him.

Help your students identify Nehemiah's qualities and then encourage them to look to the Lord Jesus for the ability to serve the Lord and His people.

LEADING THE PEOPLE (Objective 1)

God has always provided leaders for His people. The most effective leaders lived in a close faith relationship with the Lord. Helping young people grow in their relationship with the Lord Jesus should be one of the goals of a Lutheran high school. Some of our future church leaders are being prepared by God's Holy Spirit right now in your classes.

1. A leader needs to spend time in prayer. Nehemiah did so frequently. Ask your students what they think Nehemiah was praying about in the various references **(Neh. 1:4; 2:4, 12; 4:4-5, 9; 6:9)**.

2. Nehemiah was a careful planner. Sometimes we think that it's wrong to plan carefully as if it's an insult to God. People say, "Have faith!" Have your students read **Ps. 37:5; Prov. 16:9;** and **Luke 14:28.** God wants us to be good planners, but He also wants us to commit those plans to Him.

3. While planning is one part of good leadership, carrying out the plan is another. Some people think that leadership means dumping the work on someone else. Jesus taught that a leader is first a servant to those who follow **(John 13:1-17)**. Can you imagine what would have happened if Jesus had been a pompous king who expected us to save ourselves? **Neh. 4:6** and **4:23** show that Nehemiah was a good leader <u>and</u> a hard worker.

4. Nehemiah committed himself to God's law. He knew its value and importance. He knew what the breaking of God's law had done to God's people in generations past **(Neh. 13:23-27)**.

5. Ask, **What does giving credit to God for the completion of the wall show about Nehemiah's relationship with the Lord?** (It shows that Nehemiah knew that he was dependent on the Lord and happy with the Lord's involvement in his life.)

SECURING THE CITY (Objective 2)

When you think of "church" workers, do you usually think first of pastors and teachers and music directors--the professional workers? Nehemiah was a <u>layperson</u>, a professional food taster for Artaxerxes. But he was also a child of God. When something needed doing, he spoke to the Lord and made himself available. According to **Eph. 4:12** God's apostles, prophets, evangelists, and pastor-teachers were given to **prepare God's people for works of**

service. Have your students discuss this passage and the context in which it is found. Are they getting the idea that God has important plans for their lives? Do they understand that God needs lay workers in His service as well as professional workers?

1. Once Nehemiah decided to do something about the problems in Jerusalem, he had to get a leave of absence. Of course he followed his normal pattern when he prayed, planned, and presented his request to the king. Artaxerxes could have denied his request. Ask the students, **What might Nehemiah have done if his request had been denied?** If they think he would have been angry or if he would have pouted, have them read **Neh. 2:1.** Nehemiah had not been sad in the several months between hearing the news and seeing his prayer answered. Now that's confidence and patience!

2. The wall in Jerusalem was a mess. It was broken down and its gates had been burned.

3. Who are the people who intimidate students in your school and prevent the body of Christ from expressing itself? Without mentioning names, ask the students to hold these people up before God in prayer and ask God to deal with them.

Nehemiah had a creative strategy for dealing with troublemakers. He armed the workers so they could drop what they were doing at the sound of a trumpet and defend themselves. This is exactly what the U.S. Navy did during World War II with its Construction Battalions (Seabees). Seabees had to defend themselves against the Japanese as they hurried to build essential air strips in the South Pacific. This example may help the students understand what Nehemiah accomplished.

4. Of course Nehemiah did not overlook prayer to depend only on his own plans **(Neh. 6:9).**

Nehemiah also dealt with spiritual problems. Discuss those listed in **Neh. 5:1-13** and **13:1-28** as time permits.

PRAISING THE LORD (Objective 3)

The abrupt ending of the **Book of Nehemiah** is almost anticlimactic. Nehemiah asked God to remember him with favor. God thought enough of Nehemiah to include the account of his service in the Holy Scriptures.

An important celebration did take place in Jerusalem, but it was over the Lord and His law. The people could celebrate with joy because they were now secure in the Lord.

If time allows, ask the students to prepare a celebration of joy in the Lord. Divide the class into several groups of equal size and give your student groups about 10 minutes to decide on one thing they could do to celebrate and express their joy over what God has done for them. (They may wish to read a psalm, a favorite verse from Scripture, or a proclamation they write themselves. They might want to lead a praise-prayer or a song of celebration. Allow them to be creative, but have some suggestions ready. Allow each group a few minutes to present and lead its celebration.)

The people of Jerusalem celebrated because they now understood the Law. Someone has said that "the essence of education is realizing that you didn't know that you didn't know." If that is true, a lack of enthusiasm for God is in part the result of ignorance over what He has done for us and said to us. Spend a few minutes asking the students to share something that God taught them in this course that was especially meaningful.

Two folk songs directly relate to this session. "God Gives His People Strength" from Hymns for Now III (St. Louis: The Lutheran Church--Missouri Synod, 1972) is printed in the Student Book for this session. Another folk-song you might be familiar with, "The Joy of the Lord" from Rejoice in Jesus Always (Costa Mesa, CA: Maranatha House Publishers, 1973) clearly states the theme of this session. If you are musically inclined and if time permits, sing with your students. If you're not musically inclined, consider asking a musical friend to record one or both of these songs on a cassette for your class's use.

Praise the Lord!

Bibliography

Abbot, Walter M., et al. Bible Reader. New York: Bruce, 1969.

Biblical Archaeological Society. Biblical Archaeological Review. Washington, DC: Biblical Archaeological Society.

Blaiklock, E. M., ed. The Zondervan Pictorial Bible Atlas. Grand Rapids: Zondervan, 1969.

Commission on Theology and Church Relations, The Lutheran Church--Missouri Synod. Comparative Study of Bible Translations and Paraphrases. St. Louis: The Lutheran Church--Missouri Synod, 1977.

Creation Research Society. "The Sky Has Fallen"; impact pamphlet no. 128. San Diego: Creation Research Society.

Halley, Henry H. Halley's Bible Handbook. Grand Rapids: Zondervan, 1976.

Hunter, John E. Judges and a Permissive Society. Grand Rapids: Zondervan, 1975.

Keil, C. F. and F. Delitzsch. Biblical Commentaries on the Old Testament. Grand Rapids: William E. Eerdmans, 1950.

Kretzmann, Paul E. Popular Commentary of the Bible (Vol. 1: The Old Testament). St. Louis: Concordia, 1923.

LaHaye, Tim and John Morris. The Ark on Ararat. New York: Nelson, 1976.

Lewis, C. S. The Screwtape Letters. Cleveland: Collins, 1979.

Morris, Henry M. The Bible and Modern Science. Chicago: Moody, 1956.

Rehwinkel, Alfred M. The Flood. St. Louis: Concordia, 1951.

Tenney, Merrill C., ed. The Zondervan Pictorial Bible Dictionary. Grand Rapids: Zondervan, 1969.

Thaxton, Charles B., et al. The Mystery of Life's Origin. New York: Philosophical Library, 1984.

Trinklein, Frederick E. The God of Science. Smithtown, NY: Exposition Press, 1971. (Order from Frederick E. Trinklein, 131 Brookville Rd., Brookville, NY 11545.)

Woolley, Leonard. The Sumerians. New York: Norton, 1965.

Woolley, Leonard. Ur of the Chaldees. Ithaca: Cornell, 1982.

Get Acquainted Form

Following are suggestions for the get acquainted form that you may wish to prepare for session 1.

Name

Address

Telephone Number

I enjoy (including hobbies)

I live with (family situation; names and ages of sisters and brothers)

I earn spending money by

I attend church at

Other schools I have attended (including grades)

I have taken lessons in

I belong or have belonged to (clubs, societies)

I picture God as

Portions of the Bible I have read are

When I finish school, I hope to

My greatest fear is

My greates joy comes from

22-2260

Printed in U.S.A.

ISBN: 0-570-01531-6

www.ingramcontent.com/pod-product-compliance
Lightning Source LLC
LaVergne TN
LVHW061244100826
845148LV00008B/1025

* 9 7 8 0 5 7 0 0 1 5 3 1 4 *